TENNESSEE DIVORCES 1797–1858

Taken from 750 Legislative Petitions and Acts

Gale W. Bamman, C.G.
Debbie W. Spero

Copyright 1985, Gale W Bamman
Nashville, Tennessee

Reprinted with written permission from
Gale W. Bamman

Janaway Publishing Inc.
Santa Maria, California 2023
All rights reserved

ISBN: 978-1-59641-481-5

INTRODUCTION

Divorce was a last resort for unhappily married persons in the early 1800s because of the ensuing shame, embarrassment, and ostracism. Nevertheless, when a marriage could no longer be tolerated, a divorce was sought, either through the courts, or by petitioning the Tennessee General Assembly for a decree.

The petitions abstracted for this compilation account for only a small number of the divorces which were requested during 1797-1858. The others were brought before the superior courts between 1799-1809, then from 1809-1835 in the circuit courts, and since 1835, either in the circuit or chancery courts. There are many legislative divorce petitions which haven't survived, or else haven't as yet been processed, and thus aren't available for study.

We have tried to keep our abstracts of the sometimes lengthy petitions as close to the originals as possible, and have placed in quotation marks any data extracted word for word. Our explanatory comments have been placed in parentheses. Names were found to be spelled a variety of ways, sometimes within the same petition. We have shown those several spellings.

A FEW WORDS OF CAUTION:

1) Do not assume that the surname the female requested to use at the dissolving of the marriage was her maiden name. We found many mentions of second marriages of widows and widowers.

2) Do keep in mind that the accused party usually was given no chance to make a statement in his own defence when the petition was reviewed by the Legislature. A petition may be entirely accurate or only partially accurate. Certainly statements by neighbors and relatives, as well as many accompanying signatures, tend to lend credibility to some petitions. But, for an example of opposing remarks made by a husband in his petition and then by a wife in hers, read the petitions of David McNabb and Pebby McNabb.

3) When the words "upon proof" accompany the Legislature's decree, the divorce was not considered final until proof was presented in court, and the case tried there.

For the generous help and assistance that we received at the Tennessee State Library and Archives, we wish to thank Fran Schell, Reference Librarian, Marylin Bell, Senior Archivist, and Florence Langford, Assistant Archivist.

EARLY TENNESSEE DIVORCE LAWS

The United States Constitution left complete authority over marriage and divorce legislation to the separate states, and the first state constitutions, by omitting the subject, left the matter of divorce to the legislatures. Thus, each state had the freedom to develop its own divorce legislation. (1)

In 1799 the Tennessee General Assembly gave the authority to grant divorces to the superior courts, located in the districts of Mero, Hamilton, and Washington. However, both prior to this act and until 1835, divorces and privileges of feme sole were granted by the General Assembly. (2) (Feme sole is a term used to indicate a single woman, or a woman whose marriage has been dissolved by death or divorce, and also a woman who has been judicially separated from her husband.) (3)

The researcher seeking information on a divorce in Tennessee between 1796 and 1835 should be aware that although the great majority of the divorce cases were heard in the courts, a large number of divorce and feme sole petitions were brought before and were acted upon by the Tennessee General Assembly.

Valid grounds for a divorce in 1799 were:

a) Impotence, or being incapable of procreation;
b) When the married partner knowingly entered into a second marriage, "in violation of a previous vow made to a former wife or husband, whose marriage is still subsisting;"
c) Adultery;
d) "Wilful and malicious desertion or absence without a reasonable cause, for the space of two years." (4)

It was further enacted in 1799 that "if any husband or wife upon a false rumor, apparently well founded, of the death of the other, (where such person has been absent for the space of two whole years) has married or shall marry again, he or she shall not be subject to the pains of adultery, but it shall be at the election of the party remaining single, at his or her return, to insist to have his or her former husband or wife restored, or to have his or her own marriage dissolved, and the other party to remain with the second husband or wife, if the suit is instituted within one year after such return." (5)

---

(1) The Encyclopedia Americana, (Danbury, Connecticut: Grolier, Inc., 1984), Vol. 4, p.215.
(2) Tennessee Code, Annotated, (Charlottesville,Virginia: The Michie Company, 1980). Vol. 1. Constitution. Art. XI, Section 4. p. 737.
(3) Henry Campbell Black, Black's Law Dictionary. (St. Paul, Minnesota: West Publishing Company, 1951), p.745.
(4) Acts of Tennessee, 1799, Chapter XIX, Section 1, p.48.
(5) Ibid., Section 3, pp.49-50.

The person requesting a divorce had to meet certain conditions:

a) He or she must have been a resident of the State of Tennessee for at least one year prior to the filing of the petition;
b) The petition had to be presented along with an affidavit, taken upon oath before the judge of the superior court or before some justice of the peace in the county where the petitioner resided, that the facts contained in said affidavit were true, and that said petition was not made out of levity.
c) A woman could not petition the courts in her own name, but had to petition by her "next friend." (A married woman in this time period of 1796-1835, suffered the civil disability of being unable to sue in her own person.) (6)

Consequently, if a woman wished to instigate a divorce suit in the courts, she had to find some male to represent her there, perhaps an attorney, but certainly someone who could and would accompany her to the court where the suit was to be heard. Since the court may not have been held in the county in which she lived (prior to 1809), that may have placed a hardship on her. Additionally, there would have been financial costs involved in a court suit.

There was another avenue open to her, however. She could send a written petition to the Tennessee General Assembly, where it would be read by the representative from her county. (7) The petition would then be referred to a committee (in 1797, the Committee of Propositions and Grievances) for consideration. Upon that committee's recommendation, a bill would be drawn up and then would on three occasions be read in both the Senate and the House. If the bill was passed, it was then enrolled. (8) The enactment would subsequently appear in the Acts of Tennessee. (9)

The General Assembly took one of four approaches to a bill and petition for divorce or feme sole:

a) It dismissed the petition, and refused to act upon it; or
b) It decreed a divorce from bed and board, in which instance the woman was granted the privileges of a feme sole.
    In addition to the grounds listed earlier, the following were grounds for a legal separation:
    1) Malicious abandonment of a wife, or turning her out of doors;
    2) Cruel or barbarous treatment endangering her life;
    3) Offering such indignities to her person as to render her condition intolerable and thereby forcing her to withdraw. (10)

---

(6) Ibid., Section 2, p.48
(7) See example in Senate Journal, 1825, p.69
(8) See example in Senate Journal, 1797, pp.57,60,68,70,77,78.
(9) See example in Acts of Tennessee, 1797, p.92.
(10) Acts of Tennessee, 1799, Chapter XIX, Section 9, p.52.

c) It decreed that the marriage be dissolved. However, if the divorce had been granted because of adultery, the person who had been guilty could not marry, during the life of the former husband or wife, the person with whom the said crime was commtted. If it was the wife who had been guilty of adultery and if she was proven even to cohabit with said person, she could not then alienate her property. (11)

d) It recommended a divorce upon proof, in which case the divorce suit had to be taken into court.

In 1807 the General Assembly repealed the Act of 1799, and then revived it in 1809, changing the jurisdiction of divorce cases from the superior courts to the circuit courts, and specifically, the circuit court of the county where the petitioner resided at the time of filing the petition. (12)

In 1819 the laws were further amended, and an additional ground for divorce was added:

"If a woman shall be in a state of pregnancy with a child of color at the time of marriage, it shall be lawful for the circuit court to grant a divorce." (13)

When the Tennessee Constitution was rewritten in 1835, the circuit courts and the chancery courts were given the SOLE jurisdiction over divorces. The jurisdiction of the Legislature in granting divorces or feme soles was REMOVED, and its authority in such matters was reduced to the degree that it "may authorize the courts of justice to grant divorces for such causes as may be specified by law, but such laws shall be general and uniform in their operation throughout the State." (14)

After 1835, petitions for divorce, though reduced as to number, continued to be presented to the General Assembly, but no decrees were made on these.

My remarks and interpretation of the early laws have been reviewed by C. Edward Coomer, Attorney at Law, Nashville, Tennessee.

Gale W. Bamman
Certified Genealogist
June 1985

---

(11) Ibid., Section 6, p. 51.
(12) Acts of Tennessee, 1809, Chapter LXLVIII, Sections 1-2, p.217.
(13) Acts of Tennessee, 1819, Chapter XX, Section 2, p. 45.
(14) Tennessee Constitution, Article XI, Section 4.

EXPLANATION

PETITION SOURCES:

Tennessee State Library and Archives, Nashville, Tennessee:

Microfilm: Legislative Petitions, Reels #1 through #20.

Manuscripts Division: Undated Boxes of original Legislative Petitions; Record Group 60, Box 14, Folder 35; Sneed Family Papers, AC 992, Box 4.

SOURCE FOR DIVORCE ACTS AND GRANTS OF FEME SOLE:

Acts of Tennessee, 1796-1835.

ARRANGEMENT OF ABSTRACTED PETITIONS:

Name of Petitioner:
The petitioner was the offended marriage partner, but occasionally a petition was written by a third party, on behalf of the offended party. These instances have been so identified. When the husband and the wife mutually requested a divorce, the person assuming the larger portion of the petition was listed as the petitioner.

Date of Petition:

When stated in month, day, and year, this states the date the petition was signed in the presence of a justice of the peace, or a judge, or in the absence of such witnesses, reflects the date of the petition.

County:

The county stated is usually the county where the petitioner had lived for at least one year prior to the filing of said petition. Some petitions contained no mention of a county.

WORDING OF THE ABSTRACTS:

When statements by persons other than the petitioner accompanied the petition, these were generally reiterating the remarks of the petitioner; hence, we didn't abstract these, unless they contained additional data.

The many signatures accompanying the petitions were not extracted by us; however, we did note those which bore the same surname as the petitioner, or the maiden or former name of the wife.

IDENTIFICATION OF SOURCES:

Following the petition abstracts are numbers representing first, the petition number, and second, the year of the petition. Following Acts of the Legislature are the year and page number.

ABSTRACTS FROM LEGISLATIVE PETITIONS AND ACTS OF TENNESSEE:

AARON, RACHEL   1825   STEWART COUNTY
Rachel is the wife of JOHN AARON of Stewart County. She is to have the privileges of a feme sole.
Acts of TN, 1825, p.152

ADAMS, MARTIN   2 October 1812   DAVIDSON COUNTY
Martin petitions for a divorce from his wife MARTHA. He says that she left him October 1806. They had been married nearly 10 years when she left. Supporting statement made by John Overton, Travellers Rest.
51-2-1812

ADAMS, MARTIN   1812   no county stated
The marriage bonds are hereby dissolved between MARTIN ADAMS and wife, MARTHA.
Acts of TN, 1812, p.66

ADAMS, NANCY   1833   no county stated
The marriage bonds are hereby dissolved between NANCY ADAMS and TODD R. ADAMS. Nancy is to resume her maiden name of FARIS.
Acts of TN, 1833, p.117

AITHEY, SARAH   August 1822   BLEDSOE COUNTY
Sarah's husband is ELIJAH AITHLEY, who contracted and gave her a venereal disease. She left him. She has children (number not stated) from a previous marriage. Elijah is "a man of morally and infamous character, having been long confined in jail on a charge of murder."
56-1822

ALLEN, CALLOWAY   1833   COCKE COUNTY
Marriage bonds are hereby dissolved between Calloway Allen and his wife, SARAH.
Acts of TN, 1833, p.99

ALLEN, GEORGE WASHINGTON   18 October 1825   MARION COUNTY
George W. Allen of Marion County was married to ANN WALKER of Blount County in 11 May 1805. She left him in September of 1816.
114-1825

ALLEN, LUCY W..   1827   WHITE COUNTY
Lucy is the wife of John W. Allen of White County. She is to have the privileges of a feme sole.
Acts of TN , 1827

ALLEN, POLLY D.   1827   no county stated
Polly is the wife of LEVI P. ALLEN, a lunatic. She may, with Mathew Rybourn, the guardian of Levi P. Allen, make deeds to John Walker of Montgomery County, Tennessee for certain lands in said county and also to certain lands in Dyer County, Tennessee.
Acts of TN, 1827

ALLEY, MARY   24 November 1823   RUTHERFORD COUNTY
Mary is the wife of WILLIAM ALLEY of Rutherford County. She is to have all the privileges of a feme sole, except that of intermarrying with another man.
Acts of TN, 1823, p.227

ANDERSON, EDMUND R.   21 October 1825   DAVIDSON COUNTY
On 1 April 1823 in Limestone County, Alabama, Edmund was married to ELIZA
PEETE, then a citizen of Limestone County, Alabama. She was pregnant when
they married, by another man; so he took her and her possessions back to her
father in Alabama and left her.
Supporting statement by David R. Cole that Ben Peete, father of Eliza, said
that Doc Anderson shouldn't live with Eliza, and that Eliza was seduced
previous to her marriage by her brother-in-law and became pregnant.
163-1825

ANDERSON, EDMUND R.   1825   no county stated
The marriage bonds are hereby dissolved between Edmund R. Anderson and his wife,
ELIZA ANDERSON. Edmund is to be restored to all the privileges of an unmarried man as though he had never been married to Eliza.
Acts of TN, 1825, p.211

ANDERSON, ELIZABETH   1833   BEDFORD COUNTY
Elizabeth is wife of WILLIAM ANDERSON. Elizabeth is granted all the privileges of a feme sole, except that of intermarrying with another man.
Acts of TN, 1833

ANDERSON, HENRY   1831   no county stated
The marriage bonds are hereby dissolved between Henry Anderson and his wife,
FANNY.
Acts of TN, 1831, p.218

ANDERSON, SALLY (SARAH)   29 September 1831   DAVIDSON COUNTY
Sally Anderson is the daughter of a widowed mother, living now "as she has
done for a large number of years in the town of Nashville." In 1830 Sally
went to Columbia in Maury County to visit a sister who is married and lived
there at that time. While there she was urged by her brother-in-law to marry
WILLIAM L. ANDERSON. She was not willing to marry him; among other reasons
he was too old for her, being old enough to be her father. Her brother-in-law
however, threatened to beat her if she didn't marry Anderson. So she consented. When the time of the marriage came near, she again said she didn't
want to marry Anderson. Her brother-in-law beat her. She was forced to
marry him, but she told him she would not cohabit with him.
199-1831

ANDERSON, WILLIAM   6 January 1830   MAURY COUNTY
This file contains a letter of 6 January 1830 from William Anderson to Thomas
Claiborne of Nashville, counselor of Mrs. Bigby and her daughter, to whom
William was married sometime ago. "She can petition the legislature for a
separation. I have nothing more to say on the subject, but to grant her her
request."
99-1831

ANDERSON, SALLY   1831   DAVIDSON COUNTY
A divorce is hereby granted Sally Anderson from her husband, WILLIAM ANDERSON.
Acts of TN, 1831, p.218

ASHBURN, REBECKA   September 1831   OVERTON COUNTY
Rebecka was married ca 1828 to JOHN ASHBURN in Overton County. They lived
together about 11 months. She accuses him of adultery. He left her ca 1829.
She has "a father who has a large family and is poor." Her father expects
to leave Tennessee soon, and she wants to go with him. She wants a divorce
and to have the rights of a single woman again.

Supporting statements by Celia Fisk, David Collier, and Sally Brown.
Statement by Jacob Brown that he lived within 2 miles of said Ashburn and his
wife when they parted. Statement by Jesse Brown that he lived near the Ash-
burns. Also, a paper with 11 signatures.
149-1831

                    BABB, WILLIAM   July 1822   ROBERTSON COUNTY
William Babb was married ca 1804 to ELIZABETH FITCHJEARL. They lived together
about 3 weeks, then she left him and took up with another man and refused to
return to William. The Baptist Church of Christ at Popular Spring Meeting
House, Logan County, Kentucky believes there is sufficient cause to divorce
Babb and wife. This petition is signed by E. C. Williams, clerk.
Statement by Jesse Babb that Elizabeth had been with three men after she left
William.
Statement by John L. Doyle that before Elizabeth married William, she courted
another man for a long time but when this man was absent for a long time, she
married William.
Babb's petition is accompanied by a paper with 79 signatures, including that
of Alsa Babb.
28-1822

                    BACON, CHARLES   1825   no county stated
A divorce is to be granted Charles Bacon from his wife ANN BACON, upon proof.
Ann was said to have been pregnant at time of marriage, and that the child
was a child of color.
Acts of TN, 1826, p.135

BAILEY, CATHERINE   10 July 1822   no county stated
Cahterine Bailey was a widow with five helpless children in March 1821. She
then married JOHN BAYLEY. Three months after they married, he left her, on a
borrowed horse and has never since been heard of. She was informed that
Bailey married her only to get what property she had, "which belongs to her
children," and once he found out the property belonged to the children, he
left her.
There are signatures on the petition of four neighbors who said they had
known her for 6 or 7 years.
Statement signed by M. Johnston who said he had known her for better than 5
years.
Another statement by Catherine Bailey in which she said that about 1807 she
married JOHN RAGINS. They lived together about 10 years, and at the close of
such time, he started down the river in a boat, with intention of returning to
his family, she believed. When he didn't return, she believed him dead. She
said she married John Bailey, and he left her after 3 or 4 weeks of marriage.
101-1822

                    BAKER, REV. ROBERT   October 1831   CARROLL COUNTY
Robert wants a divorce from his wife CHARLOTTE. Before their marriage, she
had prostituted herself to her own uncle, a married man.
Petition is accompanied by the signatures of 82 persons.
Statement by Bennett Maxey that Baker and his wife married 30 June 1829, and
that she had a child 17 November 1829. They parted a short time when he
discovered she was pregnant before their marriage.
Statement by Champness Madding.
Statement by William H. Bigham that Charlotte went back to her father's
house.
Another statement by Robert Baker that he married CHARLOTTE C. LYNN of Madison
County. She was pregnant by her half-uncle by marriage. The child's name is
Zimri.

Baker appeared before a Justice of the Peace in Davidson County and made oath that his petition was true.
Statement by Richard Beard, Minister of the Gospel, Carroll County that he married Robert Baker and Charlotte.
Statement by R. E. C. Dougherty, Davidson County, that Charlotte had said the baby was her uncle's, Warham Easley's.
260-1831

BAKER, ROBERT   1831   CARROLL COUNTY
A divorce is hereby granted Robert from his wife, CHARLOTTE. Zimri, son of Charlotte, is not to inherit property of Robert Baker.
Acts of TN, 1831, p.27.

BALL, ANN   no date stated   no county stated
Ann was married to WILLIAM BALL on 8 November 1824. On 21 January 1826, he left her. She has a few Negroes she had before they married. "I (Ann) was raised in Davidson County. My father was massacred by the Indians when I was a child."
Undated Box of Legislative Petitions, Manuscripts Division

BALL, EVELINA   15 September 1821   SUMNER COUNTY
Evelina was married to JAMES BALL of Sumner County in 1811. They had three children. They lived together until 1820. In 1820 James became embarrassed in his affairs and left Sumner County for the Arkansas Territory, intending, he told her, to return in a short time. He had debts when he left and the property was sold to pay those debts. He still has several unpaid debts.
69-1831

BALLARD, ELIZABETH A.   25 October 1831   WILLIAMSON COUNTY
In about 1819 Elizabeth was married to JAMES R. BALLARD. In June of 1829 he left her, and absconded from Mt. Pleasant, TN. He left her and five infant children. He took with him a woman and went to Kentucky where he and the woman now cohabit.
321-1831

BANTY, NANCY   5 September 1832   KNOX COUNTY
In about 1828 Nancy was married to PETER BANTY. They had two children. He treated her cruelly and left her.
Another statement by Nancy Banty that upwards to five years ago, ca 1827, she married Peter Banty, ..."a stranger then lately from Kentucky." Banty left ca August 1830.
Supporting statements by Samuel Flemiker and James Badgett, Jr.
82-1832

BAREFOOT, NANCY CHOATE   1825   MAURY COUNTY
Nancy was married to DILLON W. H. BAREFOOT in 1817. About six months after their marriage, he took to rambling. She learned he was at Knoxville and left her father's home in Maury County and went ot Knoxville to try to induce him to settle down. They did, in Sequatchie Valley. He wouldn't work, so she returned to her father's home in Maury County. She tried, and again failed to settle down with him and returned to Maury County. He announced intentions to go to South America to join the patriots. They had one child. A few signatures accompany the petition.
39-1825

BARHAM, ARRILLA CAROLINE   30 December 1845   BENTON COUNTY
She was formerly Arrilla Caroline PERKINS. On 9 February 1843, she was married to JOHN A. BARHAM. She wants a divorce and custody of their child because of his abuse and because he is a gambler.

Petition is accompanied by the signatures of J. G. Sims, Margaret Sims, E. F. Wills, and C. R. Wyly.
140-1846

BARKER, BRIGGS   1833   HUMPHREYS COUNTY
On 17 September 1818 he was married to ELIZABETH in Stewart County, Tennessee. She left him ca 1827. They had two daughters. Elizabeth was the mother of two children after she left Briggs.
Petition is accompanied by the signatures of Howell W. Barker and 24 other persons.
24-1833

BARKER, REBECCA   10 September 1809   BEDFORD COUNTY
Rebecca was married ALEXANDER B. BARKER about 1807. He left her. They had one child.
Petition is accompanied by the signatures of William Adams, Samuel Fleming, and John Warner.
31-1-1809

BARTON, CYNTHIA   1833   MONROE COUNTY
The marriage bonds are hereby dissolved between Cynthia and her husband, ANDERSON BARTON. She is to be given rights of feme sole.
Acts of TN, 1833, p.4

BATTE, AMERICA R. ELIAM   28 August 1833   WILLIAMSON COUNTY
America is the daughter of Edward ELIAM, dec'd. of Williamson County. She was married to WILLIAM P. BATTE of Bedford County. They lived together 14 months. He abused and beat her.
Statements by Kinchen Pate and Polly Pate on 2 October 183.
Statement by Jane Elaim on 2 October 1833 that she (Jane) told Batte to come get America at her house, and he would not.
Statement by William Covington on 4 October 1833, and also by Michael Pitman. William P. Batte also makes a statement and says that the bad reports against him are false and that he does not want a divorce.
75-1833

BATTE, WILLIAM P.   8 October 1833   BEDFORD COUNTY
William is the husband of AMERICA R. BATTE. He asks that America's petition for a divorce from him be rejected.
Petition is accompanied by the signatures of 28 persons, including those of Frederick Batte, Sr. and Robert Batte.
Statement by Edward Gregory that he and Batte were gone to the "western" district. They started 5 February 1823 and returned 24 February 1823. They went to sell a horse, and Batte's wife left him while he was gone.
Statement by Edward C. Harrison that he and Batte went to the western district to sell horses on 5 February 1823 and returned 24th of said month. Batte's wife had left him.
267-1833

BAYLES, RICHARD   1822   no county stated
Richard is to be divorced by judge of first circuit court after petitioning same.
Acts of TN, 1822, p.113 (page missing; this data from index page of 1822 Acts.)

BEASON, NANCY   July 1822   HARDIN COUNTY
Nancy has resided in Hardin County more than one year (the time required for the filing of a petition of this nature). She was married on 7 April 1819 to JOHN W. BEASON. They lived together 1½ years, then he left her. They were living in Kentucky. She stayed in Kentucky nearly a year, but then returned to Tennessee to her father in Hardin County.
71-1822

BELL, ELIZABETH C.   22 October 1831   SUMNER COUNTY
She was formerly ELIZABETH C. ESSEX, a resident of Sumner County. In 1818 she was married to JOSEPH M. BELL of Sumner County. They lived together about nine years. He was a first rate mechanic, but gave in to habits of dissipation. In 1827 he left her and their four children and has been travelling ever since. His father lately died and left him a legacy of $200-$300. She wants a divorce and to be restored to a feme sole.
Petition is accompanied by the signatures of 7 persons who say Elizabeth is a "respectable communicant of the Methodist Church."
102-1831

BELL, ELIZABETH C.   1831   SUMNER COUNTY
Elizabeth, wife of JOSEPH M. BELL, is granted the privileges of a feme sole, except that of intermarrying with another man.
Acts of TN, 1831

BEMBRIDGE, LYDIA   July 1820   WILLIAMSON COUNTY
Lydia has long been a resident of Williamson County. She married PETER W. BEMBRIDGE in Davidson County ca 1805. They lived together eleven months, til he left her with an infant child. He returned after eight years, and they lived together again. He stayed about 3½ months, leaving her in a state of pregnancy.
Supporting statement by Melinda Parks, a neighbor.
95-1820

BERRY, PATSEY SELLERS   September 1812   MAURY COUNTY
Patsey married FRANCIS BERRY. He left about 1810, leaving her with one child. Berry was already married to widow Hamilton, who is still alive. Statement by Robert Sellars on 9 September 1812 that he'd been informed that Berry was married to widow Hamilton living on Cumberland River at Bennett's Old Ferry near mouth of Roaring River, Smith County. Another informant told Sellars that Berry had a wife in Pulaski County, Kentucky.
35-1-1812

BERRY, FRANCIS   1812   no county stated
The marriage bonds are to be dissolved between Francis Berry and his wife, PATSEY BERRY.
Acts of TN, 1812, p.21

BILES, ISABELLA   28 September 1826   HARDEMAN COUNTY
In 1808 Isabella was married to JAMES BILES in Wilson County. They lived in Warren County for seven years. They were happy together for several years, but then he squandered their property, putting them into poverty, and began to treat her cruelly. In April 1815, he left her, taking a son, their eldest child, and leaving her with three infants. She now resides with her brother.
29-1826

BILES, ISABELLA   1826   HARDEMAN COUNTY
Isabella Biles is to be granted a divorce upon proof.
Acts, of TN, 1826, p.135

BILLINGSLEY, POLLY   September 1825   ROANE COUNTY
Polly married ELIJAH BILLINGSLEY. He left in 1824, and is now a citizen of
the western district of Tennessee. She lives in Roane County.
Petition is accompanied by the signatures of 10 persons.
Supporting statement on 13 September 1825 by neighbor, Francis Erwin of Roane
County.
Also statements by John Brown, and Hugh Francis.
132-1825

BILLINGSLEY, POLLY   no date stated   ROANE COUNTY
ELIJAH BILLINGSLEY eloped from his family 5 years ago and has been living
with some woman in the western district. Polly has a Negro woman, some small
children, stock, and household property that were hers previous to the
marriage, and she wishes the right and control of these. Petition is signed
by James Buckhannon.
Petition is accompanied by the signatures of 44 persons.
74-1831

BILLINGSLEY, POLLY   1832   ROANE COUNTY
Polly, the wife of ELIJAH BILLINGSLEY, late of said county, is granted the
privileges of a feme sole.
Acts of TN, 1832

BISHOP, LUCINDA   1833   MAURY COUNTY
Lucinda is the wife of JAMES BISHOP. They were married in January 1810.
For the last 3 years, James has hardly stayed at home. She asks that her
husband would stay at home and that she be granted the right of a feme sole.
Petition is accompanied by the signatures of 19 persons.
38-1833

BISHOP, LUCINDA   1833   MAURY COUNTY
Lucinda, wife of JAMES BISHOP of Maury County, is granted the privileges of a
feme sole, except that of intermarrying with another man.
Acts of Tn, 1833

BLACK, BENJAMIN   22 October 1831   HAMILTON COUNTY
Benjamin's wife is SUSANNAH. She has been gone 12 months past and lives with
another man. Benjamin petitions for a divorce "with the consent of Susannah
Black."
Petition is accompanied by the signatures of 14 persons.
276-1831

BLALOCK, WILLIAM   7 September 1832   BLEDSOE COUNTY
William's wife is SARY. She left him 8 January 1828. She bedded with another
man previous to leaving him and is still roving about in Roane County. They
had six small children.
Petition is accompanied by the signatures of 13 men.
105-1832

BLEVINS, KITTURA   1821   no county stated
Kittura is wife of ARMISTEAD BLEVINS and is hereby granted the privileges of
a feme sole, except that of intermarrying with another man.
Acts of Tn, 1821, p.89

BOND, JESSE, JR.   14 August 1821   WARREN COUNTY
Jesse was married in February 1819 to FRANCES WILSON. She left him "about the middle of May next after her marriage."
20-1821

BOND, JOHN   14 August 1821   WARREN COUNTY
John was married to FRANCES WILSON on 14 FEbruary 1819. "On middle of May next after, she left him." She took some of his household furniture. She committed adultery and he believes she left this county in company with the same man (that she committed adultery with), for East Tennessee.
Supporting statement by John Rogers.
183-1821

BOND, SUSAN   1833   WARREN COUNTY
Susan is granted a divorce from her husband, JOHN BOND of the Indian Nation. She is to resume her maiden name of DUGAN.
Acts of TN, 1833, p.171

BOWMAN, CAUSBY   1829   WHITE COUNTY
Cosby was married to ELIZABETH HOWARD, widow of James Howard, on 25 December 1827. By his first wife, Cosby had six children, the youngest being 13 months. Elizabeth had two children by her first husband. They had been acquainted 12 or 13 years, and she knew his situation and number of his children. About 3 weeks after they married, he brought the youngest child to their home and took it to bed with him. Elizabeth left for the night and since that time has become more and more dissatisfied. He frequently got her step-father and mother to talk to her but to no avail. She bore one child by Causby. On about the first of March 1828, she left without cause except that he would not put away his children.

Isaac Taylor makes oath of Cosby's good character.
108-1829

BOYERS, MICHEL   October 1829   CLAIBORNE COUNTY
Michel's wife, MARGARET, left him ca 1822. She now lives with another man.
171-1829

BRADFORD, HENRY   12 October 1849   HENRY COUNTY
Henry was married ca 1844 to REBECCA GIMAN. SHe abandoned him and moved to Kentucky.
Petition is accompanied by the signatures of 56 "neighbors."
63-1849

BRADLEY, MARGARET   4 September 1832   DICKSON COUNTY
Margaret married JOHN BRADLEY in Dickson County in 1815. They lived together about 6 years and had 2 children. He then left her. She is informed he is living in Louisiana with another woman.
Statement by Benjamin CLARK, father of Margaret.
190-1833

BRADLEY, MARGARET   1832   DICKSON COUNTY
Margaret, wife of JOHN BRADLEY, is granted privileges of a feme sole.
Acts of TN, 1832

BRASSFIELD, SALLY   1822   no county stated
SAlly formerly was SALLY QUEENER. Her husband is THOMAS BRASSFIELD. She
asked for help from Sampson David to get a divorce. Thomas Brassfield came
in the neighborhood, worked at the saddling business as a journeyman with
____ Peterson for several months, after which he married Sally Queener. He
stayed with her about 10 days, then borrowed a horse, saying "he was going to
Knoxville to purchase some leather to set up the saddling business. He
proceeded on to Wythe County in Virginia." Daniel Queener followed him.
Brassfield refused to return. Sally had no children by him.
104-1822

BRACHER, NANCY   13 November 1819   WARREN COUNTY
Nancy married WILLIAM BRACHER of Warren County. They lived together but a
few months til he began beating and abusing her. She wants a divorce and
possession of the property and its benefits that she had before she married
Bracher .
89-1819

BRATCHER, NANCY   29 June 1820   RUTHERFORD COUNTY
Samuel Fettle makes statement that Nancy Bratcher and WILLIAM BRATCHER are
separated. Nancy's first husband, for 20 years, was Peter Adams.
90-1820

BRATCHER, NANCY   1820   no county stated
The marriage between NANCY BRATCHER and WILLIAM BRATCHER is dissolved. Nancy
Bratcher was formerly Nancy ADAMS of Warren County. "Said Nancy Bratcher
shall hereafter be called and known by the name of Nancy Adams."
Acts of Tn,1820,p.26

BREEDEN, JANE   no date stated   JACKSON COUNTY
Jane was formerly JANE PHARIS of Jackson County. In ca 1826 she married
LINSEY O.BREEDEN. They were married but a few months til he left her. He
was absent about 12 months, returned to her, stayed a few weeks, but left her
again.
Petition is accompanied by the signatures of 23 persons, plus those of John
Pharis, Delilah Pharis, William Pharis, and James Pharis.
40-1833

BREWINGTON, SARAH   1829   JEFFERSON COUNTY
The marriage bonds are hereby dissolved between SARAH BREWINGTON and her
husband, JAMES BREWINGTON.
Acts of TN, 1829, p.278

BRISON, GEORGE   1850   PERRY COUNTY
George was married ca 1826 to EASTER REED. He has a large family of children.
George and Easter separated "six or seven years ago."
173-1850

BRITTON, SARAH   November 1829   HAYWOOD COUNTY
Sarah is married to JOHN BRITTON. Her father is Anguish MCKIVER. Sarah says
that her husband has been gone for better than two years.
Statement by A. Hay(?), a neighbor that has lived neighbor to Anguish McKiver
for 2 years, says that John has never been there, and it is reported that he
has been twice married since he left Sarah. Everything he left he was sold
to pay debts, with some still unpaid.
Statement is accompanied by the signatures of 4 persons.
284-1829

BROOKS, JOAB   10 September 1831   FRANKLIN COUNTY
Joab is husband of SARAH BROOKS.
Statement by John Lowrey that SArah had a baby at his house and said that it was one of his son's children.
338-1831

BROOKS, JOAB   27 September 1831   WARREN COUNTY
Joab was married 15 August 1821 or 1822 to SALLY BURTON in Blount County. He lived with her ca 18 months. She then left him and took up with William Loury with whom she lived in adultery 12 months and had a child by him and then left Loury and took up with another man. She is now separated from this man and is living with her mother who has likewise separated from her husband. Sally has been gone from him (Joab) about 8 years.
27-1831

BROOKS, WILLIAM   22 August 1821   WARREN COUNTY
William is married to ELIZABETH. She left him in 1819. When he married Elizabeth, he was a widow with some small children. She treated him and his children cruelly and was guilty of frequent acts of adultery. She had a child that was not his.
Petition accompanied by the signatures of 11 persons.
Statement by John Foster and Polly Foster that sometime in March last, James Holloway and Elizabeth satyed at their house and acted like man and wife.
Petition of ELIZABETH BROOKS: William left her and she is not guilty of adultery or ill temper as he said. She says that the male child that William says was not his IS his, and she charges him with adultery. She asks not to be divorced. Her statement is dated 24 September 1821 and is accompanied by the signatures of 25 persons.
43-1821

BROWN, FRANKLIN M.   14 November 1833   BEDFORD COUNTY
Petitioner is E. W. Brown and he says that FRANKLIN M. BROWN and POLLY ANTHONY were married 8 January 1826, and that on 16 April 1826, she delivered a fine looking child. They separated, then tried again to live together, but could not.
Statement by Mary Brown of Bedford County.
Statement by Katherine Brown, who says she was present the day the child was born, and says that since that time Polly has had another child.
Petition is accompanied by the signatures of 5 persons.
110-1833

BROWN, FRANKLIN M.   1833   BEDFORD COUNTY
Franklin M. Brown was married in January 1826 to POLLY ANTHONY of Bedford County. About 4 months after they married, she had a child, not Franklin's. Polly said it was the child of her cousin, Alfred Anthony.
257-1833

BROWN, GABRAEL R.   1831   WILSON COUNTY
Gabrael says that his wife, ELIZABETH, left without cause and for the last 15 months has been living in a base way with Ill(?) Lane in City of Nashville. Petition is accompanied by the signatures of 16 persons.
82-1831

BROWN, HENRIETTA   1820   DAVIDSON COUNTY
Henrietta is wife of THOMAS BROWN. He left her 2 years and 7 months ago.
From her best information, he has been in North Carolina. Henrietta and
Thomas have been married 4 years and 11 months, "during which time he has not
lived with me 6 months..." She said she married with parental disapproval.
She has two small children. She wants a divorce and her name as it was
before her marriage- HENRIETTA BRECHEN.
Statement by Sabrina Farrow.
Petition is accompanied by the signatures of 9 persons.
99-1820

BROWN, PHILLIP   26 September 1821   LINCOLN COUNTY
Phillip was married on 15 June 1820 in Lincoln County to POLLY THOMPSON.
They lived in Lincoln County near Fayetteville until "the 26th day of April
last past," when she left and went to her father's in Lincoln County. Her
father is William Thompson. Phillip's trade is saddle making.
Statement is signed by several citizens of the area.
51-1821

BRUINGTON, SARAH   1829   JEFFERSON COUNTY
Petition of Sarah Bruington and Samuel Willson. Sarah was married ca 1809 to
JAMES BRUINGTON. He left after about one year and took up with another
woman. She heard he was dead, and she married Samuel Willson. They have
been living together about 13 years (since about 1816) and have 6 children.
Lately, they heard that James Bruington is alive and living with another
woman. Sarah wants a divorce from James Bruington. She and Samuel Willson
wish to be (legally) married.
Petition is accompanied by the signatures of 62 persons, "citizens of Cocke
and Jefferson Counties."
137-1829

BUCKHANNON, JOHN W.   10 September 1829   BEDFORD COUNTY
John was married to OBEDIENCE TURNAGE ca 1824 in Williamson County. In 1827
he was convinced that she was guilty of adultery. They had had children
(number not stated). He left her ca 1827. She has not reformed since he
left her, but has had a child about 8 months since, which is not John Buckhannon's.
Petition is accompanied by the signatures of two neighbors: John T. Neil and
J. W. (N.?) O'Neal.
213-1829

BUCKNER, DANIEL   29 September 1826   COCKE COUNTY
Daniel Buckner is now and has been for many years a citizen of Cocke County.
Some years ago, he married POLLY HAMPTON of said county. They lived together
some time in said county, then moved to "the Missouri," where they lived til
she left his bed. He returned to Cocke County. He wants a divorce. He
caught her in the act of adultery, and she has been absent from him for more
than two years. She has remarried.
Petition is accompanied by the signatures of 18 persons, "neighbors of Daniel
Buckner and some of us members of the church of which he is the pastor."
Statement by Benjamin Holland that he lived in Missouri and saw the house
where Polly and her "new" husband live.
77-1826

BUCKNER, JULIANA   1825   HUMPHREYS COUNTY
The marriage bonds between Juliana Buckner and VIRGIL BUCKNER are to be dissolved, upon proof, and Juliana is to be restored to all the privileges of a feme sole.
Acts of TN, 1825, p.264

BULLARD, LUCY   18 November 1833   GILES COUNTY
LUcy Bullard was formerly LUCY CAVELL(?). She married JOSEPH BULLARD ca 19 (19?) years ago. Joseph left Lucy " about 15 years since." She heard he was dead, and she remarried 7 November 1833 to Richard Jamor (Joiner?) in Giles County. Lucy wants a divorce from Joseph Bullard.
Petition is accompanied by the signatures of 18 persons.
Another statement by Lucy is that she married Bullard ca 1814. They lived together 6 or 7 years before he left. After her second marriage, it was rumored that her first husband was still alive. She wants a divorce.
263-1833

BULLARD, LUCY   1833   GILES COUNTY
The marriage bonds between LUCY BULLARD and her husband, JOSEPH BULLARD, are hereby dissolved. "The marriage heretofore solemnized between the said Lucy and Richard Jamor (is to) be....made valid."
Acts of TN, 1833, p.106

BULLFIN, MARY 1827   WILLIAMSON COUNTY
Mary Bullfin, wife of THOMAS BULLFIN, is granted the privileges of a feme sole.
Acts of TN, 1827

BULLOCK, DANIEL   1827   WHITE COUNTY
The marriage bonds between Daniel Bullock and wife, LYDIA BULLOCK, to be dissolved upon proof that Lydia abandoned him.
Acts of TN, 1827, p.191

BURLESON, HELKIEN   1833   no county stated
The marriage bonds are hereby dissolved between Helkien Burleson and his wife, CELIA BURLESON.
Acts of TN, 1833, p.61

BURNS, SALLY   29 July 1820   no county stated
The property of Sally Burns, wife of WILLIAM BURNS, is not subject to his debts or to his disposition in any manner.
Acts of TN, 1820, p.111

BURNS, SALLY   1825   RUTHERFORD COUNTY
"...It shall be the duty of the circuit court of Rutherford County to ascertain whether WILLIAM BURNS has for more than seven years abandoned his wife, Sally Burns, and upon proof to dissolve marriage between them.
Acts of TN, 1825

BURRUS, POLLY   10 September 1821   SMITH COUNTY
Polly Burrus was formerly POLLY WALKE. She was married ca 1811 to MICHAEL BURRUS. He mistreated her, and drank and gambled. They separated ca 1818, and she and her three children lived with her father.
Petition is accompanied by the signatures of Anthony Walke and a few others.
27-1821

BURTON, ELIZABETH   undated   BLOUNT COUNTY
Elizabeth Burton is wife of THOMAS BURTON. He left her for 2½ years and has
taken up residence in the Cherokee Nation. She has several small children.
Petition includes signatures of 7 persons, plus that of William Burton.
Undated Box, Legislative Petitions, Manuscripts Division (among 1820 papers)

BUTLER, SALLY   undated   no county stated
Sally Butler is the wife of EDWARD L. BUTLER. He left her and went to Kentucky.
He was guilty of providing no support for her while they lived together.
Petition is accompanied by the signatures of 19 persons.
Undated Box, Legislative Petitions, Manuscripts Division (among 1829 papers)

BUTLER, WILLIAM HENRY   3 September 1829   MONROE COUNTY
On 23 October 1823 William Henry Butler was married to USILLER LAWSON. They
lived together until 23 October 1824. She left at that time and since has had
two children by another man or men.
Statement by Usiller Butler Butler, formerly Usiller Lawson, relinquishing all
claims to William H. Butler, dated 7 September 1829.
Supporting statements by JOseph Callaway and Akellis Slapp.
221-1829

BUZBY, THOMAS   1799   GRAINGER COUNTY
The marriage bonds are hereby dissolved between Thomas Buzby and his wife,
MARY BUZBY.
Acts of TN, 1799, p.53

CABLER, JOHN L.   11 November 1833   DAVIDSON COUNTY
JOhn was married in 1817 in Davidson County to CHRISTIANA CORBIT, also a
citizen of Davidson County. They lived together happily for three years, but
then she changed in her conduct and feelings toward him, and refused to live
with him. They now have been apart for 23 years.
54-1833

CAHAL, REBECCA   no date stated RHEA COUNTY
Rebecca was married in 1831 to JAMES CAHAL in Rhea County. They lived together
until 1832, when he was charged with larceny and was jailed. He broke jail
and fled from justice. She requests thaty her name be changed to REBECCA
BEDWELL.
97-1833

CAHAL, REBECCA   1833   RHEA COUNTY
The marriage bonds between Rebecca Cahal and her husband, JAMES CAHAL, are
hereby dissolved. She is to resume her maiden name of REBECCA BIDWELL.
Acts of TN, 1833, p.13

CALDWELL, DAVID   1797   BLOUNT COUNTY
The marriage bonds are hereby dissolved between David Caldwell and his wife,
ELIZABETH CALDWELL.
Acts of TN, 1797,p.92

CALDWELL, SINDERELLA   24 March 1832   SUMNER COUNTY
Petition is Abraham Standfield. Sinderella Caldwell was raised in Sumner
County, Tn from about age 7, by her father, Abraham Standfield, where she
lived until 6 years ago, when she was married to WILLIAM B. CALDWELL, a citizen
of Maury County, TN. She was forced to go back to her father's, where she now
resides. She was age of 18 years at the time of the marriage and has had two

two children by said marriage. After they'd been married two years, he began drinking and kept bad company, and treated her cruelly, and threatened her life. He hired a wagon, took her to Sumner County and left her. After 3 months, he returned and promised to do better. She again removed to Maury County to live with him, but he resumed his ill ways after about a month. She learned of his illicit behaviour with one Elizabeth Lampkins. Sinderella left him again and returned to her father's. She has learned that Caldwell sold his land for $325.00, his Negroes for $425.00 each, and his stock and tools. William B. Caldwell's father is William H. Caldwell. She wants a divorce.
141-1832

CALLAWAY, ALLEN   1833   COCKE COUNTY
The marriage bonds are hereby dissolved between Allen Callaway and wife, SARAH CALLAWAY.
Acts of TN, 1833, p.99

CALLIS, MARTHA (PATSY)   1827   WILSON COUNTY
Martha is wife of ABEL CALLIS. He is in the habit of drunkeness and does not support her and their two children. She petitions for the privileges of a feme sole.
205-1827

CALLIS, MARTHA   1827   WILSON COUNTY
Martha Callis, wife of ABEL CALLIS, is granted the privileges of a feme sole, except that of intermarrying with another man.
Acts of Tn, 1827

CAMPBELL, JOHN   1820   KNOX COUNTY
The bonds of matrimony are hereby dissolved between John Campbell of Knox County and MARGARET J. McRhea.
Acts of TN, 1820, p.24

CAMPBELL, WILLIAM   1822   COCKE COUNTY
William's wife is MARY. She left him in 1820 and went off with a John Hammons of Cocke County. She left 4 small children.
Petition is accompanied by the signatures of 10 persons.
96-1822

CANNON, JAMES A.   1855   HENRY COUNTY
James was married in Henry County, Tn on 9 September 1855 to MARY A. M. WIMBERLEY, also a citizen of Henry County. One month after their marriage, Mary had a child that was not James A. Cannon's.
Petition is accompanied by the signatures of 52 persons, including that of Lewis Wimberley.
43-1855

CANTRELL, JOHN   2 October 1825   HAWKINS COUNTY
When he was about 20 years of age, John Cantrell, on 26 December 1824, was married to ANNY JOHNSON, who was then living with her uncle, James Watkins of Warren County, TN. Her father was present and consented to the marriage, after which he invited us to go home with him to Hawkins County in order to receive some parental gifts. She left him, John, 25 January 1825. Reports have it that she lives with another man in Warren County.
Petition is accompanied by the signatures of 37 persons, plus those of Benjamin Cantrell, Peter Cantrell, Moses Cantrell, Sampson Cantrell, and James Cantrell.
Statement made in Hawkins County 30 January 1825 and signed by several,

including Thomas Johnson, father of said Anna Cantrell, and by Mary Johnson, Sarah Johnson, Abner Johnson, the stepmother, sister, and brother of said Anna Cantrell, concerning Anny's leaving her husband.
32-1825

CANTWELL, LEWIS   16 September 1833   no county stated
Lewis's wife is JEAN CANTWELL. Both ask for divorce, on separate petitions. Jean signs her petition as JANE CANTWELL.
47-1833

CAPERTON, POLLY B.   1826   FRANKLIN COUNTY
Polly, wife of HUGH CAPERTON of Franklin County, is granted the privileges of a feme sole.
Acts of TN, 1826

CAPS, BENJAMIN   1824   DAVIDSON COUNTY
BEnjamin was married ca 1810 to SALLY MAULDIN, both of Davidson County. Sally left him in September 1821. She then lived with a William Carnahan. Benjamin adds that he thought she was a wi.dow but learned that her husband is still living.
13-1824

CAPS, SARAH   1820   DICKSON COUNTY
Sarah is wife of FRANCIS CAPS, late of Dickson County. She was married to Francis in April of 1818. They lived together til September 1818. He didn't give her any support and contracted several debts.
56-1820

CARD, ELIZABETH   1827   BEDFORD COUNTY
Elizabeth Card, wife of WILLIAM CARD, is granted the privileges of a feme sole.
Acts of TN, 1827

CARDWELL, ELIZABETH   26 July 1822   MARION COUNTY
ELIZABETH FERGUSON, otherwise Elizabeth Cardwell, was married to WILLIAM E. CARDWELL on 25 March 1819. She believes he has a former wife still living. He left her (Elizabeth) 15 January 1821, leaving her with an infant.
Statement by John Rice of Washington (County?) that Elizabeth Ferguson is the daughter of Alexander Ferguson, Esq.
Statements by Roswell Hall and Easter Hall that they were acquainted with William E. Cardwell while living in Washington and that Cardwell said he was married before, but that his wife had lived only 5 weeks after their marriage.
   However, Roswell and Easter still believe he had a wife in Kentucky and that she is still living.
113-1822

CARMICHAEL, JOHN   20 July 1822   COCKE COUNTY
John was married ca 1802 to MARGARET. They lived in MOntgomery County in Virginia for 15 years. Then they moved to Tennessee, he "having procured a contract in the Mail Department of the United States from Asheville, North Carolina by the way of Newport, petitioner's residence, to the Hazelpatch in Kentucky." Margaret refused to go with him to Tennessee. So, he left her in Virginia, "possessed of cattle, sheep, hogs, etc. and also in possession of a farm, being the dower of his said wife of the land of a former husband..." John returned to Virginia and found she had destroyed the greater part of the property he'd left her and had contracted debts. She decided to go with him to Tennessee, and they settled in Newport. She complained for 3 years against him for bringing her out of Virginia. Last winter he took her to visit in Virginia, and when he got ready to start home, she refused to go. John is

now 65 years of age.
Petition is accompanied by the signatures of 82 persons.

Statements by Mrs. Katherine Thomas and Mrs. Susanna Camron.
63-1822

      CARPER, ADAM 2 October 1833 DAVIDSON COUNTY
Adam's wife is SUSANNA, who left him October 1828. She has refused to return to him.
Petition is accompanied by the signatures of 28 persons.
Statement by Susanna Carper that she agrees to be divorced.
138-1833

      CARR, SUSAN D. 1827 MAURY COUNTY
Upon proof that Susan and her husband (not named) have lived separately and apart three years, the court is to decree her a divorce and change her name to SUSAN D. SMITH.
Acts of TN, 1827, p.185

      CARROLL, ANN 1829 DAVIDSON COUNTY
The marriage bonds are to be dissolved between Ann and her husband, NATHAN CARROLL, upon proof that he deserted her and for more than 5 years did not support her or his family, and had married another woman.
Acts of TN, 1829, p.259

      CARRUTHERS, WILLIAM 1807 SMITH COUNTY
The marriage bonds are hereby dissolved between William Carruthers and his wife, MARY CARRUTHERS.
Acts of TN, 1807, p.85

      CARSON, JOHN 1825 MONROE COUNTY
John was married on 5 August 1819 to CYNTHIA SPILLMAN. They had one child, after which she "refused to perform any of the duties which devolve upon the wife..."
Petition is accompanied by the signatures of several persons, including William Carson and John Carson, Sr.
191-1825

      CARTWRIGHT, WILLIAM 1809 no county stated
The marriage bonds are hereby dissolved between William Cartwright and his wife, POLLY CARTWRIGHT.
Acts of TN, 1809, p.18

CARVER, NANCY W. 2 November 1826 WILSON COUNTY
Nancy was married to BENJAMIN CARVER in 1821. He has left her several times and did not provide for her when he was with her. He has again left her. She has three small children. She petitions for the privileges of a feme sole. She has a small legacy bequeathed her by her deceased father.
Petition is accompanied by the signatures of 13 persons.
54-1826

      CARVER, NANCY W. 1826 WILSON COUNTY
Nancy, wife of BENJAMIN CARVER, is granted the privileges of a feme sole, except that of intermarrying with another man. She can sue for divorce.
Acts of TN, 1826

CASEY, NATHANIEL   1827   HARDIN COUNTY
A dissolution of the marriage is to be granted, upon proof of adultery on the part of his wife, CHINA CASEY.
Acts of TN, 1827,p.196

CHAMBERS, JOEL   28 August 1827   no county stated
Joel was married ca 8 March 1826 to MARGARET HULL. In the summer of 1826 she left him and has not returned. He believes her to be guilty of adultery.
42-1827

CHAPLAIN, ELIZABETH   30 September 1829   WEAKLEY COUNTY
Elizabeth was married ca 1822 to MOSES CHAPLAIN. She has had three children, two of which are now living. They lived together until ca 1828. At that time Moses became acquainted with a young woman in the neighborhood and then began to abuse Elizabeth. Moses left ca 6 weeks ago and took the young woman mentioned above with him. Before he left, Moses sold property to the brother-in-law of the girl he ran off with. He sold an occupant claim of about 200 acres for $6.00 to William Fowler. She wants a divorce and to get preference to the occupant claim.
Petition is accompanied by the signatures of 47 persons.
215-1829

CHERNY, JOHN   September 1833   GRAINGER COUNTY
John was married in November 1815 to SARAH SCAGGS. They lived together as man and wife until last few months. He cites as misconduct by his wife as: intoxication, her willful waste of his property, and committing adultery. They have three children that he is trying to raise. He feels he would be greatly delayed in court through ordinary means.
Statement by Elizabeth Seamore, involving Sarah's actions with one Thomas Dyer and one George Isom.
Statement by Barnett L. Mullins, involving Sarah's actions with James Dail.
Statement by James Sharp, who worked for John Cherney, involving Sarah with William Ferguson.
Statement by Moses Skaggs, age 39, Grainger County, that he has lived near John Cherney, who married his sister Sarah, for last 10 years.
Statement by Charles Skaggs, Grainger County, that he has lived with John Cherny for 8 years, and that John married his (Charles') sister Sarah, and that she has lived with her father since 1 January.
Statement by Lydia Popejoy that John Cherney married her sister.
Statement by Elizabeth Skaggs that Sarah Cherney is her daughter and that Sarah was involved with one David Smith. Sarah went off last January with one George Isom and said that she never intended coming back.
Statements by Harvey Wallis, William Hinds, age 36, Grainger County, and Jane Hinds.
155-1833

CHESNEY, JOHN   1833   GRAINGER COUNTY
The marriage bonds are hereby dissolved between John Chesney and his wife SARAH .
Acts of TLN, 1833, p.17

CHILDRESS, SARAH   1821   GILES COUNTY
Sarah, wife of NATHANIEL G. CHILDRESS of Davidson County, is to be granted the privileges of a feme sole, except that of intermarrying with another man.
Acts of TN, 1821, p.215

CHISHOLM, JOHN   1799   KNOX COUNTY
The marriage bonds are hereby dissolved between John Chisholm, late of Knoxville, and his wife, PATTY.
Acts of TN, 1799, p.53

CHOWNING, JOHN SR.   1825   ROBERTSON COUNTY
The marriage bonds are to be dissolved between John and his wife, MARY, upon proof of desertion by her for the past two years.
Acts of TN, 1825, p.277

CLARK ELIZABETH   22 September 1829   FRANKLIN COUNTY
Elizabeth in 1808 in Knox County was married to SAMUEL CLARK. They lived together 10 or 12 years and he then abandoned her and her two sons, the only children she has living. She says Samuel is a vagabond and lives sometimes in Lincoln County and sometimes in Alabama.
230-1829

CLARK, ELIZABETH   1829   FRANKLIN COUNTy
The marriage bonds are to be dissolved between Elizabeth and her husband, SAMUEL CLARK, upon proof.
Acts of TN, 1829, p.61

CLARK, JOHN G.   28 September 1833   ROANE COUNTY
John, a citizen of Roane County, was married on 12 October 1830 to WINNEY JAMES. On 24 May 1831 she delivered a child that he believes was begotten before their marriage. He had no sexual knowledge of her before their marriage. From affidavit of midwife, the child seemed to have come to full term. After the birth, John returned Winney and her child to her father. Statements by Robert Campbell, Rebeccah Ausborn, Marthy Scoggins, and D. C. Scoggins, all of Roane County.
104-1833

CLAY, MARTHA A. S.   1832   RUTHERFORD COUNTY
Martha is granted a divorce from her husband, SAMUEL CLAY. She is to resume her maiden name of MARTHA EDWARDS, and is given the privileges of a feme sole.
Acts of TN, 1832, p.97

CLEMENTS, LUTHER M.   1833   FRANKLIN COUNTY
Luther Clements is asking for rights of a feme sole for his wife because his father-in-law, Thomas Howard, wants to give property to his wife but wants her (Luther's wife) to hold the land as a feme sole.
216-1833

CLEMENTS, FLORINDA   1833   no county stated
Florinda, wife of LUTHER M. CLEMENTS, is granted the privileges of a feme sole, except that of intermarrying with another man.
Acts of TN, 1833.

CLENDENNEN, JOHN   September 1831   WARREN COUNTY
In July 1825 John was married to ELIZABETH HERNDON. They lived together 7 or 8 months. She left him. A short time after she left, she married William Kelley of Rhea County, where they now reside. Since she married Kelley, she's had two children. John Clendennen wants a divorce and the same privileges as if he'd never married Elizabeth.

Statement by William Brown, Justice of the Peace for Warren County, TN that he solemnized the rites of matrimony between Elizabeth Herndon and William Kelley.
Statement by Charles Clabough that he saw William Kelley bedded with Elizabeth in June 1830 when he (Charles) "was coming from the state of Georgia and slept at the house of said Kelley."
110-1831

          CLENDENNEN, JOHN   9 September 1831   WARREN COUNTY
Affidavit of Jonathan McMahon that he was present and heard William Brown solemnize the rites of matrimony between William Kelley and Elizabeth Herndon. Brown had a license to do same. He (Jonathan) believes Elizabeth was at the time wife of John Clendennen.
166-1831

          CLENDENNEN, JOHN   1832   no county stated
A divorce is granted John Clendennen from his wife, ELIZABETH.
Acts of TN, 1832, p.110

          CLEVENGER, THOMAS S.   2 September 1833   JEFFERSON COUNTy
Thomas was married 11 December 1829 to SARAH KIMBRO of Jefferson County. They lived together five months, then she left him and is living with James Davis of said county, and has been for nearly 18 monhts.
Statement by Daniel R. Murphy.
Statements by George Clevenger and Elizabeth Clevenger, William Ballenger and Hannah Ballenger, of Jefferson County.
Statement by Martha Bose that Davis and Sarah have had a child.
153-1833
155-1833-8

          CLEVENGER, THOMAS S.   1833   no county stated
The marriage bonds are hereby dissolved between Thomas Clevenger and wife Sarah.
Acts of Tn, 1833,p.92

          CLIFFORD, BRIDGET   15 October 1827   DAVIDSON COUNTY
Bridget married PATRICK CLIFFORD, a shoemaker, in Nashville in January 1823. Three or four months after their marriage, she discovered he was a man of "violent passions." He beat her and was in the habit of getting intoxicated. She became ill and he gave her medicine he had taken himself and had gotten from a Dr. Fisher. When she didn't get well, another physician (a resident physician of the town), a Dr. Pugsley, said what she was ill from was something she'd gotten from her husband who must have gotten it form a woman of bad character.
91-1827

          CLOSE, NANCY   1832   BLEDSOE COUNTY
The marriage bonds between Nancy Close and her husband SAMUEL CLOSE are to be dissolved upon proof that he deserted her for a space of two years.
Acts of TN, 1832, p.84

          CLOSE, NANCY   1827   BLEDSOE COUNTY
Nancy, wife of SAMUEL S. CLOSE of Bledsoe County, is granted the privileges of a feme sole.
Acts of TN, 1827

COBB, SARAH   14 September 1821   SUMNER COUNTY

Sarah was married 20 April 1817 to GEORGE COBB. She lived with him 4 months, then he left for Virginia to see his father living in Henry County, 11 miles below Henry courthouse. He never returned. She heard he was only 3 miles away on a horse belonging to a colored man named Peterson Stewart. This black man and another man, William P. Carr, went to see Cobb's father in Henry county, Virginia. They learned there was a Cobb there but he was not the father of George Cobb and didn't even know George Cobb. She said George told her his name was really CHEALLEY and that she had been deceived about his name being George Cobb. Sarah wants a divorce and her name changed back to SARAH BURNLEY.
Petition is accompanied by the signatures of william P. Carr and Aseaneais Dalton.
170-1821

COMPTON, SARAH   31 October 1833   HENRY COUNTY

Sarah is wife of JOHN COMPTON. He left her.
Statements by John Blakemore, Milton H. Marr, and Samuel Blake that John was accused of dishonesty and that maybe that was why he left Sarah.
112-1833

COMPTON, SARAH 1833   HENRY COUNTY

Sarah was married to JOHN COMPTON in Davidson County. After about 2 months of marriage he left her and was gone about 3 months. He returned and they lived together ca 12 months. He left again and has not returned. She has since learned he left the country to avoid prosecution for stealing corn.
185-1833

CONNER, HANNAH   1824   LINCOLN COUNTY

A divorce is to be granted Hannah from her husband JOHN B. CONNER upon proof that he deserted her for a space of two years and has made no provision for her support or that of her children.
Acts of TN, 1824, p.112

CONWAY, THOMAS JR.   1831   OVERTON COUNTY

In January of 1831 Thomas Conway was married to FRANCES POTEET. He was age of 18 years and one month when he was married. Two months after they married, she left him, "declaring she never would live out of her father's house again." Her father set off for Indiana in March and took her with him. She had a child on the way. Thomas says it is not his. He says she was 25 years old when they married and pregnant by another man.
Petition is accompanied by the signatures of 25 persons.
180-1831

CONWAY, THOMAS   1831   OVERTON COUNTY

Thomas Conway is hereby granted a divorce from his wife, FANNY.
Acts of TN, 1831, p.218

COOK, SALLY   18 July 1820   RUTHERFORD COUNTY
Sally was married to JOHN F. COOKE ca 4 July 1815. He left her with two
children. She had considerable property when they married, but John squandered it. Her husband is also guilty of adultery.
Statement by Archibald Harris, Benjamin Hasten, Thomas Pettypool, John Nelson,
and Hardy Pope.
93-1822

COOK, SALLY   1822   RUTHERFORD COUNTY
Sally Cook, wife of JOHN F COOK, is granted the privileges of a feme sole.
Acts of TN, 1822

COOK, SARAH   1827   CARTER COUNTY
The judge of the circuit court is to take cognizance of the application for
divorce of Sarah Cook of Carter County from her husband, JOHN COOK, and upon
proof of ill treatment or adultery on his part or absence with no cause, to
dissolve the marriage. Sarah is to return to the name SARAH BURNS
Acts of TN, 1827, p.262

COOK, WILLIAM   6 October 1827   BLOUNT COUNTY
William's wife, MARY COOK, left 3 May 1815 and took up with John Allen, and
has lived with John ever since. She has had several children by Allen, and
William has not seen her within 10 years.
Petition is accompanied by the signatures of 6 persons.
98-1827

COOPER, CELIA   25 October 1825   RUTHERFORD COUNTY
Celia Cooper was formerly CELIA WHEELER. She married EDWARD COOPER in March
1825. He mistreated her and then left the country after being found guilty
of various misdemeanors and impropriety of conduct. She asks for a divorce
and to have maiden name back. She has lived in the county 8 or 9 years.
Petition is accompanied by the signatures of several persons.
160-1825

COOPER, JAMES   23 July 1822   ANDERSON COUNTY
James' wife is SARAH . She committed adultery with John McGee and James H.
Wilson. John McGee's wife had not been dead long when he and Sarah Cooper
committed adultery. Sarah Cooper was SARAH ASHLOCK. She married James Cooper
on 24 August 1817.
Statement by Anderson Runnolds, Betsy Childers, Peggy Cooper, Matty Webb, and
John Cooper.
Petition of James Cooper is accompanied by the signatures of 60 persons and
also the signature of John Cooper, Sr.
Statement by Sarah Cooper, agreeing to be divorced from James.
4-1822

COOPER, NANCY   7 September 1823   no county stated
Nancy, formerly NANCY JONES, married ca 1818 or 1819 WILLIAM COOPER. He
mistreated her and then left her.
Petition is accompanied by the signatures of Richard Jones and Stephen Jones.
70-1823

CORBAN, ELIZABETH   30 November 1831   MONTGOMERY COUNTY
Elizabeth is the wife of BENNET B. CORBAN. He left her in October of 1830
"to go to Natchez, as he stated, for the purpose of collecting money." He
left her with 2 small children. She is now living with her father.
Petition is accompanied by the signatures of 10 persons.
188-1831

CORBITT, MICHAEL   1848   WHITE COUNTY
Michael petitions for a law that when a man and wife are separated and stay apart for 5 years they shall then be divorced.
235-1848

CORDING, JACOB   15 September 1821   MONTGOMERY COUNTY
Jacob Cording in 1812, a citizen of Beaufort County, North Carolina, was married to MARY NORMAN. They lived together 12 months. Mary was guilty of adultery. She got a venereal disease and communicated it to Jacob. On 21 January 1813 they separated. He moved to Montgomery County, Tennessee and has been an inhabitant of that county 3 years last June.
Statement by William James that he lived in the same neighborhood as Jacob in North Carolina in 1812.
177-1821

COUNTS, RACHEL   1812   no county stated
Rachel is hereby divorced from her husband, JOHN COUNTS.
Acts of TN, 1812, p.66

COX, PHEBE   1833   ANDERSON COUNTY
Phebe is hereby divorced from her husband, JOHN COX.
Acts of Tn, 1833, p.77

CRAWFORD, SAMUEL   27 September 1833   MAURY COUNTY
Samuel married MARY SELLERS 6 January 1829 in Maury County. After they'd been married 3 months, she left him but returned upon his request. She left again, for 2-3 weeks, but again returned. She continued to run off every so often but would return. ON 3 April 1831 she left and has not returned since. He accuses Mary of adultery. She has children, one of which is a female, crippled from birth.
Statement by Dickson Sellers, James Rutledge, James Sellers, and David Dodson.
10-1833

CRAWFORD, SAMUEL   1833   MAURY COUNTY
The marriage bonds between Samuel and his wife, MARY, are hereby dissolved.
Acts of TN, 1833, p.16

CREACY, NANCY   25 September 1827   WILLIAMSON COUNTY
Nancy was married in February 1807 to JOHN CREACY of Williamson County, a silversmith. Her father, Dan HILL, rented a house in Franklin for them and furnished John with tools to carry on his business. In about 1 or 1½ years, John commenced drinking, gambling, and abusing her. He left and everything was sold to pay his debts, even that that had been purchased by her father. John returned in 5 months. Her father fixed them up again, but John continued as he had before and in about 18 months had spent everything. She left him to go to her father's because John did not provide for her. John moved to Columbia, quit drinking, and did good at his trade. She went to live with him. In one year he started drinking again. He left her and their infant son several times. After about 2 years and 9 months, her father moved her to a piece of land near his farm where she has since stayed. John came with her and stayed 5 or 6 years, treating her cruelly before he left her with 2 small children. He was gone upwards of 3 years but returned to the neighborhood. She refused to lived with him. Her father recently died. John still comes to her house and threatens her, and once she had to go to her brother's house.
Statement by Elizabeth Spencer, a neighbor; Harry R. W. Hill, Elizabeth Almstead, Robert P. Currins, Garner McConnico, and John Buchanon, all of Williamson County, and by Martha Hill of Davidson County.
227-1827

CREACY, NANCY   1827   WILLIAMSON COUNTY
The marriage bonds between Nancy Creacy and her husband, JOHN CREACY, are to
be dissolved upon proof of his desertion and neglect to support his wife.
Acts of TN, 1827,p.120

CRENSHAW, ELIZABETH L.   1827   WILLIAMSON COUNTY
The marriage between Elizabeth Crenshaw and her husband, DANIEL CRENSHAW is to
be dissolved upon proof he deserted her and neglected to support her and
was convicted of horse stealing.
Acts of TN, 1827,p.210

CRENSHAW, HARRIET P.   1833   FRANKLIN COUNTY
The marriage of Harriet P. Crenshaw and her husband, DANIEL W. CRENSHAW is hereby
dissolved and rendered utterly null and void. Harriet is to resume her
maiden name of WHITNEY.
Acts of TN, 1833, p.8

CUNNINGHAM, JOHN   1809   KNOX COUNTY
The marriage bonds are hereby dissolved between John Cunningham and his wife,
ELIZABETH.
Acts of TN, 1809,p.18 (2nd Session)

DAFT, LANEY   1831   HICKMAN COUNTY
Laney on 17 March 1828 wass married to JOHN DAFT of Hickman County. He
committed many misdemeanors against her and left and has been gone 4 years or
longer. She sued for divorce in the circuit court in 1830 and from "report
current she had good grounds to believe said Daft was dead, which suit was
dismissed." She wants a divorce and hereafter to be known as LANY TROWELL.
Petition is accompanied by the signatures of 32 persons.
353-1831

DAVENPORT, JOHN   1831   HUMPHREYS COUNTY
John was married in 1829 to JANE ASH. She left right after their marriage
and refused to live with him. He was a widower at the time of his second
marriage, with 2 small children.
Petition is accompanied by the signatures of 43 persons.
268-1831

DAVENPORT, JOHN   5 September 1832   HUMPHREYS COUNTY
John became a widower sometime in 1829, and in December 1829, he was married
to JANE ASH. On the eve of the marriage, she refused communion with him and
left and has since removed with her parents to Illinois.
Petition is accompanied by the signatures of 25 "neighbors."
96-1831

DAVENPORT. JANE   1833   HUMPHREYS COUNTY
Jane was married 3 December 1829 to JOHN DAVENPORT. They separated right
after the marriage, for nearly 5 years now. They cannot get along.

Petition is signed by both John Davenport and Jane Davenport.
Petition is accompanied by the signatues of 7 persons.
66-1833

DAVENPORT, JOHN   1833   no county stated
The marriage is hereby dissolved between John Davenport and wife, JANE DAVEN-
port.
Acts of TN, 1833, p.62

DAVIS, ELIZABETH   1833   WILSON COUNTY
Elizabeth Davis, wife of ROBERT C. DAVIS, is granted the privileges of a feme sole, except that of intermarrying with another man.
Acts of Tn, 1833

DAVIS, JOHN   27 August 1832   OVERTON COUNTY
Petitioner is Nathaniel Townsend, who says that John Davis wants a divorce from his wife, LITTITIA DAVIS. LIttitia keeps going off to her father's house.
Petition is accompanied by the signatures of 17 persons.
77-1832

DAVIS, MARY   20 July 1819   BEDFORD COUNTY
Mary was married ca 1791 in Granville County, North Carolina to JESSE DAVIS. He abandoned her on 25 December 1816. She has been in Bedford County, TN for 10 years. When they married she had a Negro woman who has since had 11 children, and this was the greater part of Jesse's property at their marriage.
  Mary's father died ca 1799, and she received 2 other Negroes, a girl and a man. Jesse sold the girl for 200 acres where he lives now, in Bedford County. He also sold the man for another Negro man. Jesse was cruel to her. He threw her out 25 December 1816; he endangered her life and she's had to go to the neighbors. She is old, infirm, and has rheumatism. Jesse has much real and personal property, and she believes he is going to dispose of it so that she won't get any of it.
Statements by Timothy Sugg and Noble L. Majors.
(Petition was addressed to the 6th Judicial Circuit in Bedford County. It was rejected by this court and referred to the General Assembly.)
84-1819

DAVIS, NANCY W.   1821   no county stated
Nancy's husband is THOMAS C. DAVIS. He declines to live with her, and kidnapped her children from a grammar school.
Petition is accompanied by the signatures of 10-15 persons.
141-1821

DAWSON, DAVID B.   28 September 1826   FRANKLIN COUNTY
David was married in the summer of 1823 to ESTER WEEKS, daughter of Charles Weeks of Franklin County, in a forced marriage. Some men came and got him and took him to her father's house where a justice of the peace was waiting. David was 17. After they married, he found out she was given to intoxication and was a common prostitute. He left her.
196-1825

DEADERICK, GEORGE MICHAEL   1817   no county stated
The marriage bonds are hereby dissolved between George Michael Deaderick and his wife, POLLY.
Acts of TN, 1817, p.15

DEAR, NANCY   1812   no county stated
The marriage bonds are hereby dissolved between Nancy and her husband, GOODALL DEAR.
Acts of TN, 1812, p.66

DEATHERIDGE, DIANAH   August 1831   GREENE COUNTY
About 14 years ago, Dianah's husband, RUSSELL DEATHERIDGE, left her and married another woman.
Statement by Jonathan Dearee.
256-1831

DENNIS, ELIZABETH   10 October 1826   OVERTON COUNTY
Elizabeth was married in June 1820 to AZARIAH DENNIS of said county and
continued to live with him in Overton County until 17 June 1826 when she left
because of his cruel treatment towards her. When she married said Dennis she
had con. derable sums of money, but he has spent it. She wants the marriage
annulled and to "be restored to all the rights and immunities incident to a
state of celibacy."
Statement by Joanna Robertson concerning Dennis' cruelty to Elizabeth.
Statement by Dr. Michall Gabbort that he attended Elizabeth during her during
her sickness.
Statement by Jonathan Whiteside that he took food to Elizabeth during her
sickness and that she was not cared for by her husband.
Statement by Alfred Robertson that he'd heard Dennis threaten to beat Elizabeth.
151-1826

DENTON, EDWARD   October 1833   WILSON COUNTY
Edward in latter part of 1831 was married to SUSAN SMITH, a widow then of
Wilson County. She was impotent and "badly ruptured." Her condition was
diagnosed by a Wilson County doctor, Dr. McWhirter.
Petition is accompanied by the signatures of 48 persons.
Statement by Dr. S. C. McWhirter that Susan had had 2 children by her first
husband, and that childbirth may have caused her rupture.
29-1833

DENTON, EDWARD   1833   WILSON COUNTY
The marriage bonds between Edward and his wife, SUSANNAH, are hereby dissolved
and forever annulled.
Acts of TN, 1833, p.51

DEPRIEST, POLLY T.   1819   WILLIAMSON COUNTY
Polly was married 13 November 1817 to CHARLES C. DEPRIEST. They had one
child. He gambled and drank to such extent that "he has spent and made away
with all the property that I had when we were married." She accuses him of
adultery and asks for a divorce and that her name be changed to POLLY TURLEY
EDWARDS.
Statements by James Patton, Robert Patton, John Patton, Tilman Clark, and
Robert Sharp.
57-1819

DEPRIEST, POLLY T.   1819   no county stated
Polly is hereby divorced from her husband, CHARLES C. DEPRIEST, and she "shall
hereafter be named Polly T. EDWARDS."
Acts of TN, 1819, p.162

DEWEESE, MORGAN   July 1822   WHITE COUNTy
Morgan married AGNES LON. They lived together 2 years and then she left him,
refusing to return. She has committed acts of adultery.
Petition is accompanied by signatures of 12 persons.
Statements by John Cash and John Carpenter that they had seen Agnes with a
man named Thomas Sherley last winter.
Statement by William Usrey.
98-1822

DICKSON, SAMUEL   11 July 1822   OVERTON COUNTY
SAmuel was married ca 1812 to ANN MILLER. Ann has committed adultery and left the bed and board of Samuel for the past 12 months.
Statement by John Briggs that in summer of 1821 he saw Ann with Hugh Miller.
Statement by Susannah Boswell that in August 1821 Ann left Samuel and said she was going to East Tennessee to live and that she wouldn't return, and that Samuel should never have a divorce if she could help it.
Statement by Philip Jones that he saw David Collins and Ann Dickson in bed together.
Statement by Ann Miller that she (Ann) came to live with the Dicksons in March of 1821.
Statement by Polly Miller that Ann Dickson was at her house in May 1822 saying she would not live with Samuel again and that she would keep him from getting a divorce.
Statements by Hugh Miller and James Boswell.
46-1822

DICKSON, SAMUEL   6 October 1823   OVERTON COUNTY
Samuel is husband of ANN DICKSON. She left in 1821 and moved to McMinn County where she married John Combs in 1822 or 1823, and they continue to live together in Fentress County.
Petition is accompanied by the signatures of 10 persons.
Statement by David Neuman, Justice of the Peace for McMinn County that he married John Combs and Ann Dickson January last.
232-1829

DILLEHAY, STERLING   11 November 1831   HUMPHREYS COUNTY
Sterling's wife is POLLY. They lived together for 4 years. On 3 June 1828 she left him and his home in Reynoldsburgh and ever since has lived in Nashville.
Petition is accompanied by signatures of 6 neighbors in town of Reynoldsburgh and by 9 others who were neighbors from Hurricane Creek in Humphrey's County (his "old neighbors").
230-1831

DILLIARD, GABRIEL   30 October 1833   SUMNER COUNTY
Gabriel was married to SARAH J. JONES in 1820 in Sumner County. Ca 1 January 1825 she left him and left Tennessee ca 1831. They have been separated nearly 9 nears.
Petition is accompanied by the signatures of 4 men.
Statement by Zach. Talley.
273-1833

DODD, JOHN   1822   GREENE COUNTY
The marriage bonds between John Dodd and wife, SARAH, are hereby dissolved.
Acts of TN, 1822, p.124

DODSON, FORTUNE   12 November 1831   no county stated
Fortune was married 27 March 1828 to PATIENCE FIELD, widow of Bennett Fields, dec'd. She stayed with him til 20 May 1828, then left him and has not returned.
Petition is accompanied by the signatures of 12 persons.
103-1831

DODSON, JEHU   11 September 1824   WARREN COUNTY
Jehu's wife is NANCY. They were married ca 1811. About two years ago last April she left him. She returned after about two years, but stayed only a few days and left again. She was formerly NANCY CHRISTIAN of Warren County.

Statements by Martin Dodson, Elijah Dodson, Obedian Ginnings, Elizabeth
Ginnings, Jesse Ginnings, Leah Ginnings, and Elizabeth Dodson.
Statement by Jay McGregor that he lived ca 2 miles from Dodson.
143-1821

DOOLEN, SUSAN   21 October 1833   FRANKLIN COUNTY
Susan was married in 1829 to THOMAS J. DOOLEN. They lived together two
years. He has left and has been guilty of adultery. He left April last.
Susan has a Negro girl that belongs to her.
Statement in Bedford County by John Gowen that Thomas J. Doolen did execute a
deed of trust to him and Susan Doolen, his wife, for her benefit in February
to the following Negroes: a boy named Step, a boy named Spence, and a girl
named Eliza. Gowen understood that Doolen had made a similar deed of trust
to Thomas Finch of Franklin County, but asked to have it returned to him
after making the deed of trust to Gowen. Step and Spence were hired to
William Malgrew, and were stolen away in the night, Gowen suspects by Doolen;
they were taken from the county and sold. In April, Thomas J. Doolin with
his brother, Jordan Doolin, and a James Armstrong attempted to take away
from Susan the Negro girl Eliza. After Dolin left the country, his effects
were taken by the "officers" and sold for said Doolin's debts.
Statement by Joseph Hickerson, resident of Franklin County, that Susan at the
time of her marriage to Doolen was a widow with considerable property, both
real and personal. "Doolen had nothing." Doolen left and said he was bound
for Texas. He has recently been seen prowling about the neighborhood, "as is
generally believed for the purpose of stealing the only remaining slave. I
heard him say he had sold 8 or 10 of his wife's slaves. When he returned
lately, he was on foot."
Statement by James Wilson, William Wilson, and William Howard, all of Warren
County.
Petition is accompanied by the signatures of 28 persons.
99-1833

DOOLIN, SUSAN   1833   no county stated
The marriage between Susan Doolin and THOMAS J. DOOLIN is hereby dissolved,
and Susan is to resume her maiden name of SUSAN WHITEHEAD.
Acts of TN, 1833, p.98

DOOLEY, WILLIAM   September 1825   MCMINN COUNTy
William's wife is MOURNING DOOLEY. She left him and took up with Samuel
Shelton and lived with him as man and wife. William and Mourning have four
children.
Statement by David Shelton and Zebedee Shelton.
143-1825

DOSSETT, RODAH   September 1831   CAMPBELL COUNTY
Rodah was married ca 1827 to MOSES DOSSETT. They lived together better than
one year, then he left her. She is informed he is living with another woman
out towards the Ohio. At the time of her marriage and a long time before
that, she lived in Campbell County.
Statement by Nimrod Miller and William Heatherly that Rodah and Moses lived
together nearly 2 years before he left.
292-1831

DOUGHERTY, MARGARET S.   1827   no county stated
Margaret was formerly MARGARET HAMILTON. Her husband is CORNELIUS R. DOUGH-
ERTY. He became a habitual drunk, treated her cruelly and now lives in open
adultery with Mary Lynch. Margaret wants a divorce and to have the rights of
a single woman.
Petition is accompanied by the signatures of 10 persons.
185-1827

DOYLE, HARDY, CAPT.   October 1819   FRANKLIN COUNTY
Hardy is a merchant. His wife is BETSY J. DOYLE. She has been seen in the streets waving weapons and shouting profanities, is said to have been in low company, and has spread lies. She mistreated her step-son, Samuel H. Doyle. They moved to Winchester in December 1817.
Statement by Hardy Doyle, further, that he married in State of Georgia in October 1807 BETSY S. LUMKIN. She was peaceful until 1810; they removed to Tennessee in 1815 and settled at Stone Fort in Franklin County. He has sons and a daughter; some of these are by Betsy. Hardy asks for a divorce.
Statements by these men of Winchester: Leo C. Tarrent, Samuel B. Moore, Nathaniel Hunt, James H. Bradford, and John C. Pryor.
Statement by James Russey and wife Polly that they'd lived next door to the Doyles for about 10 months.
Statements by Robert Sharp, Thomas Hill, William Brittain and H. M. Davidson.
Statement by Daniel Eaves regarding the partnership of Capt. William Britton and Capt. H. Doyle.
139-1819

DRAKE, SARAH   16 October 1821   DAVIDSON COUNTy
Sarah as married 14 May 1810 to JOHN DRAKE. They lived together about seven years. She had three children by him, two of which are with her now. He left her ca 1818.
Statement by Ephraim H. Foster.
181-1821

DUNCAN, JOHN   3 October 1831   MORGAN County
John was married 14 August 1830 to ELIZABETH MILTON, then of Anderson County, but lately of Morgan County. They moved from Anderson County to Morgan County shortly after their marriage. On 31 August 1831 she became intolerable, ill natured, and said she couldn't bed or live with him anymore and left him.
Petition is accompanied by the signatures of 32 persons.
Statement by Thomas Jack.
51-1831

DUNCAN, RAWLY   8 September 1823   ANDERSON COUNTY
Rawly's wife is MARY DUNCAN. Mary left her husband and family (one son is mentioned) in 1811, and traveled in company with John Cole. She now lives with Cole as man and wife, and has had several children by him.
Statements by John Gibbs, John Sharp, Jr., and Abby Sharp.
152-1823

DUNN, WILLIAM   25 October 1826   SMITH COUNTy
William's wife is POLLY H. DUNN. She left sometime in the month of November and placed herself under the protection of John D. Wood. Sometime in May past, she moved to Henry County, "Obine River." William thinks she married John Wood.
Petition is accompanied by the signatures of 16 persons.
Statements by Polly Barnes and William L. Howell.
74-1826

DUNN, WILLIAM   18 October 1829   SMITH COUNTY
William was married in the forepart of October 1825 to POLLY. She left him and took protection under John Wood of Smith County and lives with Wood as his lawful wife, though well known to be in a state of adultery.
Petition is accompanied by the signatures of 23 persons.
117-1827

DYER, AHASMERUS   2 October 1821   SUMNER COUNTY
Ahasmerus was married in 1809 to LUCRETIA BRYANT. In March 1818 he had to go
to North Carolina and did not return home (which was in Christian County,
Kentucky) until November 1818. He found his wife living in adultery with
Elijah Whitney. In April 1819 she had a child and said it was Elijah's.
Ahasmerus presently lives in Sumner County, and is informed that his wife
lives in Lincoln County.
171-1821

DYER, MARTHA   1822   RUTHERFORD COUNTY
Martha Ann is the wife of WILLIAM H. DYER. She is to have the privileges of a
feme sole.
Acts of TN, 1822

EAVES, ESTHER   17 November 1853   WAYNE COUNTY
Esther was married to CLARK EAVES in August 1852. They lived together three
weeks, then Clark left. She wants a divorce and her name changed back to
ESTHER HERRELSON. Petition is accompanied by the signatures of 19 persons,
including William M. Herrelson, William Eaves, J. G. Herrelson, and Andrew
Eaves.
42-1853
43-1853 (This is same petition, from Montgomery County.)

EDWARDS, JOHN W.   1827   GILES COUNTY
John was married in 1812 to NANCY BROWN of Giles County. They lived together
about 6 years and had 4 children, during which time they would disagree and
part for short intervals. About 1817 he could no longer take his wife's
insults and violent temper and so made over all his property to George Brown,
the father of his wife, in trust for her and their children. She left and
went to live with her father. He gave her nine Negroes and other property.
John, however, was deceived by his father-in-law and was stripped of every
piece of property he possessed. Nancy filed her petition for divorce in Giles
County in 1826. He intended to let her have the divorce, but before they came
to court she ran off with Jason Hopkins.
Petition is accompanied by the signatures of 116 persons.
133-1827

EDWARDS, LEWIS   1809   no county stated
The marriage bonds between Lewis Edwards and his wife, MARY EDWARDS, are hereby
dissolved.
Acts of TN, 1809, p.18

ELDRIDGE, SAMPSON   1807   OVERTON COUNTY
The marriage bonds between Sampson and his wife, FRANKY, are hereby dissolved.
Acts of TN, 1807, p.85

ELLIOTT, SARAH   21 September 1825   WILLIAMSON COUNTY
SARAH PORTER was married 19 February 1822 to AMOS ELLIOTT in Williamson County,
where she yet resides. This was Sarah's second marriage and she'd had four
children by her first marriage. Amos left her on 24 July 1822. He went to
North Carolina. He mistreated her, and she says her only hope of support is a
small legacy left her by her father in the State of North Carolina which her
husband is trying to obtain. Sarah's brother-in-law Thomas Neal was executor
of her father's estate.
Statement by W. S. Webb.
141-1825

ELLIOTT, SARAH   1825   no county stated
The marriage bonds between Sarah and her husband, AMOS ELLIOTT, are hereby dissolved.
Acts of TN, 1825, p.155

EMTREE, ELISHA   1807   CARTER COUNTY
The marriage bonds between Elisha and his wife, ANNIS EMTREE, are hereby dissolved.
Acts of TN, 1807, p.85

ENGLAND, JESSE   1807   WHITE COUNTY
The marriage bonds between Jesse and his wife, MATILDE ENGLAND, are hereby dissolved.
Acts of TN, 1807, p.85

ENGLISH, ELIZABETH   1820   SMITH COUNTY
The marriage bonds between Elizabeth and her husband, WILLIAM ENGLISH, are hereby dissolved. Elizabeth English was formerly ELIZABETH TITTLE.
Acts of TN, 1820, p.97

ERVING, NARCISSA   4 November 1833   GIBSON COUNTY
Narcissa, of Gibson County, was married 19 December 1820 to KINCHEN A. WILBOURNE of Gibson County. They lived in Bedford County for some time, then moved to Henderson County, where they lived til 25 July 1828-1829, at which time he left her. After he was gone two years, she got an attorney to bring a suit for divorce. It was issued in Gibson County. She thought Kinchen was dead. On 18 October 1831 she was married to William Erving of Gibson County. She is now informed and believes that Kinchen is alive and living in Mississippi.
212-1833

ESSARY, SALLY   13 October 1831   HUMPHREYS COUNTY
Sally, of Humphreys County, was married in 1829 to JOSEPH ESSARY. HE beat her and treated her cruelly and did not provide for his family. He threw her outt of his house, and she begged him to let her stay as she was a considerable distance from her family and had three fatherless children by her former husband, Joel Pool, who had died. She went to a neighbor's and stayed. She then left and with her 3 children went to some friends' and relations'. Petition is accompanied by the signatures of 19 persons.
345-1831

EVANS, ELIZABETH   1831   HUMPHREYS COUNTY
The marriage bonds between Elizabeth Evans and her husband, ALFRED EVANS, are to be dissolved upon proof that he deserted her and left the state for the last two years and has failed to support her.
Acts of TN, 1831, p.80

EVERITT, SUSANNAH   1826   RHEA COUNTY
Susannah is the wife of SIMEON EVERITT. In 1824 she had had two children and was due again in December. He left her and married another woman and said he didn't plan to return. She now has three children to care for.
Petition is accompanied by the signatures of 34 persons.
76-1826

FAGAN, ELEANOR   1825   SULLIVAN COUNTY
Eleanor is the wife of JAMES FAGAN and is granted the privileges of a feme sole except that of intermarrying with another man, and can sue for divorce.
Acts of TN, 1825.

FALLS, MARTHA   1832   ROANE COUNTY
Martha is wife of THOMAS FALLS and is granted privileges of a feme sole.
Acts of TN, 1832

FALVEY, JOHN F.   19 September 1821   ROANE COUNTY
John was married in 1815 (1818?) to ISABELLA DONNELLY in Norfolk, Virginia. They moved to Kingston, Tennessee in June 1820. She left him that year and proceeded to go to Huntsville.
Statement by Hugh Fulvey.
25-1821

FARMER, JOHN   27 August 1823   SMITH COUNTy
John was married 20 April 1808 to FANNY H. ALLEN. On 20 November 1821 she left him. She became pregnant when he was absent from the state, and it was said by William Cox. She said she was going with the said Cox when she left John and John had heard she has married or is living with another man since she left John.
Statements by neighbors: Zephaniah Orange, Elizabeth R. Orange, Absalom Cox, and Judith H. Cox.
Statements by Benjamin Moore, Elizabeth Thomas, and C. T. Thomas.
Statement by Adcock Hobson that he was acquainted with John and his wife in Virginia.
104-1823

FARMER, ELIJAH   2 September 1831   MARION COUNTY
This petition is filed by Ephraim Prigmore of Marion County, who has been acquainted with Elijah Farmer, now a resident of Marion County for the last 5 or 6 years and has been living with a woman by the name of ELIZABETH SAMPLES as man and wife, and has three children by her. Ephraim says that he has known Elijah from his youth in Blount County until he became a man, and that Elijah had told him that he (Elijah) had married POLLY BLANKENSHIP and had left her. Elijah asked Ephraim to keep it concealed.
33-1831

FARMER, POLLY   4 September 1831   no county given
Polly is wife of ELIJAH FARMER. He left her ca 1824. She has children (the number not stated). She was formerly POLLY BLANKENSHIP.
Petition is accompanied by the signatures of 35 persons.
354-1831

FARNEY, SUSAN   1826   MAURY COUNTY
A divorce is to be granted upon proof in circuit court of Maury County if proven that SAMUEL FARNEY has absented himself from his wife, Susan, for 15 months without cause. Her name wouldd then be changed to SUSAN MOORE.
Acts of TN, 1826, p.62

FARR, GEORGE   October 1821   RUTHERFORD COUNTY
George was married in 1808 to ELEANOR GASSAWAY, and had several children by her. They lived together til 1817 when he was driven from her. She had a violent temper. She left Tennessee in 1821-1822 and went to Illinois where she lives in adultery. She has been absent ca 18 months. She took some of his property with her when she left.
Petition is accompanied by the signatures of 10 perons.
Statement by Robert R. Patrick that Eleanor is living in Gallatin County, Illinois in open adultery with Joseph Hale. He has seen them "going to frolics and other places together, this said Eleanor Farr's brother and sister gave me the same information."
152-1821 (Date is questionable. A similarly worded petition was filed in 1826. See 98-1826)

FARRAR, RACHEL P.   1833   MAURY COUNTY
Rachel Farrar, formerly RACHEL P. REYNOLDS, was married to WILY FARRAR in
Maury County. Not long after their marriage they moved to the Western District. After they were there a few months, he left her and went off with a
lewd woman to Nashville, recognizing the lewd woman as his wife for several
months. He then returned to Rachel and took her first to Nashville, then to
Franklin, and then he went back to the lewd woman in Nashville. Rachel had an
infant child, and tried to go to her husband in Nashville, but he was living
with the lewd woman, so she returned to her father in Maury County. Wily left
the state with the lewd woman, and Rachel has not heard from him in years.
Rachel is the daughter of a Revolutionary Soldier who died some months since.
232-1833

FARROW, LUCINDA   1831   SULLIVAN COUNTY
Lucinda was formerly LUCINDA LLOYD. In the fall of 1829, JOHN G. FARROW came
to Sullivan County recommending himself as a schoolmaster and succeeded in
getting a school. After teaching 9 months, he was married to Lucinda. In a
few days after their marriage he informed her that she was his 17th wife. In
13 days he left the country to parts unknown. She has not heard from him
except a letter from St. Louis, Missouri dated 19 Augsut 1830 to Mr. William
Childers of Sullivan County, in which he states that "when he left this county
he went on to South Carolina and had a difference with and killed his brother-
in-law and was then taking his escape to Texas."
Statement by Robert W. Torrell and Joseph Powell, Sr.
Petition is accompanied by the signatures of 18 persons.
168-1831

FICKLE, MARGARET   1827   SULLIVAN COUNTY
The marriage bonds between Margaret and her husband ABRAM B. FICKLE are to be
dissolved upon proof that Abram has been convicted as deputy postmaster of
taking money out of a letter in the post office. Margaret would then be
constituted the sole guardian of their son, Robert P. Fickle.
Acts of TN, 1827, p.196

FICKLE, MARGARET   October 1829   SULLIVAN COUNTy
Margaret petitioned in 1827 for a divorce from her husband, ABRAHAM B. FICKLE,
because he had been convicted of taking money out of a letter while acting as
assistant or deputy post master in Blountville and had been sentenced to 10
years' imprisonment. She didn't get her divorce in 1827, but in December 1827
a law was passed making it lawful for her to file her petition for divorce in
Sullivan County and if above charges against Abraham had been carried out she
shouldshould get her divorce. She wants a divorce and her name to be changed
to MARGARET RHEA.
150-1829

FICKLE, MARGARET   1829   SULLIVAN COUNTy
Margaret is to be granted a divorce from her husband, ABRAM B. FICKLE, upon
proof and the names of Margaret Fickle and her son, Robert P. Fickle, to be
changed to MARGARET RHEA and Robert P. Rhea.
Acts of TN, 1829, p.61

FICKLE, MARGARET   22 August 1831   SULLIVAN COUNTy
Margaret is petitioning for a divorce from her husband, ABRAHAM B. FICKLE.
She applied for same in 1827, and on 13 December 1827 an act was passed requiring her to file her petition in the circuit court of Sullivan County and prove
that Abraham had been convicted as deputy postmaster of taking money out of a
letter and was sentenced to two years' imprisonment. She at that time was

unable to get her divorce because of decision of Sullivan County Circuit
Court. In 1829 she petitioned the legislature again for a divorce, but again
the courts refused. She has not seen Abraham for more than 5 years, but has
been informed that he lives in Jonesboro and is dissolute. She wants to be
separated from him for life so that she can provide for herself and her son.
She wants a divorce and to change her name to her former name of MARGARET RHEA
and her son's name of Robert P. Fickle to Robert Preston Rhea.
150-1831   Witnessed by Samuel Rhea, Justice of the Peace.

FIELDS, DENSON   17 September 1813   OVERTON COUNTy
Denson was married in March 1808 to RACHEL PETTY. After 3 months he was
informed that she had been married previously to another man. Denson lived
with Rachel about 3 months and discovered she would go to bed with another
man, William Pettry.
1-1-1813

FINNIE, ELIZABETH D.   1824   DAVIDSON COUNTy
The marriage bonds are to be dissolved upon proof that Elizabeth has been
deserted for more than 7 years past by her husband, JAMES FINNIE, and that he
has failed to support his wife and child.
Act sof TN, 1824, p.129

FIRESTONE, WILLIAM   1831   McMINN COUNTy
On 28July 1825 William was married to SARAH LATTIMORE in McMinn County where
he has ever since resided. After only a few weeks of marriage, she tried to
kill him with a broad axe and later tried to poison him, a fact since admitted
by her to James Smith and Charles Bunch. In August 1828 he was informed by
George Thompson and Elijah Cantrell that while he was absent from home, William
L. Taylor committed adultery with her. On 11 February 1829, William saw
Taylor enter his house, and William caught Sarah and Taylor in the act of
adultery. He drove Sarah from his house. William wants a divorce.
122-1831

FISHER, BENJAMIN   1827   LAWRENCE COUNTy
The marriage bonds between Benjamin FIsher and his wife, PEGGY FISHER, are to
be dissolved upon proof of desertion for more than two years and of adultery.
Acts of TN, 1827, p.196

FLETCHER, POLLY   1822   WILSON COUNTY
Polly was married ca 1808 to EDMOND FLETCHER. They had four children, all now
of tender age. He left her for one year or more and then returned, and after
remaining with her for some time, left her again. He stayed in a state of
continual intoxication. Polly is reduced to a state of starvation by the
imprudence of his conduct. Edmond left outstanding debts which officers of
the law are trying to collect from her.
Petition is accompanied by the signatures of 12 persons.
106-1822

FLETCHER, POLLY   1822   WILSON COUNTY
Polly, the wife of EDMUND FLETCHER, is granted the privileges of a feme sole.
Acts of TN, 1822

FLY, CALEB   22 September 1832   MAURY COUNTY
Caleb was married ca 1824 to MARY HESTON. They lived together 2 years, then
Mary deserted him.
Petition is accompanied by the signatures of 70 persons.
129-1832

FLY, CALEB   1832   MAURY COUNTY
The marriage bonds between Caleb Fly and his wife, MARY FLY, are to be dissolved upon proof of desertion of Mary.
Acts of TN, 1832,p.26

FONVILLE, JOHN B.   27 October 1827   GIBSON COUNTY
John was married in 1825 to EVELINA RUTHERFORD. She was of a bad disposition, treated her children with cruelty and barbarity, and he could not live with her. He wants a divorce and the rights of a single man.
127-1827

FORD, MARY   1829   SULLIVAN COUNTY
Mary was married ca 1809 to LOID FORD of Sullivan County, "with whom she lived many years." (Remainder of this petition is too dim to decipher.)
262-1829

FORD, MARY   1827   no county stated
Mary Ford is granted the privileges of a feme sole.
Acts of TN, 1827

FORMWALT, AURELIA   November 1827   GILES COUNTY
Aurelia Formwalt, formerly AURELIA WHITE, was married in 1822 to WILLIAM B. FORMWALT and lived with him until May 1826 in Pulaski, Giles County, when he left her. He treated her cruelly and left her with their one child. She wants a divorce.
Petition is accompanied by the signatures of 12 persons.
Statementsby Fountain Lester, James Patterson, William R. Davis, Henry I.
132-1827   Cooper, and Thomas Underwood.

FORMWALT, AURELIA   1827   GILES COUNTY
The marriage bonds between Aurelia and her husband JOHN B. FORMWALT are to be dissolved upon proof of his desertion and failure to support his wife.
Acts o TN, 1827, p.122

FORMWALT, AMELIA G.   1829   GILES COUNTY
The marriage bonds between Amelia and her husband WILLIAM B. FORMWALT are to be dissolved upon proof of his desertion and failure to support his wife.
Acts of TN, 1829, p.219

FORMWALT, NANCY B.   no date stated   KNOX COUNTY
Nancy B. Formwalt, a resident of Knox County from infancy to the present time, was married 9 January 1817 to JOHN H. FORMWALT, then of Knox County. She was 15 years old at the time of her marriage. They lived together but a short time before he began mistreating her, and being drunk. She left him and went to her mother's and stepfather's home in Knox County. Nancy and John then tried a reconciliation, but he treated her the same and she again left and returned to her stepfather's, where she has resided the last 7 or 8 years. John lived for some time in Alabama but then returned to Tennessee. She asks for her former name to be returned to her.
Undated Box 1, 1825-1834, Legislative Petitions, Manuscripts Division

FORMWALT, NANCY B.   1825   KNOX COUNTY
The marriage bonds between Nancy B. and her husband JOHN H. FORMWALT are to be dissolved upon proof that John has not provided support for Nancy for a space of 7 years.
Acts of TN, 1825, p.261

FOSTER, JOHN   no date stated   HARDEMAN COUNTY
John, ca 4 or 5 years ago, being only 17 years old, "was deluded by DARCAS CANNON of Illinois, a base woman, who proposed to him, swearing two children to him if he would not marry her, notwithstanding the fact that the eldest must have been born before your petitioner was over 12 years old." JOhn, being young, poor and a widow woman's son, was persuaded to marry Darcus"in order to escape the penalty of the law which she threatend him with..." He left her.
Undated Box, Legislative Petitions, Manuscripts Division

FOSTER, NANCY   1822   SMITH COUNTY
Nancy, wife of EDWARD FOSTER, is granted the privileges of a feme sole. Edward has been absent since 27 February 1821.
Acts of TN, 1822

FOSTER, THOMAS   October 1821   CARTER COUNTY
Thomas was married in Carter County in July 1818 to JEMIMA ODLEBY. For some time he was in the service of John Nave in driving a team, which "occasioned his absence much from home." Thomas says that Jemima left with Henry Cook in fall of 1819 and proceeded to French Broad near Gordon's Iron Works, where they are now living. Cook offered Thomas 50 acres if Thomas would go and take back his wife and live with her. Thomas refused.
Statement by John Lyon that Henry Cook commenced working as a hammerman in the forge of Mr. John Nave in April 1819. He worked there until the spring of the following year. Jemima lived in adultery with Cook, and she left with Cook. Statements by Hezikiah Dannelly and Nancy Dannelly.
176-1821

FREELING, LUCY   1 September 1832   MADISON COUNTY
LUcy is wife of JOHN H. FREELING. Both had property previous to their marriage to each other. Lucy asks for privileges of a feme sole. Both John H. and Lucy sign the petition.
95-1832

FREEMAN, ELIZABETH   1827   no county stated
Elizabeth, the wife of HAMLEN FREEMAN, is granted the privileges of a feme sole.
Acts of TN, 1827

FREEMAN, JOHNSON   7 October 1831   CLAIBORNE COUNTY
Johnson accuses his wife, JANE FREEMAN, of fornication. They have no children. Statement by Melinda Chumley that Melinda lived at Freeman's house from September 1829 til February 1830, and that Jane was guilty of fornication, having seen Jane with Isaac A. Farris. Jane told Melinda she (Jane) was guilty of fornication with Benjamin Matlock and her own cousin, John Campbell. Jane laid in the woods with her cousin Campbell on the day Johnson killed hogs with her (Jane's) brother Jacob.
Statement by Lewis Chumley and Mary CHumley and Hannah Huffaker, and Phoebe Hicks.
147-1831
364-1831

FREEMAN, MARIA   10 December 1847   WILSON COUNTY
Maria was formerly the widow of Mathew Dew who died at his residence in Lebanon in 1828 or 1829, leaving her with 4 children and a "comfortable estate." Ca 1832 or 1833 she was married to JOSEPH P. FREEMAN. Joseph has spent nearly all her property. She wants privileges of a feme sole. She now depends for support on a house and lot in Lebanon, her dower from death of her first husband.

Petition is accompanied by the signatures of 2 persons.
46-1847

     FRY, MARTIN 31 August 1831 GREENE COUNTY
Some years ago, Martin was married to LETITIA WALKER. He accuses her of adultery.
Statement by Elizabeth Champlain, Sr. of Greene County that she lived with the Frys for 5 weeks during the summer of 1830 and that when Martin was absent, a man would come to his house.
Statement by Dr. Joseph E. Bell of Greene County that Letitia had come to him for medicine for a disease caused by one Andrew Kennedy.
255-1831
35-1833

     FULLERTON, WILLIAM 1812 no county stated
The marriage bonds between William and his wife, AGNES FULLERTON, are hereby dissolved.
Acts of TN, 1812, p.21

     FUSSELL, SUSAN 10 November 1823 DAVIDSON COUNTy
Susan, the wife of HARRISON FUSSELL, is granted the privileges of a feme sole and is constituted guardian to her children.
Acts of TN, 1823, p.174

     GALLAHER, MARY ANN 1809 no county stated
The marriage bonds between Mary Ann and her husband WILLIAM GALLAHER are hereby dissolved.
Acts of TN, 1809, p.18

     GARDENHIRE, NANCY 1807 ROANE COUNTY
The marriage bonds between Nancy and her husband, GEORGE GARDENHIRE, are hereby dissolved.
Acts of TN, 1807, p.85

     GARDNER, HENRY 5 October 1821 ROBERTSON COUNTY
Henry was married in 1813 to MARY L. CARNEY of Montgomery County. He was of Robertson County. She lived with him until 14 July 1816, when she left and returned to her father's home. She returend to Henry's house on 13 August 1816 and took eher Negroes, and on 17 August 1816 she took from his house all the property she'd brought with her to his house when they were married. She refuses to return or "to receive a portion of his property and agree to live separate and undisturbed lives which (he feels) would be conducive much more to the happiness of both parties living as they do in the same neighborhood."
Statements by William A. Earl and Elias Fort, Jr.
188-1821

     GARROTT, BENJAMIN 1832 OVERTON COUNTY
The marriage bonds between Benjamin and his wife, ELIZABETH GARROTT, are to be dissolved upon proof that she left Benjamin and Overton County and went to some other county or state in company with Hugh St. Clair, a free man of color.
Acts of TN, 1832, p.83

     GARTIN, DAVID 25 September 1827 CAMPBELL COUNTY
DAvid was married in 1818 to HESIAH BREWTON of Campbell County. They lived together happily for 18 months, then he returned home late one night and found her asleep in their bed with another man. David left her. He said he could not prove his statement.
273-1837

GEORGE, RACHEL   7 October 1841   no county stated
Rachel was formerly RACHEL STEEL. She was married to JESSE GEORGE. They
lived together until 6 January 1839. He treated her so badly that she left
him and went to her mother's. she has a son, now 2 years, 10 months old.
Jesse now lives in Mississippi. She is afraid he will take her son. She
wants custody of the child and wants his name changed to william Steel. His
name is presently William Steel George.
Petition is accompanied by the signatures of 28 persons.
16-1841

GIBSON, HARRIET H. 11 July 1820   STEWART COUNTY
Harriet's husband is HENRY GIBSON. Harriet wants a divorce because of Henry's
neglect of business, his cohabiting with other women, his abuse of her, and
because he discharged her from his premises for finding her out of his house.
Shortly after that, he removed to Kentucky with all his Negroes (10) and his
horses. He has lived in Kentucky ca 12 months and still lives there. The
balance of property he left behind was sold to settle his debts. She has 5
children.
Statements by C. B. Wilson and William curl.
98-1820

GIBSON, HARRIET   1B22   STEWART COUNTY
Harriet, the wife of HENRY GIBSON, is granted the privileges of a feme sole.
Acts of TN, 1822

GIBSON, PRISCYLLA M.   12 September 1829   JEFFERSON COUNTy
PRISCYLLA M. PARROTT was married 19 April 1825 to DENNIS GIBSON of Jefferson
County. On 18 September 1825, Dennis left and has been gone since.
Petition is accompanied by the signatures of 5 persons.
53-1829

GIBSON, PRISCILLA   1829   JEFFERSON COUNTY
The marriage bonds between Priscilla and her husband, DENNIS GIBSON, are to be
dissolved upon proof of desertion for two years by Dennis.
Acts of TN, 1829, p.97

GLADDIN, JOHN   12 November 1841   GREENE COUNTY
John petitions for a divorce from his wife REBECCA BALL GLADDIN.
Petition is accompanied by the signatures of 15 persons.
9-1841

GOLDEN, WILLIAM   30 september 1833   MCMINN COUNTy
William was married 8 March 1832 to LUCINDA FIELDS of McMinn County. She was
4 months pregnant when he married her, but he did not know it at that time.
When she confessed it, he left her.
Petition is accompanied by the signatures of 25 persons.
118-1833

GORDEN, THOMAS   1820   WILLIAMSON COUNTy
The marriage bonds are herebydissolved between Thomas and his wife POLLY
GORDON.
Acts of TN, 1820,p.108

GOWER, ELISHA   6 September 1832   DAVIDSON COUNTy
Elisha is a citizen of Davidson county and has been since 1780. In 1807 he
was married to JEMIMA PATTERSON. After only a short time, Jemima left and
went to her brother's in Dickson County where she stayed the latter part of
1810. She returned to her husband but only for a short time and then went
back to Dickson County, and he has not seen her since. Ca 1814 she was married
to Stockley Humphreys, a resident of Dickson County. she had 6 children by
Stockley. She is presently living with, as he as been told, and married to
(blank) Runnells, a very near relation of hers in Dickson County.
126-1832

GOWER, ELISHA   1832   DAVIDSON COUNTY
The marriage bonds are herebydissolved between Elisha Gower and his wife,
JEMIMA GOWER, formerly JEMIMA PATTERSON.
Acts of TN, 1832, p.37

GRACE, DAVID   1809   possibly CARTER COUNTY
The marriage bonds between David and his wife, ELIZABETH GRACE, formerly of
Carter County, are hereby dissolved.
Acts of Tn, 1809,p.59

GRAHAM, REUBEN P.   21 June 1822   DAVIDSON COUNTy
On 4 March 1818, Reuben was married to NANCY THOMAS in Nashville. She committed adultery and became a prostitute in Nashville.
Petition is accompanied by the signatures of about 15 persons.
111-1822

GREEN, DANIEL   1833   HAWKINS COUNTY
Daniel was married some 13 years ago in Virginia to MARY MCCAWLY. A short
time afterwards, she became dissipated. They remained in Virginia til 1828,
then moved to Hawkins Countywhere he now lives. For the last 5 years, they
have lived together very little on account of her vicious habits, but he has
paid her board wherever she did live, and has paid the debts contracted by
her. They have no children. She had lived in Claiborne, Hawkins, and Grainger
Counties, and now is living in Kingston, leading an adulterous life.
Petition is accompanied by the signatures of 22 citizens of Rogersville,
Hawkins County and 18 citizens of Rutledge, Grainger County.
Statement in Grainger County by John Easley, age 24, on 1 August 1833.
Statement by James Cheek, age 28.
281-183 3

GREEN, DANIEL   1833   HAWKINS COUNTY
The marriage bonds between Daniel and his wife, MARY GREEN, are hereby
dissolved.
Acts of TN, 1833, p.35

GREEN, MARTHA SMITH   19 September 1829   WILLIAMSON COUNTY
Martha, formerly MARTHA DENSON, daughter of WILLIAM DENSON of Williamson
County, was married to THOMAS C. GREEN on 10 January 1828. Thomas used cruel
and abusive language towards her and accused her wrongly of being intimate
with one of her relations and with his Negro man Jim. On the 2nd Sabbath in
July, 1828, a Negro woman came to their house, and Thomas began handling the
Negro in an indecent manner. Martha ordered the Negro girl out, but Thomas
went after her, and was gone 1½ hours. He returned to their house and admitted
to being carnal with said Negro girl. In August of 1828 Thomas beat Martha.
She carried the marks of his beating 20 weeks. She tried to escape to her

father's house the day after he beat her, but he sent his Negroes and dogs after her and made her return. She then became very ill. Shortly after, her half-brother, Col. Kearney, came and persuaded Thomas to let her go to her father's to be near the physician. She lay ill 18 weeks. While she was ill, Thomas abused her mother and oldest sister. She asks "the General Assembly to pass an act for her benefit, securing the right of all the property she may hereafter acquire by honest industry or donation of friends."
106-1829   Petition signed by Robert Henderson, and R. McGavock.
138-1829

GREEN, MARTHA SMITH   1829   WILLIAMSON COUNTY
Martha, the wife of THOMAS C. Green, is granted the privileges of a feme sole.
Acts of TN, 1829

GREENWOOD, JOHN   6 February 1825   RHEA COUNTY
(This is not a petition, but is a file consisting of three letters.)
First letter:
    Written by James Townsend of MOrganfield, Union County, Kentucky, addressed to William Smith, Postmaster, Smiths Crossroads, Rhea County, Tennessee, regarding John Greenwood who lived for some time at Smith's house, but has now returned to his wife and child in Morganfield. Rumors are that he has a wife in or near Rhea County. "Is this true?" John left Kentucky because he resisted an officer. His wife will live with him now if he has not married in Tennessee.
Second letter:
    Written by James Townsend to william Smith, and states that Townsend is dismayed from Smith's reply to his first letter, and his saying that Greenwood does have a wife in the Rhea County area. Townsend suggests that the Rhea County wife should file a bill in chancery for a divorce. Greenwood was married "here in Kentucky six years ago this summer" to MISS BETSY PARKER. He left her with child when he went off; he was compelled to go off, as he had struck an officer.
Third letter:
    Written by John Greenwood 19 February 1825 and addressed to Smith's cross Roads, Rhea County,Tennessee and asking that someone go to Nancy and explain how he was delayed and that he expects to get hom by the middle of May. He and Elisha Parker were having troubles in some other town. (The outside of the letter has the name NANCY LOUDWICH written in one corner.)
216-1825   (See petition of NANCY LAUDERDALE.)

GREER, GEORGE   25 October 1823   HENRY COUNTY
George was married in 1813 in Stewart County to RACHEL GELY. In September 1818 she left him and married Briant Guin and went down to Natchez.
Petition is accompanied by the signatures of 17 persons.
84-1823

GREER, NANCY   6 September 1831   MCMINN COUNTy
Nancy, formerly NANCY FARLESS, was married ca 1828 to CASWELL GREER. She was ..."almost in a state of infancy." They separated and have lived separate 2 years and 6 months. She wants a divorce, her name changed to Nancy Farless, her former name, and to "have and to hold any property she may have and manage the same in her own name."
In another statement by Nancy, she says Caswell treated her badly and she saw him in bed with another woman.
Petition is accompanied by the signature of James C. Greer.
Statement by James Farless.
8-1831

GRIFFIN, SARAH   1831   HENRY COUNTY
Sarah, wife of JESSE W. GRIFFIN, is granted the privileges of a feme sole, except that of intermarrying with another man.
Acts of TN, 1831

GRIGGS, SARAH   1827   HENDERSON COUNTY
Sarah, wife of WILLIAM GRIGGS, is granted the privileges of a feme sole, except that of intermarrying with another man.
Acts of TN, 1827

GROVES, SARAH   1833   SUMNER COUNTY
Sarah, wife of HIRAM GROVES of Sumner County, is granted the privileges of a feme sole, except that of intermarrying with another man.
Acts of TN, 1833

GRUBBS, LENA   October 1826   RUTHERFORD COUNTY
Lena was married to THOMAS GRUBBS in Rutherford County in April 1825. He lived with her until October following and then left her. He treated her cruelly. She has to depend upon her own ambitions and the kindness of an aged parent for support.
Statement by Hannah Mosely and Rebecca Crawford.
Statement by Nancy Underwood that Thomas carried a knife about saying he was going to kill himself, but Lena feared he would kill her.
100-1826

GRUBBS, SINE   1826   no county stated
Sine, wife of THOMAS GRUBBS, is granted the privileges of a feme sole, except that of intermarrying with another man.
Acts of TN, 1826

GRUBBS, SENE   1827   RUTHERFORD COUNTY
Sene, wife of THOMAS GRUBBS, is to be granted a divorce upon proof of desertion by Thomas for 2 years.
Acts of TN, 1827, p.60

GUTHERY, ALLEY   1 June 1820   SULLIVAN COUNTY
Alley was married 13 September 1814 to WILLIAM GUTHERY of Sullivan County. On 13 September 1818 William left her. In February 1819 William was committed to the jail of Blountville for horse stealing.
Statements by Elihu Embree and William Smith, acknowledged in Washington County, Tennessee.
Statement by William CAIN, father of Alley Guthrey.
40-1820

GUTHRY, ELEANOR   1820   SULLIVAN COUNTY
The marriage bonds between Eleanor Guthry, formerly ELEANOR COEN, of Sullivan County, and WILLIAM GUTHRY of said county, are hereby dissolved.
Acts of TN, 1820, p.26

GUTTRY, POLLY   1833   no county stated
The marriage bonds are hereby dissolved between Polly Guttry and her husband, PEYTON H. GUTTRY.
Acts of TN, 1833, p.77

GWYN, JINCY C.   30 October 1843   HENRY COUNTY
Jincy is wife of THORNTON P. GWYN. She wants feme sole. She has "several" children.
Petition is accompanied by the signatures of 54 persons.
29-1843

HACKNEY, JACOB   6 September 1827   KNOX COUNTY
In 1821 or before, Jacob was married to SARAH FISHER of Knox County. She left
him.
Statement by James McLemore that Jacob and Sarah arrived about 5 years ago,
that they lived in Knoxville a short time and parted, and that they have been
apart ever since.
Statement by Bowling Smith and Allen Perry.
Further statement by Jacob Hackney that his wife broke her marriage vows with
a man named Doughty.
219-1827

HALE, JOHN   13 August 1827   no county stated
In April of 1822 John was married to ANNA BROWN. Ca April 15 last, she left
him and eloped with a certain George Pasinger. John believes she is guilty of
adultery with George.
69-1827

HALL, MICHAEL C. A.   December 1831   OVERTON COUNTY
Michael was married in October 1830 to HOPY SIMCOCK. Since that time he has
found out that she was married twice before she married him. He did know that
she was married once before she was married to him and that that was to a Mr.
Simcock, her first husband, but he understood that Mr. Simcock was dead.
Since their marriage he now believes both of her husbands to be living.
The circuit court of Overton county at its September term 1831 "found a bill
of presentment against...Hopy Simcock for living with a man contrary to the
statues made...."
Petition is accompanied by the signatures of 19 persons.
15-1831
21-1831 (This petition says date of marriage of Michael to Hopy was 15 August
1829 in Overton County.)

HALL, WILLIAM   29 August 1832   HINDS COUNTY, MISSISSIPPI
William is husband of PHEBE HALL. Phebe separated from him ca 1 August 1829.
She is of a bad reputation and associates with women of ill fame.
Statement by William Ross.
49-1832

HALL, WILLIAM   5 October 1833   FRANKLIN and RUTHERFORD COUNTIES
William lived in Franklin County as early as 1809. HIs wife, PHEBE HALL, was
cruel to him. In 1826 he moved to Mississippi. She continued to be cruel to
him and was wasteful of what he earned, and was unfaithful to him. Hall
returned to Tennessee early in 1830 and has since settled permanently in
Rutherford County. Phebe left him ca 1829.
Petition is accompanied by the signatures of 42 persons, "citizens of Franklin
and Rutherford Counties."
Statement by Giles Richeson and Frances Richeson that in 1820 they were living
at Stone Fort Mills near William Hall.
Statement by Gabriel Jones and Polly Jones that they lived near Hall at Stone
Fort Mill.
84-1833

HALL, WILLIAM   1833   no county stated
The marriage bonds are hereby dissolved between William and his wife, PHEBE
HALL.
Acts of TN, 1833, p.139

HALL, SAMUEL   September 1833   WEAKLEY COUNTY
Samuel was married in July 1813 in Caldwell County, Kentucky, where he then resided, to POLLY HUGGINS. They lived together 7 years. She committed adultery with Robert Ritchie. There are 4 children of this marriage, but the father of these are not known for certain. In 1822 Samuel went off to Middle Tennessee with 4 or 5 horses to sell them and remained in Franklin County some 18 months, intending to return to his wife and children if her conduct was reformed. Only 2 of the children are now alive. Samuel is "yet" a middle-aged man. He has not been financially able to petition the courts of chancery. Petition is accompanied by the signatures of 84 persons, including that of James Hall.
Statement of Joseph Cooke of Weakley County that Samuel and Polly have been separated the last 11 years, and that Polly is now and has been for a long time living with one William Mahon as man and wife in this county. She has had 4 children since she married william Mahon.
Statement in Henry County by James Hall.
Statement of (illegible) on Henry County, that he knew Samuel Hall in Lincoln County (state not given).
178-1833

HALL, SAMUEL   1833   WEAKLEY COUNTY
The marriage bonds between Samuel and wife, POLLY HALL, arehereby dissolved.
Acts of TN, 1833, p.72

HALLUM, NANCY   1833 CARROLL COUNTY
Nancy, wife of MORRIS HALLUM of Carroll county, is granted the privileges of a feme sole, except that of intermarrying with another man.
Acts of TN, 1833, p.44

HAMILTON, WILLIAM   28 September 1832   BLOUNT COUNTY
In October 1828 William was married to NANCY MORRISON in Blount County. They lived together three months. She left him and he hears now that she cohabits with any and all.
Statement by John Coulter.
225-1831

HAMLET, CYNTHIA   16 October 1821   WARREN COUNTY
Cynthia, formerly CYNTHIA MILLER, in December 1814, while then living in White County, was married to WILLIAM HAMLET of White County. They had 2 children. In 1816 he began to treat her cruelly by beating her. Friends of hers persuaded her to leave him. She didn't want to do that and decided to try to change him. He grew worse during 1817-1819. In April 1819 he left her. She had just managed to get some food and clothing when in May or June 1819 he returned to White County where she still lived and took everything she had. He left again and in July 1819 was in Maury County. She has heard he plans to return again and take everything she has managed to get since he left. She wants a divorce.
Statements by Jane Miller and James Miller.
187-1821

HAMMAND, ELIZABETH   22 November 1826   WHITE COUNTY
She is married to GEORGE HAMMAND of White County. She has had 1 child. George beat her and treated her cruelly. He was suspected of horse stealing, and in Sumner County was tried and found guilty. He was put in jail, and she has not heard from him for ca 2 years. She wants a divorce.
Elizabeth signs the petition as ELIZABETH DISHAWN.
3-1826

HAMMOND, ELIZABETH   1826   no county stated
Elizabeth, wife of GEORGE HAMMOND, is granted the privileges of a feme sole, except that of intermarrying with another man.
Acts of TN, 1826

HANDY, ELIZABETH   1820   SMITH COUNTY
The marriage bonds are hereby dissolved between Elizabeth and her husband, ISHAM HANDY, of Smith County. Elizabeth was formerly ELIZABETH TITTLE.
ACts of TN, 1820, p.97

HANKS, JOHN A.   28 August 1833   LINCOLN COUNTY
JOhn was married in 1823-1824 in Campbell county, Virginia to FRANCES F. MASON. They lived together untila year ago when he learned she was inconstant and unfaithful to him. In 1830 he moved to Lincoln Conty and asked her to live with him therer but she refused to go. they've been apart ever since. Statement by Lucy Hanks of Lincoln County.
64-1833

HARDEMAN, MARY ELIZABETH   26 October 1833   RUTHERFORD COUNTy
MARY ELIZABETH PURSELL was married 29 July 1824 in Prince Edward County, Virginia to JOHN HARDEMAN of BUckingham County, Virginia. They settled in Buckingham County, Virginia. After 4 or 5 months of marriage, he beat and mistreated her. In March of 1828 he left her and went to Georgia. After he left her, she went to Prince Edward County, Virginia to John Pursell's, her brother. On 6 November 1831 she moved with her brother to Rutherford County, TN. They arrived there on 17 December 1831. She wants a divorce and to be restored to the privileges of an unmarried woman.
230-1833

HARDEMAN, MARY ELIZABETH   1833   no county given
The marriage bonds are hereby dissolved between Mary Elizabeth and her husband, JOHN HARDEMAN.
Acts of TN, 1833, p.121

HARDIN, CATHERINE   1823   SEVIER COUNTY
Catherine is granted the privileges of a feme sole, except that of intermarrying with another man and can apply to the circuit court for a divorce. (Name of husband is not stated.)
Acts of TN, 1823, p.144

HARLIN, NANCY   1827   HICKMAN COUNTy
Nancy, wife of JEREMIAH HARLIN, is granted the privileges of a feme sole.
Acts of TN, 1827

HARMON, GILLY   2 OCtober 1833   DICKSON COUNTY
Gilly was married in August 1828 to LEWIS HARMON. They lived together til May 1829. Then he wished a final separation and did move out. He has lived with 2 other women since then and has 2 or 3 children.
Petition is accompanied by the signatures of 18 persons.
9-1833

HARMON, GILLY   1833   DICKSON COUNTY
Gilly, wife of LEWIS HARMON, is restored to the rights of a feme sole. The marriage bonds between Gilly and Lewis are hereby dissolved.
Acts of TN, 1833, p.52

HARMON, JANE   1827   BLEDSOE COUNTY
In February 1822 JANE HUTCHISON was married to JOHN HARMON, both of Bledsoe
County, where she now lives. She lived with John until November 1823, when he
left her. She does not know where he is, and has heard by some that he remarried and by others that he died sometime ago in the Arkansas Territory.
Petition is accompanied by the signatures of 16 persons.
277-1827

HARP, MARIA   1831   DAVIDSON COUNTY
The marriage bonds are to be dissolved between Maria and her husband, NATHANIEL
HARP, upon proof that Nathaniel has deserted her for the past 3 years and has
failed to support Maria and her two children.
Acts of TN, 1831, p.79

HARPER, ELIZABETH   1833   SUMNER COUNTY
Elizabeth was married to JOSEPH HARPER 25 years ago in Sumner County. He
abandoned her 20 years ago. She had a daughter by him, Nancy, who still lives
with her. Joseph went to Kentucky and married and is still married to this
other woman.
Statement by 7 citizens of Sumner regarding the petition of Noah Cotton and
Elizabeth Harper.
Statement by Noah Cotton that he has had the following natural children by
Elizabeth Harper: Sophia, Harriett, Zelda, John M., James L., and Talitha,
Mary, and Alexander T. Harper and wants to legitimize them and change their
names to Cotton, and wishes to change the name of Elizabeth's child by Harper--
Nancy, also to Cotton. Noah and Elizabeth have been living together about 18
years.
259-1833

HARPER, ELIZABETH   1833   no county stated
The marriage bonds are hereby dissolved between Elizabeth and her husband,
JOSEPH HARPER. Elizabeth is to resume the name of COTTON and all eight child-
ren's names are to be changed to Cotton. "They (the children) shall enjoy all
the rights and privileges as heirs of Noah Cotton of Sumner County."
Acts of TN.1833, p.50

HARRIS, AMEY   1822   OVERTON COUNTY
Amey on 17 March 1814, she being a feme sole, married ANDREW HARRIS. He left
after 3 months of marriage. He returned after being gone for about 12 months
and wanted her to take him back. She received him back (she "had an infant
child by then"), and only a short time after they started living together
again, he began to ill treat her and left her again and took up with Peggy
Howard and lived with her in adultery. He later took her (Amey) to the Indian
Nation and left her in a camp among "savages." She got back to Overton County,
but Andrew refused to live with her.
Petition is accompanied by the signatures of 40 persons.
110-1822

HARRIS, AMEY   1831   GREENE COUNTY
Amey, wife of WILLIAM HARRIS of Greene County, is granted the privileges of a
feme sole, except that of intermarrying with another man.
Acts of TN, 1831

HARRIS, JOURDEN   1825-1826   JACKSON COUNTy
Jourden was married when he was 18 years old to REBECCA EMBRY. She left him
ca 1823-1824 and went to the Western District.

Petition is accompanied by the signatures of 50 persons.
Statement by Patsy Embry and Anna Harris.
Statement by Robert Harris and 8 other persons that Rebecca had left Jackson
County with her father, John Embry, to go to the Western District.
109-1825
186-1826

HARRIS, JOURDEN   1826   JACKSON COUNTY
The marriage bonds are to be dissolved between Jourden and his wife, REBECCA
HARRIS, upon proof that Rebecca has deserted him for more than 2 years.
Acts of TN, 1826, p.89

HARRIS, JULIA G.   1822   RUTHERFORD COUNTY
The marriage bonds are hereby dissolved between Julia G. Harris, formerly Julia
G. MARSHALL, and her husband, GEORGE E. HARRIS.
Acts of TN, 1822, p.49

HARRIS, MARY   1827   no county stated
Mary is wife of RICHARD C. HARRIS   "Several years ago" her husband treated
her so cruelly she left him. He was also guilty of adultery and was the
reputed father of several children. She wants a divorce and the rights of a
feme sole.
48-1827

HARRIS, MARY   1827   MAURY COUNTY
The marriage bonds are to be dissolved between Mary Harris and her husband,
RICHARD C. HARRIS, upon proof of adultery by Richard. Mary "may change her
name as she desires."
Acts of TN, 1827, p.185

HAWES, TABITHA T.   1827   JACKSON COUNTY
Tabitha T. Hawes, wife of WILLIAM HAWES, is granted the privileges of a feme
sole.
Acts of TN, 1827

HAYWORTH, ABSALOM   4 October 1829   no county stated
On 14 March 1826 (?) Absalom was married to SARAH LONG, and has since resided
in city of Augusta and state of Georgia. He accuses his wife of harsh treatment and bad temper towards him. This is his second marriage, and he has 2
daughters who were approaching womanhood when his first wife died. He also
has other children. He carried his second wife to South Carolina to see her
relatives, and she refused to go back home with him. He left her, with money,
at her brother's. He feels she never will return. She has been away more
than 18 months, and he understands she now lives near Mobile, Alabama.
Petition is accompanied by the signatures of 18 persons.
224-1829

HEARN, MILLEY   1827   WILSON COUNTY
Milley, the wife of GEORGE HEARN, JR. of wilson county, is granted the privi-
leges of a feme
Acts of TN, 1827

HENDERSON, JOHN   October 1827   WARREN COUNTY
In October of 1824 John was married to POLLY THOMAS of Warren county. Since
that time she has been "greatly of lewdness" with James Holson.

Statement 5 July 1827 by Polly Henderson: "I, Polly Henderson, wife of John Henderson, son of Robert Henderson, now living in Warren County on Stones River".....grants John his freedom and says she does not plan to return to him. Witnesses by James Holson and John Barrott.
171-1827

HENDERSON, JOSEPH, JR.   1825   GREENE COUNTY
The marriage bonds are to be dissolved between Joseph and his wife, SARAH HENDERSON upon proof that Sarah has been guilty of acts of incontinence with any other person or persons before marriage with Joseph and that she was pregnant previous to that marriage.
Acts of TN, 1825, p.308

HENDERSON, POLLY   1821   MORGAN COUNTY
Polly was married in August 1818 to CARTER HENDERSON, at that time a citizen of Morgan County. On 11 July 1819 he left her and went off with Sally Dalton. Since he's left Polly, she went to live with her father, John DAVIS, in Morgan County.
Petition is accompanied by the signatures of 23 persons, and also by John M. Davis and Thomas Davis.
96-1821

HENDRY, CHLOE   2 September 1813   WASHINGTON COUNTy
Chloe was married in early life to WILLIAM HENDRY. They lived together many years until she had evidence of his having committed adultery, and he did not deny having issue from this woman. Better than 7 years ago, he left Chloe and left Washington County and went to Greene County, where he has taken another wife. William allows Chloe sufficient alimony.
28-2-1813

HENLEY, RHODA   31 August 1821   ROBERTSON COUNTy
RHODA BYRNS was married ca 1807 to ISAAC HENLEY of Robertson County, where they then lived. About 1817 he left and she heard he was in Missouri where he has taken up another woman to be his wife and has children. Rhoda asks for a divorce and that her name be restored to RHODA BYRNS.
52-1821

HICKERSON, ELLINOR   1831   SUMNER COUNTY
Ellinor, wife of EZEKIEL HICKERSON is granted the privileges of a feme sole except that of intermarrying with another man.
Acts of TN, 1831

HICKLIN, MARY T.   8 October 1821   MAURY COUNTy
Mary T. was married 28 October 1818 to AVERY M. HICKLIN. She lived with him til 22 April 1819 when Avery "left her in a delicate position." He had but little property, only what he received when he married her, and he left her with debts so that all the property was sold to pay his debts. Some larger debts are still unpaid. She wants a divorce and to have her name changed to MARY T. HUNTER.
Statement by David Craig, Samuel H. Smith, and Tilman A. Crisp that A. M. Hicklin is now residing in Kentucky.
42-1821

HICKLIN, POLLY   1824   MAURY COUNTy
The marriage bonds are to be dissolved between Polly Hicklin and her husband, AVERY M. Hicklin, upon proof of desertion by Avery for more than 5 years and

that he failed to support Polly or her child, Henry W. Hicklin. "The said
Polly Hicklin shall hereafter be called by the name of POLLY HUNTER, and her
child, Henry W.Hicklin, shall be called by the name of Henry W. Hunter."
Acts of TN, 1824,p.129

              HICKMAN, SNOWDEN   24 October 1827   WILSON COUNTY
Snowden is husband of MILLY HICKMAN. She left him in summer of 1823. She
went to John W. Nichols' to live. Also, in 1823 she came with 9 or 10 men
armed with clubs and brought a wagon and took by violence all the property
that she had before she married Snowden. She left Wilson County and moved to
Fayette County, near Summerville.
Statement by Elijah Truett.
294-1827

              HICKMAN, SNOWDEN   1827   WILSON COUNTY
Themarriage bonds are to be dissolved between Snowden and his wife, MILLY
HICKMAN, upon proof of desertion for more than 2 years by Milly.
Acts of TN, 1827, p.110

              HICKMAN, WILLIAM   October 1829   MAURY COUNTY
William is husband of POLLY HICKMAN. She left him and eloped with John West.
Statements by Nancy Meaders and Nazareth Meaders.
Petition is accompanied by signatures of 57 neighbors.
268-1829

              HICKMAN, WILLIAM   1827   GILES COUNTY
The marriage bonds are to be dissolved between William and his wife, POLLY
HICKMAN, upon proof of desertion by Polly and her elopement with another man.
Acts of TN, 1827,p.121

              HICKS, STEPHEN   August 1833   WARREN COUNTY
In October of 1829 Stephen Hicks was married to JANE TAYLOR, both of Warren
County. She lived with him til July 1830, then left him and refuses to return.
Statements by John Reeves, Josiah Capshaw, and Francis Cantrell.
Statement by Henry Hicks that he heard "...William Taylor say that Jane Hicks
and William Wats have agreed to live together, ...and that William Taylor,
Jane's father, said in his church that he should have killed...Jane ...had he
not been prevented..."
199-1833

              HILL, CAROLINE   28 November 1829   MAURY COUNTY
Caroline is wife of BENNET HILL. Ca 1828 Bennet proposed marriage to her.
When asked what prospects he had for a livelihood, Hill told Caroline's father
and her brother that he had 2 Negroes coming from his uncle, an old bachelor
in North Carolina, that he had $1,000.00, a legacy from his aunt which he
would be in possession of "this fall," and that he had $300.00 to get a place
to live. Hill's health was not good. Within a day or two after their union,
CAroline was informed by Hill's close connections that Hill was a swindler in
all of the above, that he was no good and would not work. Caroline wants a
divorce and her name changed back to her original name, CAROLINE FRASER.
Statement by Robert Hill, Carolina Hill, and D. N. Fraser, before J. H. Fraser.
59-1829
303-1829

              HILL, ELIZABETH   19 August 1825   FRANKLIN COUNTy
Elizabeth was married ca 1815 to ALFRED HILL. He left her after about 4
months and now lives in Alabama with another woman. She is too poor to apply
to the courts for relief.
112-1825

HILL, LEWIS   29 July 1822   BEDFORD COUNTY
Lewis says that both he and his wife, SEINA HILL, want a divorce and that they have already parted.
Statement on 6 July 1822 by Cyna Hill in Wilson County that she declares her marriage void.
108-1822

HINES, JOHN B.   1841   JOHNSON COUNTY
John B. is husband of ELIZABETH HINES. She left him ca February 1839 and emigrated to lower part of North Carolina.
105-1841

HOGAN, JANE   1833   PERRY COUNTY
Jane was married ca 1826 in Perry County to WILLIAM HOGAN. They lived together 3 days and nights, then he left her and went somewhere on the Ohio or Mississippi and has not returned.
Petition is accompanied by the signatures of 20 persons.
167-1833

HOLDWAY, HUGH B.   1 November 1851   SCOTT COUNTY
Hugh B., at age 19 was married June 1847 to REBECCAH NEWPORT. He enlisted in the U.S. Army in September 1847 against Mexico. Returning home in August of 1848, he found his wife living with Mr. Philie Begly. In July 1851, his wife left the state with a B. Embrey and went to Kentucky.
Petition is accompanied by the signatures of 50 persons, including J. W. Holdway.
74-1851

HOLLEY, JOHN   30 september 1827   LINCOLN COUNTY
John was married in Lincoln county on 15 June 1821 to CELIA ODUM. they lived together until 2 years ago, when she left without cause, and continues to refuse to live with him. He requests a divorce.
Petition is accompanied by the signatures of 35 persons, including Sion Holley, David Holley, Mary Holley, and William Holley.
197-1827

HOLT, SARAH   8 September 1825   GREENE COUNTY
Sarah was married 1 July 1800 to JOSEPH HOLT. They lived together until 24 November 1822, when he left Tennessee, taking with him a girl of infamous character named Catherine Smith, whom he claims for his wife. Sarah Holt has no relations, and was raised as an orphan girl by James Galbraith, Esq., a citizen of Greene County, to whom she has returned since her husband left her.
205-1825

HONEYCUT, ELIZABETH   25 November 1845   MORGAN COUNTy
Elizabeth is wife of ROBERT HONEYCUT and requests a divorce.
Petition is accompanied by the signatures of 6 persons.
37-1845

HOOKINS, MARY   1845   ANDERSON COUNTy
Mary requests a divorce from her husband, WILLIAM "BILLY" HOOKINS. They have 2 children. She has suffered physical abuse.
Petition is accompanied by the signatures of 24 persons.
25-1845

HOOPER, MARY S.   August 1823   PERRY County
Mary S. was married in 1812 to CLARENDER HOOPER of KEntucky, she being then
nearly 16 years old. Sometime after their marriage, they moved to Illinois.
They were happy for several years til she found out her husband was maintaining
a correspondence with Cynthia Merritt who lived in their neighborhood. He
privately made arrangements to dispose of all his property before eloping with
Cynthia. He conveyed all of his property to a brother of Cynthia's. Clarender
then left Mary with 3 infant children. Mary told her problem to her father,
then a citizen of Humphreys County, Tennessee. With his help, she left Illinois and moved to Tennessee where she has since resided. Clarender left Mary
in 1821. Mary's father recently died.
129-1823

HOOPER, MARY S.   1823   PERRY COUNTY
Mary Hooper is granted the privileges of a feme sole, except that of inter-
marrrying with another man, and can petition for a divorce.
Acts of TN, 1823, p.116

HOPSON, SALLY   1835   no county stated
Sally was married about 1810 to HARROD HOPSON. They had 12 children. Harrod
left her in 1832 and is living with another woman.
Petition is accompanied by the signatures of 9 persons.
89-1835

HOPSON, SALLY   1831   CLAIBORNE COUNTy
Sally, wife of HARROD HOPSON, is granted the privileges of a feme sole, except
that of intermarrying with another man.
Acts of TN, 1831

HORNBERGER, PHILIP   1812   no county stated
The marriage bonds are hereby dissolved between Philip and his wife, ALICE
HORNBERGER.
Acts of TN, 1812, p.66

HORTON, WILLIAM   30 October 1833   CARROLL COUNTY
William was married on 13 November 1828 to PATSEY,"MARTHA". She left him in
February 1829.
Statement by S. F. Ellin that Patsy had said that William wouldn't let her
children live with them. William denied it and said he'd offered to let her
son, about 16 years old, come to live with them. Patsy also had a daughter
10-11 years old.
Statement by John Parker.
219-1833

HOWARD, BENJAMIN   1825   ROANE COUNTy
Benjamin was married to MAHALY MCCOMAC. After 2 years of marriage, she eloped,
leaving husband and child, and going off with another man.
Petition is accompanied by the signatures of 50 persons, including Reuben
Howard, Alexander Howard, and James Howard.
127-1825

HOWETH, JOHN 28 August 1832 HAMILTON COUNTy
John is married to AQUILLA. She left him in January of 1831.
Petition is accompanied by the signatures of 13 persons.
107-1832

HUFF, ANN   1822   no county stated
ANN GILBREATH was married in 1812 to JOHN HUFF. He married her with a view to defraud her of her estate, and whom he soon after abandoned. She is granted the privileges of a feme sole, except that of intermarrying with another man.
Acts of TN, 1822

HUGHLETT, JOHN   1820   HICKMAN COUNTY
JOhn and his wife, TEANY HUGHLETT, have been married "a considerable number of years." They have no children. They have "secret reasons" for wanting a divorce. Both sign the petition.
Witnessed by Robert Totty, Jr. and John Estes.
Petition is accompanied by the signatures of 15 persons.
45-1820

HULME, SUSAN   1822   WILLIAMSON COUNTY
Petition is written by Susan's father, Stephen CHILDRESS. In 1812, she, SUSAN CHILDRESS of Williamson County, was married to THOMAS HULME. In 1820 she was forced to separate from him. She wants rights of a feme sole.
61-1822

HULME, SUSAN   1822   WILLIAMSON COUNTy
Susan, wife of THOMAS HULME of Williamson County, is granted the privileges of a feme sole except that of intermarrying with another man during the lifetime of her said husband.
Acts of TN, 1822

HUMPHREYS, MARY   1823   CARTER COUNTY
Mary was appointed the guardian of her husband, JESSE HUMPHREYS, in 1821. In 1823 she was authorized to contract and be contracted with, as a feme sole in all matters relating to the stock or produce of the farm of her said husband.
Acts of TN, 1823, p.102-3

HURT, ELIZABETH   17 October 1831   WHITE COUNTY
Elizabeth was married to ISAAC HURT in Tennessee. They had 3 children. Before the birth of the third child, Isaac took up with Peggy Fulser and got a venereal disease. After the third child was born, Isaac took up with and kept Suckey Hill in Warren County. He gave Elizabeth the venereal disease. He drove Elizabeth from his home to her father's. She understands that Isaac wants a divorce but she does not want one. She says he left her.
42-1831

HUSTON, RACHel   1826   ROBERTSON COUNTY
Rachel, wife of WILLIAM HUSTON, is granted the privileges of a feme sole.
Acts of TN., 1826

HUTCHESON, AMBROSE   1818, 1820, 1821   ROBERTSON COUNTY
Ambrose Hutcheson of Robertson County was married ca 1799 to SARAH GOSSETT of Montgomery County. He accuses her of extreme intoxication, a very abusive tongue, and says she leaves and runs him into debt. Once, when she had come back to him, she sold all of his household property in his absence. She then left again and went to her father's in Montgomery County. It has been nearly 2 years since she left.
Statement by R. Murphy that he'd known Ambrose before and since his marriage.
STatement by William M. Bell and William H. Earle.
Undated Box, Legislative Petitions, Manuscripts Division
91-1820
40-1821

IRICK, JANE N.   7 October 1854   KNOX COUNTy
Jane was married in June 1851 in Knox County to JAMES IRICK. She has 2 infant children. She claims ill treatment by her husband, adultery by him with Polly Ann Norwood and she wishes an injunction to prevent his taking away her children or the property in her possession. She was formerly JANE H. BROWN, and has lived in Knox County since her birth. James, at time of their marriage, was a resident of Knox. Jane left him at one point and lived with her mother, who then and still does reside in Knox County. James has left the country. (This divorce suit was heard in Knox County Circuit Court 17 February 1855.)
Jane N. Irick vs James Irick
Decree: Jane is to be returned to status of a feme sole and that she take the name of Jane N. Brown, and that all property be divested out of James Irick and in Jane N. Brown. The children's names are to be changed to Mary Jane Brown(age 3 years), and Joseph Brown (age 14 months). Sheriff's statement: "...defendant not to be found in my county." Mary Brown was the security for Jane N. Irick in this cause.
Sneed Family Papers, Mss. Ac.#992, Box 4, Manuscripts Division

ISAACS, ELIZABETH   27 October 1829   LINCOLN COUNTy
Elizabeth is wife of JOHN W. ISAACS. She wants a divorce and her name to be changed to ELIZABETH GATTIS.
117-1829

ISAACS, ELIZABETH   1829   LINCOLN COUNTY
The marriage bonds are to be dissolved between Elizabeth Isaacs and her husband, JOHN W. ISAACS, upon proof that John "...abused and chastised her and wholly ceased to extend support and protection to her." Elizabeth's name shall be changed to her maiden name of ELIZABETH GATTIS.
Acts of TN, 1829, p.220

JACK, JEREMIAH   1829   GREENE COUNTY
The marriage bonds are hereby dissolved between Jeremiah and his wife, CATHERINE JACK.
Acts of TN, 1829, p.173

JACKSON, ISABELLA   31 August 1827   GREENE COUNT
Isabella was married 12 October 1815 in Greene County to JOHN JACKSON. They lived together until ca first of April 1818. John left at that time and she is informed he went to the State of Missouri. He has never returned. While they lived together his treatment towards her was cruel. They had one child.
82-1827

JACKSON, ISABELLA   1827   GREENE COUNTY
Isabella Jackson is granted the privileges of a feme sole. (husband's name not stated)
Acts of TN, 1827

JAMESON, HOSEA   1819-1821   MAURY COUNTY
Hosea is husband of NANCY JAMESON. She left him 20 August 1819. They have three small children, 1 an infant 3 months old, and the 2 other small children. She went to the state of Alabama.
Petition is accompanied by the signatures of 28 persons.
Statement by six persons that Nancy will not return to live with her husband.
102-1819
41-1821

JARRETT, ELIZABETH A.   1833   BEDFORD COUNTY (see last page for this omission.)
         JARRETT, ELIZABETH A.   1833 BEDFORD COUNTY
The marriage bonds are hereby dissolved between Elizabeth A. and her husband, GEORGE L. JARRETT.
Acts of TN, 1833, p.162

         JENKINS, SARAH   1821   no county stated
Sarah is wife of JEREMIAH JENKINS. He treats her cruelly and she asks for a divorce.
Petition is accompanied by the signatures of Abraham Lillard, Josiah Harrison, and William Jiles.
99-1821

         JENNINGS, AGNES   1826   LINCOLN COUNTY
Agnes Jennings is granted the privileges of a feme sole. (Husband's name is not stated)
Acts of TN, 1826

         JETT, JOHN F.   October 1858   KNOX COUNTY
MARY ANN ROLAND was married in Knox County on March 1858 to JOHN F. JETT, both residents of Knox County, where they both still live. Mary proved to be pregnant at the time of the marriage, by another man. She has been guilty of adultery since the marriage. John F. makes plea on 5 February 1859 to circuit court of Knox County that he is unable financially to bear the expenses of a lawsuit and is entitled to a divorce.
Sneed Family Papers, AC#992, Box 4, Manuscripts Division

         JIAMS, WILLIAM L.   September 1821   SUMNER COUNTY
William L. was married in 1817 to SALLY GROOMS. She left after they'd been married for about 2 months. She returned, stayed about 2-3 months, then left again. They lived like this for 2 years, until she left and has been gone for more than 2 years. She has been with other men. He has no heir by her. William had 1 child by his first wife, who died before he married Sally.
Petition is accompanied by the signatures of 47 persons.
97-1821

         JOHNSON, ASHLEY   1833 BLOUNT COUNTY
The marriage bonds are hereby dissolved between Ashley and his wife, SOPHRONIA JOHNSON, formerly SOPHRONIA WRINKLE.
Acts of TN, 1833, p.20

         JOHNSON, CALVIN   12 September 1832   JACKSON COUNTY
Calvin is husband of SARAH JOHNSON. Because they disagree with each other, they have separated about 4 times, but have tried to work things out. They cannot, and "by the mutual consent of each other and by the ...agreement of our parents..." they ask for a divorce.
Signed by Calvin Johnson and by Sarah Johnson.
Petition is accompanied by the signatures of 4 persons, including William Johnson, Martha Johnson, James Goldsby, and Elizabeth Goldsby. All signed with an X.
42-1832

         JOHNSON, WILLIAM   23 SEptember 1831   ROBERTSON COUNTY
William was married in 1809 in Wilson County to SARAH ROSE. They lived together until 1820 when she left without cause. Her father, Bazel Rose, took her to his house, where she lived ca 2 years, then her father removed to Missouri and Sarah remained in "said county" for about 2 years. William has not seen her for last 5 years. William is a member of the Baptist Church of

Robertson County and has lived in Robertson County at least 15-20 years, say witnesses, including C. Johnson and John Johnson.
91-1831

JOHNSTON, NARCISSA   17 July 1820   RUTHERFORD COUNTY
Narcissa was married May 1815 to JOHN JOHNSTON. They lived together in Murfreesboro until ca March 1816, when he left. They have one child. Narcissa heard that John is married and living in Ohio. When he left Narcissa, he was much in debt.
Statement by Narcissa's father, George Haynes.
65-1820

JONES, CATHERINE   1820   HAWKINS COUNTY
The marriage bonds are hereby dissolved between Catherine and her husband, JOEL JONES.
Acts of TN, 1820, p.26

JONES, JAMES   3 OCtober 1821   WARREN COUNTY
James is husband of ELIZABETH JONES. They are residents of Warren County. They both petition for a divorce. They have lived separate for several years, for singular causes "known to ourselves."
Petition is signed by James Jones and by Elizabeth Jones.
Letter from Elizabeth to James dated September 1821, in answer to his letter asking her to go to Alabama to live with him has reply that she will live with him only if he will live within 5 miles of Jesse Trires.
19-1821

JONES, JANE   18 September 1823   SUMNER COUNTY
Jane was married in March 1818 to WILLIAM JONES of Sumner County. They lived together in the counties of Smith and Sumner for nearly 2 years. In January 1820 he left. She believes he now keeps a brothel in New Orleans. They have one child.
Witnesses to petition are Daniel Cochran, Solomon Brown, and David Kirby.
Statement by Rowland Hodges and Jacob Brown, Sr. that William has been absent from his wife Jane 3 years and 8 months, after living with her nearly 2 years. While living with Jane, William did not apply himself to earning a living.
6-1823
8-1823

JONES, JANE   1823   SUMNER COUNTy
Jane Jones, wife of WILLIAM JONES, is granted the privileges of a feme sole, except that of intermarrying with another man, and can petition for a divorce in the circuit court of Sumner County.
Acts of TN, 1823

JONES, JULIA   1831   DAVIDSON COUNTY
The marriage bonds are to be dissolved between Julia Jones and her husband, DEMPSEY JONES, upon proof that she has been deserted by Dempsey for more than 2 years.
Acts of TN, 1831, p.80

JONES, MARTHA A. R.   1819   DAVIDSON COUNTY
Martha was married 19 December 1816 to ALEXANDER A. JONES. AT the time of her marrriage she was possessed of a considerable estate, both real and personal, the gift of her father, John COCKRILL, Sr. of said county. Alexander tried to coerce her into signing over her land to him.
Petition is accompanied by the signatures of 36 persons.
50-1819

JONES, MARTHA A. R.   1819   DAVIDSON COUNTY
The marriage bonds are hereby dissolved between Martha A. R. Jones and her husband, ALEXANDER W. JONES. Martha was formerly MARTHA A. R. COCKRILL.
Acts of TN, 1819, p.11

JONES, POLLY   1822   no county stated
Polly Jones is granted the privileges of a feme sole, except that of intermarrying with another man. (Her husband's name is not stated.)
Acts of TN, 1822, p.156

JONES, RHODA   10 October 1829   FENTRESS
Rhoda was married in July 1827 to LEWIS JONES. They lived together 4 or 5 months. He spent his time in idleness and dissipation. He abused her and left her with a child not more than 8 days old. He took a woman of ill fame and started to leave the country with her.
Statement by Nelly Groom who had known Rhoda since Rhoda was a small girl, and stated that Lewwis said he came from Virginia. Nelly helped them get back together, but Lewis deserted Rhoda again. Lewis also sold all the property (land, cattle, mare, and household furniture) that Rhoda had managed to acquire before their marriage through her own industry.
Statements by Asa Johnston, John W. Simpson, Elizabeth Atkinson, Jr.
136-1829

JONES, SUSANNAH   1821?   WILSON COUNTy
Susannah was married to DAVID JONES in North Carolina. They lived a few years in that state, during which time he drank. She left her parents and other relations and came with him to Wilson County, Tennessee. He had promised to quit drinking but continued to do so, and in about 2 years, he spent all they had. On 6 March 1818 he left her with 2 children, one ca 6 weeks old. Petition is accompanied by the signatures of 12 persons.
Undated Box, Legislative Petitions, Manuscripts Division

JORDAN, LUCRETIA   1822   no county stated
Lucretia, formerly LUCRETIA POOL, is granted the privileges of a feme sole. (Her husband's name is not stated.)
Acts of TN, 1822

JUSTICE, ESTHER   1821   no county stated
Esther is wife of WILLIAM JUSTICE. He ran away from Tennessee in the fall of 1819, leaving her poor. All his property was sold soon after his leaving. She had 7 or 8 small children, 1 an idiot and 1 lame with a white swelling. She believes he went to Missouri and married another woman. He passed some counterfeit bank notes.
98-1821

KEARNEY, LUCY D.   1812   no county stated
The marriage bonds are hereby dissolved between Lucy D. and her husband, HENRY G. KEARNEY. Lucy is to receive one-third of the real and personal property as alimony.
Acts of TN, 1812, p.21

KEELING, THOMAS S.   17 October 1833   WAYNE COUNTY
In November 1830 Thomas S. was married to LAVINA ARCHER, he being age 19. May May 1831 he was going to move to Maury County, but she refused to go and has not lived with him since. He wants a divorce and to be at liberty to marry again if he wants to.
8-1833

KELLY, REBECCA 27 August 1833   county not stated
REBECCA HAMILTON was married in 1806 to JESSE KELLY. He has neglected her and
failed to support her and their 2 children. He left her and has been absent
more than 20 years.
Petition is accompanied by the signatures of 14 persons.
121-1833

KELLY, REBECCA   1833 WASHINGTON COUNTy
The marriage bonds are hereby dissolved between Rebecca and her husband, JESSE
KELLY.
Acts of TN, 1833, p.65

KENNEDY, HUGH   1812   KNOX COUNTy
Hugh was married in 1807 to ELEANOR WALKER. After six months' marriage,
Eleanor had a child, of whom Hugh was not the father. Hugh left.
8-1-1812

KENNEDY, HUGH   1812   no county stated
The marriage bonds are hereby dissolved between Hugh and his wife, ELEANOR
KENNEDY.
Actsof TN, 1812, p.66

KENNEDY, JAMES   24 August 1819   Pleasant Cove, WARREN COUNTY
James resided in Pendleton District, South Carolina for more than 20 years,
having filled the place of Lieutenant and Captain more than 8 years. He has
served as a captain under Generals Graham and Jackson in the Creek expedition.
Previous to the above, he has served the United States in the Corps of Archi-
tects and Engineers as a non-commissioned officer and a cadet 3½ years in the
years 1794-1797. He now teaches school. His first wife died leaving seven
children. He married his second wife, HANNAH COMMINS, in South Carolina on 5
February 1818. On 7 November 1818 he moved to Tennessee. When he left South
Carolina, his wife refused to come.
105-1819

KERSEE, ELIZABETH L.   6 October 1821   SUMNER COUNTY
Elizabeth was married on 10 November 1818 in Sumner County to CHAMPNESS KERSEE
of said county. He left her and their one infant child.
Petition is accompanied by the signatures of 16 persons.
Statement by William Lauderdale, John Mills, and Peter W. Lucus.
108-1821

KEY, MARGARET C.   no date stated   SUMNER COUNTY
MARGARET C. GRAHAM of Sumner County was married on 12 January 1812 to STROTHER
KEY, a native of Virginia. At the time of their marriage, Key was possessed
of "respectable property." He got in the habit of gaming until he was reduced
to poverty. They have two children. In September 1823 he left her and has
since lived in Manchester, Tennessee. She wants a divorce and to be a feme
sole.
Petition is accompanied by the signatures of 4 persons.
Undated Box, Legislative Petions, Manuscripts Division

KEY, MARGARET C.   1831   SUMNER COUNTY
Margaret, wife of STROTHER KEY, is granted the privileges of a feme sole,
except that of intermarrying with another man.
Acts of TN, 1831

KEYE, TANDY   1821   DAVIDSON COUNTY
Tandy was married ca 1818 to DELILAH BEESLEY of Davidson County. She left after
  12 months of marriage. She has committed adultery and fornication. Tandy
has been a citizen of Davidson County about 12 years.
38-1821

KIMBROUGH, THOMAS   1821   JEFFERSON COUNTY
Thomas was married ca 1819 to ANNE SMITH, then of Jefferson County. She left
him after about 8 months of marriage.
STatement by William Hopkins and Samuel Sellars.
185-1821

KINNARD, DAVID C.   29 May 1821   WILLIAMSON COUNTy
David has been a citizen of Tennessee since he was 2 years old. In January
last, having attained the age of 20, he was married to HANNAH MILLER, a resident of of Williamson County (then and now). She committed adultery with one
of her relations who lived in the neighborhood. She admitted her guilt and
said she'd been involved with him also before their marriage. David left her
and returned her to her father.
Statement by P. F. Pearson that he delivered a letter to Hannah written by
David saying that David couldn't remain married to her.
Statement by R. Currin and David Mason that David has lived with them as a
storekeeper and clerk from August 1815, then being about 15 years of age,
until March 1820.
Petition is accompanied by the signatures of 21 persons.
101-1821

KINNARD, DAVID C.   1821   WILLIAMSON COUNTY
The marriage bonds are hereby dissolved between David and his wife HANNAH
KINNARD.
Acts of TN, 1821, p.103

LAUDERDALE, NANCY*   1825   no county stated
Nancy was married 28 December 1823 to JOHN GREENWOOD. He left on 17 January
1825 to go to Kentucky for business. He was supposed to return in 4 weeks,
but did not. On 2 March 1825 she found out that he had returned to Morganfield
in Kentucky to a former wife he had married six years ago. Nancy has one
infant daughter.
Petition is signed by Nancy Lauderdale.
142-1825
*See Petition of John Greenwood

LAWRENCE, WILLIAM R.   3 November 1833   MONROE COUNTY
William R. was married 5 August 1830 in McMinn County to REBECCAH BALLING.
She left him in 1831.
Petition is accompanied by the signatures of 9 persons.
107-1833

LAWRENCE, WILLIAM R.   1833   no county stated
The marriage bonds are hereby dissolved between William R. and his wife, REBECCA
LAWRENCE.
Acts of TN, 1833, p. 121

LEE, JACOB   1827   WAYNE COUNTY
The marriage bonds are to be dissolved between Jacob and his wife, MOURNEN
LEE, upon proof of desertion for more than 2 years and adultery by Mournen.
Acts of TN, 1827, p.196

LEUTY, ELIZABETH *   1833 no county stated
The marriage bonds are hereby dissolved between ELIZABETH MCCLURE, now called
ELIZABETH LEUTY, and her first husband, CHARLES C. MCCLURE, and the marriage
heretofore entered into and solemnized in Rhea County between DAVID LEUTY of
said county and Elizabeth McClure, at that time of the state of Alabama, but
originally of the state of TEnnessee, be and hereby is made valid.
Acts of TN, 1833, p.79
*See MCLURE, ELIZABETH.

LEWIS, MARTHA H.   1821   FRANKLIN AND WILSON COUNTIES
The marriage bonds are hereby dissolved between Martha H. Lewis and her husband,
JAMES LEWIS. The said Martha H. Lewis shall hereafter be called and known by
the name of MARTHA H. FIGURES.
Acts of TN, 1821, p.136

LEWIS, DR. SAMUEL   October 1821   WILSON COUNTY
Samuel wants a divorce from SALLY LEWIS, his second wife. He is her second
husband. He charges her with adultery. He says that they had no children,
but that he has three children of his own. He wishes Sally's name to be
changed back to SALLY CARSON, her former name.
Statement by George L. Smith that Sally signed a statement saying she consents
to being divorced. 18 May 1821.
Statement by Buckhannon James and Samuel Lewis, Jr.
Statement by John Holland and Claybourne Gunter of Warren County that they
were lately in Williamson County and in conversation heard that Sally was a
lewd, idle woman.
Statement in Rutherford County by Samuel Lewis, and statement by Sarah Lewis.
Petition is accompanied by the signatures of 32 persons,(but this part of the
petition is dated 10 June 1819 and is marked "Warren County.")
50-1821

LILLIARD, JEREMIAH   1827   MONROE COUNTY
The marriage bonds are to be dissolved between Jeremiah and his wife, SARAH
LILLIARD, upon proof that Sarah deserted him and eloped with another man.
Acts of TN, 1827, p.190

LINDSEY, NANCY   6 September 1831   LAWRENCE COUNTY
NANCY WISDOM of Lawrence County was married in said county in 1824 to JEFFERSON
LINDSEY. They lived together ca 2 years. He left her and stayed absent about
18 months, then returned and lived with her about 1 or 2 months and then left
again. He stayed away about 9 months, and again returned and stayed with her
until the first week of April 1829, when he left her again, this time leaving
her with 2 infant children.
Petition is accompanied by the signatures of 97 persons.
289-1831

LINDSY, BETSY   8 September 1825   MCNAIRY COUNTY
Betsy was married 17 June 1822 to GREEN LEE LINDSY. They moved to McNairy
County. He mistreated her and finally left her. She wants a divorce and to
have her name changed back to BETSY H. CRISP.
Petition is accompanied by the signatures of 5 persons.
215-1825

LINSEY, BETSY H.   1827   HARDEMAN COUNTY
"Be it enacted that BETSY H. LINSEY may apply to the circuit court of Hardeman
County by petition, and upon due proof that her husband has absconded her
altogether for 2 years, said court may divorce her from her husband ...if it
shall be proved that he is gone to parts unknown."
Acts of TN, 1827, p.197

LINE, WILLIAM   8 November 1821   no county stated
William is husband of ELEANOR LINE. They have been married "many years." She was unfaithful, and he left her.
39-1821

LINN, BETSEY   24 September 1825   CLAIBORNE COUNTy
Betsey was married 1 September 1824 to JACOB LINN. Jacob left October 1824 to go to salt works on Goose Creek in Kentucky. On 23 November 1824 Linn was charged with having committed different felonious acts. On 5 April 1825 he was convicted and sentenced to one year's imprisonment. He also stole several items from Daniel Garrard.
Petition is accompanied by the sigantures of 33 persons.
Enclosed with petition is a copy of the record of the circuit court of Clay County, Kentucky, showing Linn's conviction.
11-1825

LINN, ELIZABETH   5 November 1831   CAMPBELL COUNTY
Elizabeth was married ca 1824 to JACOB LINN. They lived together about 4 months, then he left her. She is informed that he has been charged and convicted with felonies more than once.
Petition is accompanied by the signatures of 8 persons.
293-1831

LINN, ELIZABETH   1831   no county stated
The marriage bonds are hereby dissolved between Elizabeth and her husband, JACOB LINN.
Acts of TN, 1831, p.208

LOGAN, CATHERINE   7 November 1831   CLAIBORNE COUNTY
Catherine is wife of DAVID B. LOGAN. He left her after 3 or 4 months of marriage to go to see his mother in Halifax in Virginia and overstayed his time. She wrote and learned that he'd not been there. Last fall, a neighbor, William English, saw him about the Ohio River. "He left me 2 years ago last February, and I expect him never to return." She was formerly CATHERINE DAVAULT.
Statements by John Mitchell and Abraham Davault.
363-1831

LOGUE, MARY   8 September 1821   no county stated
Mary was married to DAVID LOGUE on 11 September 1816. They lived together a little over 2 years. He beat her and slept with Negro women, so she left him and returned to her father's.
81-1821

LONG, JUDITH R.   20 November 1826   WILLIAMSON COUNTY
Judith R. of Williamson County was married to NICHOLAS I. LONG of Maury County on 23 May 1822. They lived together 15 months. She left him and went to her father's for asylum. He treated her cruelly. They had one child.
102-1826

LONG, JUDITH R.   1826   MAURY COUNTY?
Judith R. Long, wife of NICHOLAS LONG of Maury County, is granted the privileges of a feme sole, except that of intermarrying with another man, but "if she should hereafter live with Nicholas Long, then the provisions of this section shall be null and void."
Acts of TN, 1826

LOUDERMILK, JACOB   22 September 1831   WASHINGTON COUNTY
Jacob was married in September 1825 to DARIAS BORIN, also of said county.
They had three children. She became dissatisfied with him and returned to her
father, Joshua Borin, and finally abandoned Jacob on 15 May 1830.
Petition is accompanied by the signatures of 40 persons, including Adam
Loudermilk.
63-1831

LUMPKIN, EDMUND   9 September 1831   GILES COUNTY
Edmund was married to NANCY TASHLEY about 9 years ago in Giles County and
lived with her until July 1830 when she abandoned him.
Petition is accompanied by signatures of 65 persons.
Statement signed by 89 persons that Edmund, they believe, has treated his wife
improperly and is not entitled to a divorce from her and that she would live
with him if he would live with her.
69-1832

LUSK, SAMUEL   1833   CARTER COUNTY
The marriage bonds between Samuel and his wife, HANNAH LUSK, are to be dis-
solved upon proof that Hannah is deranged.
Acts of TN, 1833,p.20

MADDUX, NATHANIEL   September 1827   COCKE COUNTY
On 6 December 1819, Nathaniel was living in peace with his wife, ANNY MADDUX,
when she left him. She left with Philip Rains. Nathaniel applied for a
divorce at the circuit court on July 1820. He then married on 24 February
1821 to Rebecca Howard, thinking it wouldn't be hard to get a divorce from his
first wife, Anny.
Petition includes the signatures of 60 persons.
Statements by John McNabb, William Vinson, and Abraham Lillard.
198-1827

MAHON, MIRANDA   2 August 1827   WAYNE COUNTY
Miranda was married to HENRY MAHON of Hardin County, Tennessee. He has
recently left the state with his whole estate and property after having lived
in adultery with Susana Anderson, so Miranda believes. Henry made Susana
believe she was lawfully married to him. Henry threatened the life of Miranda,
and verbally abused her. She wants a divorce and her name changed to MIRANDA
WASSINGTON, her former name.
Petition includes signatures of 37 persons.
Statement by Penelope Hassell that Henry beat Miranda and her mother, Joanna
Wassington.
Statement by John Dickson that he saw Henry and Susan Anderson in bed together
and that Henry said he and Susan were married by Elijah Flanery, that Elijah
acknowledged same, and that Susan believed she was legally married to Henry.
Statement by Edward Stanford.
60-1827

MAHON, MIRANDA   1827   WAYNE COUNTY
Miranda is to be granted a divorce from her husband, HENRY MAHON, upon proof
of adultery by Henry.
Acts of TN, 1827,p.121

MALONY, HUGH   10 September 1819   GREENE COUNTY
Hugh was married 30 September 1812 to Susannah Conway, daughter of Col. Henry
Conway of Greene County. She died 4 May 1816, leaving two small children.
Hugh was remarried 30 April 1817 to POLLY EASTERDLY of Greene County. Polly
left him in June of 1817.
91-1819

MALONEY, HUGH   no date stated   GREENE COUNTY
Hugh Maloney, of Greene County, was married about "eight years ago" to Susanna Conway of Greene County. She died in 1814, leaving three small children. In 1815 he was married to POLLY EASTERLY of Greene County. She mistreated his children. She left him and is now living with another man. She has been living away from him about three years.
Undated Box, Legislative Petitions, Manuscripts Division

MANCHESTER, MARY   1829   DAVIDSON COUNTY
The marriage between Mary and her husband, WILLARD MANCHESTER, is to be dissolved upon proof of desertion by Williard and his neglect of wife and children.
Acts of TN, 1829, p.83

MANLY, LAURA   1829   HARDEMAN COUNTY
The marriage is to be dissolved between Laura and her husband CHAPMAN MANLY, upon proof of desertion by Chapman.
Acts of TN, 1829, p.109

MARLOW, JOSEPH   20 October 1827   GILES COUNTY
Joseph was married to POLLY LYNCH in Giles County ca 5 September 1826. They lived together in Pulaski until March 1827, when she left and said she would not live with him again. He has one child, seven years old, by a former wife. The former wife died. Polly went to Lincoln County and has lately been with several men (names are unknown to him). She came to his house and tried to take household articles away with her and had armed men with her.
Petition includes signatures of 71 persons.
130-1827

MARSH, NANCY   1832   FRANKLIN COUNTY
Nancy Marsh, wife of DANIEL MARSH, is granted the privileges of a feme sole.
Acts of TN, 1832

MARSHALL, SARAH G.   29 October 1833   MAURY COUNTY
Sarah G. Marshall, of Maury County, while residing at her father's house in Maury, was married to WILLIAM MARSHALL in 1821. He did not support her and was violent and savage in his treatment of her. He did wild things, like shooting a gun off in the house, etc. In January 1828 he ordered her to leave his house. She says he is impotent and incapable of procreation. She filed a petition for divorce with the circuit court of Maury County but withdrew it because of the disgraceful answer William gave to the court. She wants a divorce and the rights of a feme sole.
Statement by Abner H. Partee
26-1833

MARTIN, MARY   September 1827   WILLIAMSON COUNTy
Statement by Dr. R. C. Hancock that Mary's husband, SAMUEL N. MARTIN, had gonorrhea.
Statement by (illegible) Bailey that Samuel was given to drinking and neglected his family. This statement includes signatures of 10 other persons.
Statement by J. K. S. Webb that he had known Samuel N. Martin ever since 1813, that soon after Samuel was married to Miss Polly Alison, he started drinking. His property was frequently exposed to public sale. Samuel's father-in-law, James Allison, agreed to pay about $1800.00 to Samuel, and Samuel was to relinquish his Negro property, which James Allison then conveyed by deed of trust to Mrs. Martin and child.
236-1827

MARTIN, MARY   1827   WILLIAMSON COUNTY
Mary Martin is to be divorced from her husband, SAMUEL N. MARTIN, upon proof of adultery by Samuel.
Acts of TN, 1827, p.120

MARTIN, SALLY   1831   MONROE COUNTy
Sally Martin, wife of JOSEPH J. MARTIN, is granted the privileges of a feme sole, except that of intermarrying with another man.
Acts of TN, 1831

MASON, BENNETT   17 OCtober 1833   RUTHERFORD COUNTY
Bennett Mason in 1816 in North Carolina was married to MARTHY. In that same year he moved to Tennessee. He has six children, four he supports, and two who live with a relation of his. "Three years last past" Martha left him. Petition includes signatures of 18 persons.
229-1833

MASSENGALE, HENRY, SR.   1811   SULLIVAN COUNTY
The marriage bonds between Henry Massengale, Sr. and his wife, MARY, are hereby dissolved &"...each of them be restored to all their rights and capacities."
Acts of TN, 1811, p.45

MATTHEWS, ISAAC   23 October 1819   no county stated
Isaac Matthews was married 31 August 1806 to Toppenas. In Hopkins County, Kentucky on 23 October 1819, Isaac, in witness of two justices of the peace, James Edmiston and John N. Cunningham, questioned his neighbors, this to be used as evidence against Toppenas, who was charged by her husband as living in adultery with Robert Johnson Gulley, also a neighbor. The neighbors who were questioned were Edward Baldwin, Henry Bishop, Ann Simes, John Matthews, and Ezekiel Clinton, all of whom said they knew, or were told by Toppenas, of the adultery. Ezekiel Clinton said that Gully told him that his (Gully's) wife would not drop corn (plant corn) for him and that he had a notion of leaving her.
Statement by Isaac Mathews that he had been a neighbor some 3 or 4 years.
111-1819

MATTHEWS, ISAAC   1819   WILLIAMSON COUNTY
Isaac Matthews is hereby divorced from his wife TEPPINS.
Acts of TN, 1819, p.181

MATTHEWS, JOHN   September 1825   HAWKINS COUNTY
John is husband of REBECCA MATTHEWS. In 1817 she attempted to poison him by putting poison in his coffee. He then left her, giving her the furniture, 2 negroes, a man and a woman, and $1500.00 in cash.
Statement in Washington County, Georgia by Temperance May that Temperance thought Rebeckah had married John for his property.
Statement by Rebeckah Matthews, Senior (not Rebecca, John's wife), Washington County, Georgia.
Statement by John Matthews, Sr. and Wiley Pope, Washington County, Georgia, that John would give Rebecca four more Negroes, besides the three he had already given her (the Negro that he'd given her had had a child), and $400 and also a plantation for "her lifetime." The other property would be hers to will and dispose of as she saw cause, provided John and Rebecca were divorced.
194-1825

MAXWELL, CAPT. JAMES J.   September 1823   RUTHERFORD COUNTY
Capt. James J. Maxwell was married 11 January 1811 to ELIZABETH SPRINGFIELD. In 1815 she left him, proclaiming love for another man and saying that she

would rather be a common prostitute to another man than to be James' wife.
Petition includes the signatures of 23 persons, those who have known Maxwell
for the last 6 or 7 years, which is how long he's been in Rutherford County.
Statement by Elizabeth Matthews that while she and James lived together, it
was in disagreement. She said she couldn't live with James anymore because
she loved a man named Griffin much better.
After 9 or 10 months of marriage, Elizabeth had a daughter, but James was not
the father.
Statement by Lydia Maxwell, Elizabeth Maxwell, Jr., and John W. Maxwell.
72-1823

MAXWELL, JAMES I.   1825   RUTHERFORD COUNTY
James is hereby divorced from his wife JANE MAXWELL upon proof.
Acts of TN, 1825, p.274

MAY, SARAH   1812   no county stated
The marriage bonds are hereby dissolved between Sarah May and her husband,
JAMES MAY.
Acts of TN, 1812, p.66

MCADAMS, JACOB   23 November 1829   BEDFORD COUNTY
Jacob was married in 1826 to SARAH GOLLAHAN of Bedford County, where they have
since lived. Sarah committed adultery with Lawrence Nichols and others. She
left Jacob about about 1827.
Statement by Nancy Turpin and Matthew Turpin that sometime in 1828 they saw
Sally McAdams and Laurence Nichols in bed together in the night time.
286-1829

MCADOW, SAMUEL   1821   no county stated
Samuel is husband of PATSY MCADOW. They have separated and want a divorce.
Petition includes signatures of 211 persons, including that of Finley S.
McAdow.
48-1821

MCALPIN, THOMAS   29 November 1831   McNAIRY COUNTY
Thomas McAlpin, of McNairy County, was married in Knox County on 22 March 1792
to AGNES BROWN, then of Knox County. Agnes is high-tempered. They had a poor
marriage until 1810, then from 1810 to 1814 they lived together in a period of
friendship and unity. Since 1814 she has been contrary and ill disposed
towards him, and has refused for the last five years to have sexual intercourse with him. He says Agnes is perfectly willing for them to be divorced.
Statement by Agness McAlpin that husband's petition is true and that she is
agreeable to a divorce.
Statement by Thomas McAlpin, Davidson County, that on the day he "obtained the
clerk's certificate, I got crippled and I never expect to recover, and circumstances prevented me from forwarding the petition to the...legislature."
Petition is signed 6 August 1833, and includes signatures of 48 citizens of
Purdy, McNairy County.
87-1833

McCABE, ELIZABETH   3 September 1827   KNOX COUNTY
Elizabeth was married ca August 1822 to STARK McCABE, a citizen of Knox County.
About four months later he left, with a herd of horses, to go to Georgia.
She doesn't know whether he's dead or alive.
Oath made by Robert Murphy that Elizabeth statements are true.
296-1827

McCARDLE, SINA   1825   GREENE COUNTY
Sina, wife of JOHN McCARDLE, is granted the privileges of a feme sole, except that of intermarrying with another man.
Acts of TN, 1825

McCLANNATHAN, NANCY   1831   no county stated
Nancy, wife of LEWIS McCLANNATHAN, is granted the privileges of a feme sole.
Acts of TN, 1831

McCLURE, ELIZABETH (see LEUTY, ELIZABETH)

McCLURE, ELIZABETH   1833   no county stated
Elizabeth is hereby divorced from her first husband, CHARLES C. McCLURE. "The marriage...entered into and solemnized in Rhea County between David Leuty of said county, and Elizabeth McClure, now...Elizabeth Leuty, at that time of the state of Alabama, but originally of the state of Tennessee...is ...valid..."
Acts of TN, 1833, p.79

McCLURE, WILLIAM   16 July 1822   MONTGOMERY COUNTY
William was married July 1820 to REBECCA SMITH. William says that Rebecca had sexual relations with a Negro slave, Taff, a former slave of his that he had sold. Rebecca left and went to Illinois.
Oath by James McClure.
95-1822

McCONNEL, POLLY   1821   MAURY COUNTY
Polly McConnel, formerly POLLY POWEL, of Maury County did "some years since" marry JAMES McCONNEL of said county. Two children were born to them: Andrew Jackson McConnel and Charlotte Matilda McConnel. Afterwards, Polly, in circuit court of Maury, obtained a divorce from said James McConnell and is now desirous to retain her former name and that her children assume her former name instead of her husband's name. "Be it enacted that Polly be hereafter called and known by the name of POLLY POWEL and her children to be called by name of Powel also.
Acts of TN, 1821

McCUBBINS, PHEBE   1833   GRAINGER COUNTY
Phebe is granted the privileges of a feme sole (husband's name not stated).
Acts of TN, 1833, p.79

McCUBBINS, PHOEBE   1833   GRAINGER COUNTY
The marriage between Phoebe and her husband, WILLIAM McCUBBINS, is to be dissolved upon proof of William's desertion.
Acts of TN, 1833, p.139

McCURRY, JAMES   28 August 1833   GREENE COUNTY
James was married in 1828 to POLLY ZIMMERMAN. He was not long married before he found out that Polly had a "most turbulent and unruly temper." She wanted to go visit her father. James took her and then returned home to take care of affairs. He went back to her father's to get her but she refused to return with him. She returned to him sometime later and took all of his valuable domestic goods. She then left again and he has not seen her for three years. He heard she has had a child since she left him and that she lives in Kentucky.
213-1833

McCUTCHEN, JOHN   18 September 1809   CLAIBORNE COUNTY
Both John McCutchen and his wife, JANE MCCUTCHEN, request a divorce, for reasons best known to them.
Witnesses by John Bell, David Proffitt, and Elias Walker.
29-1-1809

McDONALD, JOHN   13 October 1827   WARREN COUNTY
John was married in 1817 (?) to LUCY HELTON. After 8 months of marriage, she left him. She committed adultery with Robert Balch. She has had 2 children and is pregnant with a third.
Statements by Archibald McDonald and Thomas Gibbs.
165-1827

McDONALD, NORMAN   27 November 1829   WHITE COUNTY
Norman was married 22 October 1812 to MILLY PERRY, he being of Wilson County. He says he can't stand her intolerable ill temper and imprudent conduct. They have children (number not stated). Milly has refused to live with him since about 1824. He supports her and the children, but she won't let him see the children.
Petition includes the signatures of 19 persons.
19-1829

McGEE, MARTHA   9 November 1829   WARREN COUNTY
Petition is written for Martha, by her next friend, Richard Forrest. Martha was married ca 1823 to CLENDENAN McGEE of Warren County. He drank a lot, was cruel to her when intoxicated. Frequently he left her and the two children. Martha's mother would take care of them when Clendenan would leave. He has been gone since ca 1827. He squandered the estate which Martha's father gave her.
4-1829

McGINNIS, ARTHUR   1841   HARDIN COUNTy
Arthur was married 25 December 1838 to MAHULAY DICUS of Wayne County, Tennessee. She left after a few days of marriage, left the state of Tennessee and is "supposed to be the wife of another man with whom she went away..."
102-1841

McGUIRE, ELIZABETH   1833   DAVIDSON COUNTY
At the November term 1832 of circuit court of Davidson County, Elizabeth filed a petition to be divorced from her husband, MERRIMAN McGUIRE. He lived in open adultery with several women and finally left Elizabeth in 1828. She did not know where he went when he left her. The judge would not grant the divorce "upon the ground alone that the suit for divorce ought to be brought in the county where the offending party resided, which she could never ascertain with certainty..."
146-1833

McGUIRE, ELIZABETH   1833   DAVIDSON COUNTY
A divorce is to be granted to Elizabeth from her husband MERRIMAN McGUIRE upon proof of desertion by Merriman. "...court authorized to take jurisdiction and to proceed .... for a divorce...as if the marriage had taken place in the state."
Acts of TN, 1833, p.149

McILROY, MARTHA   1831   WHITE COUNTY
Martha McIlroy is granted the privileges of a feme sole, except that of intermarrying with another man. (Husband's name not stated.)
Acts of TN, 1831

McINTOSH, JANE   1822   McMINN COUNTY
Jane is "authorized to have all the rights and privileges and immunities of a free white female citizen of the state of Tennessee.
Acts of TN, 1822, p.129

McINTOSH, REBECCA   1831   HICKMAN COUNTY
Rebecca, wife of NIMROD McINTOSH, is granted the privileges of a feme sole.
Acts of TN, 1831

McKEARLEY, PERMELIA   1831   JACKSON COUNTY
Permelia, formerly PERMELIA ROBERTS of Jackson County, married JAMES McKEARLEY. He left her and has lived with other women. He has two other wives. He has no occupation to provide for his family or himself. She wants a divorce and to be returned to her the privileges of a feme sole.
Petition includes signatures of 30 persons, and also James Roberts, Ridley Roberts, and Silas Roberts.
281-1831

McKEE, JOHN   1825   GREENE COUNTY
John McKee, citizen of Greeneville, was married 17 May 1803 or 1804 in Carter County, PA to ELIZA KEASLEY. In 1822 he learned his wife was guilty of improper conduct. He was at the time engaged in merchandising and tavern keeping. The two separated.
Petition includes a few signatures.
184-1825

McKEE, JOHN   1829   GREENE COUNTY
The marriage between John McKee and his wife ELIZA McKEE, of state of Pennsylvania, is hereby dissolved.
Acts of TN, 1829, p.3

MCLINN, WILLIAM   1833   ANDERSON COUNTY
The marriage between William and his wife, ANN McLINN, is hereby dissolved.
Acts of TN, 1833, p.139

McMINN, JOSEPH   16 October 1821   no county stated.
Joseph petitions for a divorce from his wife, NANCY. She left him.
Statement by wife, Nancy McMinn that she left him because of his ill treatment to her.
22-1821

McNABB, PEGGY   1822   CARTER COUNTY
In January 1822 Peggy's husband, DAVID McNABB, took up with Jane Matticks. He moved from Carter County where Peggy lived, to Monroe County, 150 miles away. David and Jane had several children, Peggy heard.
Petition includes a few signatures.
105-1822

McNABB, DAVID   May 1822   CARTER COUNTY
"Last winter ...(David) was ...called from home to transact business in the Cherokee country..." While he was gone, his wife, MARGARET McNABB, took up with William Owins of North Carolina and went off with him to Wilksborough, North Carolina. David is informed they are now living together. Margaret left David with three small children.
Statements by John McInturff, Voelit Swaner, Lucinda Dunkin, and George Slagle.
107-1822

McNABB, SAWNEY   1827   WHITE COUNTY
The marriage between Sawney McNabb and his wife, JEMIMA McNABB, is to be dissolved upon proof of desertion by Jemima.
Acts of TN, 1827, p.191

MacRAE, ALEXANDER   1 October 1829   MAURY COUNTY
Alexander MacRae was married in 1824 to MRS MARY MOODY. They lived together
one or two years before she wanted to separate. She asked him to give to her
the property he obtained with her at the time of their marriage, and he agreed.
They entered into an article of separation on 3 June 1826, and she has been
gone ever since, to the state of Alabama.
Petition includes signatures of 16 persons.
36-1829

MEDLEY, BENONI   9 September 1829   MARION COUNTY
Benoni Medley was married 14 May 1826 to MILLY WALKER, by Isaac Hicks, Justice
of the Peace for Marion County. They lived together 10 months. After that
they could not get along. Both want a divorce.
Petition is signed by both Benoni Medley and Milly Medley.
211-1829

MEDLY, BENONI   1833   WHITE COUNTY
The marriage is hereby dissolved between Benoni Medly and his wife, MILLY
MEDLY Acts of TN, 1833, p.53

MENNES, ELIZABETH C.   1821   BEDFORD COUNTY
Elizabeth is wife of WILLIAM MENNES, late of Bedford County, now of state of
Alabama, who left her and children in Bedford County. Elizabeth is granted
the privileges of a feme sole, except that of intermarrying with another man.
Acts of TN, 1821,p.215

MENESS, ELIZABETH   1822   no county stated
Elizabeth Meness, formerly ELIZABETH BURFORD, is granted the privileges of a
feme sole.
Acts of TN, 1822

MIDKIFFE, KIMBLE E.   September 1821   GRAINGER COUNTY
In 1816, Kimble E. Midkiffe, then under the age of 16 years, became acquainted
with a woman, Nancy Perenpile, who was 20 years or upwards. He left his
father's house and went into the next county with her and they got married.
He lived with her six months. She committed adultery with a man of color in
the neighborhood. Kimble left her. She has lately been delivered of an
illegitimate child, now about 9 months old, and charges a young man of the
neighborhood with being the father.
Statement by Margaret Long and by Elizabeth Purkeypile.
Statement by Rachel Purkepile that she'd heard Nancy Midkiffe say she had
slept with Walter Evens.
67-1821

MILLER, NOAH   9 October 1827   GRAINGER COUNTY
                16 August 1831
Noah's petition of 1827 states that his wife, ALICE, left him and has since
been married to another man and lived with this man for six months in the same
neighborhood as Noah, and that she is now pregnant. She also wishes to be
divorced from Noah.
Petition includes the signatures of 28 persons.
Noah's petition of 1831 states that he is now a citizen of Grainger County,
and that in April 1828 he married ALEY RICE of Hawkins County. At the time of
the marriage, he was not 17 years old. He occupied part of his father-in-law's
dwelling. In about 3 months, Aley refused to lodge with him and left him.
She then permitted herself to be courted by other men. In six months she
became the wife of another man, Mathies Nichols in Grainger County. She lived

with Nichols a few months, then they separated and she fell in with a man
named Burwell Vaden of Hawkins County, by whom she had a child.
138-1827
226-1831

            MILLER, SALLY   16 September 1824   HUMPHREYS COUNTY
Petition is prepared for Sally by her next friend, Robert Hamilton. She
states that in October 1822 she was married to HOSSEA C. MILLER, who had only
a short time previous become a citizen of Humphreys County. He had also only
recently come to Tennessee from New York. He was cruel to her. In the winter
of 1822 or the spring of 1823 Hossea took Sally with him to Carroll County,
and then they returned. Then it was learned that Hossea was married to someone
in New York. Hossea abandoned Sally and went to Nashville, where he lived a
few months and then went down the Ohio River to Orleans. They have one child.
21-1824

            MILLS, NANCY   1812   no county stated
The marriage between Nancy Mills and her husband, BIRD MILLS, is hereby dissolved.
Acts of TN, 1812, p.66

            MISINGO, SALLY   1831   CAMPBELL COUNTY
Sally was married in January 1828 to CHARLES MISINGO. They lived together 5
or 6 weeks. He left her and went to Virginia where he has since remained. He
has been gone three years.
Petition includes signatures of 5 persons and affidavits of George Peatry,
William A. Hollingsworth, Jacob Petree, and John Cliborn.
335-1831

            MITCHELL, DELANEY   14 October 1831   GRAINGER COUNTY
Delaney was married in February 1813 to ROBERT MITCHELL. They lived together
about 14 years. He was unfaithful and became unkind and cruel to her. In
November of 1827 he "turned her out of doors without a home to go to." Since
then he has been living in open adultery with one woman and sometimes with
another. He has been indicted in the circuit court of Grainger County for
such. She had 3 children by Robert, the youngest a boy now about 13 years
old. Robert has not permitted them to live with her. She wants a divorce and
to be given powers and privileges of a feme sole.
Petition includes signatures of 105 persons.
She made oath before a justice of the peace in Claiborne County that her
petition was true.
223-1831

            MITCHELL, DELANY   1831   CLAIBORNE COUNTY
A divorce is to be granted to Delany Mitchell from her husband, ROBERT
MITCHELL, upon proof that Robert was guilty of keeping other, lewd, females in
his own house. She may file in circuit court of Claiborne or Grainger.
Acts of TN, 1831, p.223

            MITCHELL, HENRYETTA   1 September 1831   WILSON COUNTY
HENRIETTA JACKSON was married 20 November 1827 to HENRY MITCHELL. He left her
"now more than 2 years since." He poisoned her but she was cured by a physician. She then moved to her parents' home, where she has lived since.
Statement by G. H. Glenn and Isaac Hunter.
Statement by Josiah Beasley and Stith T. Tarpley that Henry was determined not
to pay any of Henrietta's contracts, and set up advertisements forewarning
this. These were set up in Wilson and Sumner counties.
55-1831

MITCHELL, WILLIAM   19 October 1833   RUTHERFORD COUNTY
William Mitchell was married 26 November 1828 to JANE SHUMAKER of Rutherford County. They lived together abut seven months, then separated. In 1832 she left Tennessee and went to Kentucky with a man named Ashby, married him, and returned to Wilson County, Tennessee.
Statement of James Gilliam of Rutherford County that "the father and brother of ...Jane said to me in the fall of 1832 that ...Jane and Ashby was married in Kentucky and was at that time living in Wilson County..."
Petition includes the signatures of 28 persons, including that of James Mitchell, Sr.
231-1833

MITCHELL, WILLIAM   1833   RUTHERFORD COUNTY
The marriage is hereby dissolved between William Mitchell and his wife, JANE MITCHELL.
Acts of TN, 1833, p.136

MOORE, EDWIN S.   1812   no county stated
The marriage bonds are hereby dissolved between Edwin S. Moore and his wife, POLLY MOORE.
Acts of TN, 1812, p.66

MOORE, ELIAS   no date stated   no county stated
Elias Moore states that "some two years ago" his wife, PERMILIA MOORE, became common with other men, and she continues to cohabit with other men.
Statements by Dabney Ewell and William J. Matterson.
Petition includes signatures of 58 persons.
Undated Box, Legislative Petitions, Manuscripts Division

MOORE, ELIZABETH   21 November 1831   no county stated
Elizabeth is wife of JOHN MOORE. In 1825 he left her and went off with another woman to Illinois, where he had remained since, and she has been informed that he has married that woman.
167-1831

MOORE, ELIZABETH   1831   SUMNER COUNTY
Elizabeth Moore is granted the privileges of a feme sole, except that of intermarrying with another man. (husband's name not stated)
Acts of TN, 1831

MOORE, PERLINA   1829   LINCOLN COUNTY
The marriage bonds are to be dissolved between Perlina Moore and her husband, CHARLES MOORE, upon proof of desertion of Charles.
Acts of TN, 1829, p.109

MOORE, SALLY   1833   no county stated
Sally was married ca 1808 to NIMROD MOORE of Bledsoe County. After 5 or 6 years of marriage, he took up drinking, being sullen, and associating in gambling companies. He abused her and her children. He moved them frequently. One time he left them in McMinnville, Warren County. He went from there to Jasper in Marion County. She and the children were kicked out of a rented house in McMinnville (the rent expired), and they moved to a cabin on Cumberland Mountain. She got word to her mother and brother who came and got her and the children. Nimrod came to her mother's and she went with him to try to live in Jasper. He stayed drunk and would not support her and the family, so she went back to her mother's house, where she now lives and has for the past five years. Nimrod came to her mother's but left again to Cumberland Mountain. He took some of the children but left them at Cumberland Mountain without

anything and they ran away and returned to her. He came again and took five of her children to Jasper, and then left them again and went from there to Hamilton County. The children returned to her. Nimrod took up with another woman in Hamilton County. Last April he came to where Sally was living on her brother's land and took all of her property. Last summer he and that woman he was living with were committed to Hamilton County Jail for stealing.
52-1833

       MOORE, SALLY   1833 BLEDSOE COUNTY
The marriage is hereby dissolved between Sally Moore and her husband, NIMROD MOORE.
Acts of TN, 1833, p.118

       MOORE, SAMUEL 17 September 1827 ROANE COUNTY
Samuel Moore was married in 1826 in Roane County to ANN E. PARKS. They disagreed about things from the beginning. Then in June 1827 Ann left him with the intention of living with Jonathan Haynes, who was in the neighborhood.
Statement by ANN E. MOORE stating that she wishes also to be divorced. She states that she wishes to be known as ANN E. PARKS.
Statement by Charles Atkins that Ann Moore came to his house when she left her husband. Atkins left Ann with Haynes and Ann's two younger sisters on the side of the road.
Statement by Margaret T. Atkins.
13-1827

       MOORE, SAMUEL   1809   GREENE COUNTY
The marriage bonds are hereby dissolved between Samuel Moore and his wife, ANN MOORE.
Acts of TN, 1809, p.18

       MOORE, SARAH HAILE 22 November 1819 RUTHERFORD COUNTY
This petition is brought forth by Cage Haile and Thomas Murry. Sarah was married in 1810 to ROBERT MOORE (both were of Sumner County). They had two infant children. He got drunk and left about 1815 in pretense of going to North Carolina.

48-1819

       MOORE, SARAH   1819 SUMNER COUNTY
The marriage bonds are to be dissolved between Sarah Moore and her husband, ROBERT MOORE, upon proof that Robert was cruel to her and has long since deserted her.
Acts of TN, 1819, p.166

       MORELOCK, SARAH   1833 GREENE COUNTY
Sarah, daughter of "a very respectable farmer of Greene County," was married ca 1820 to ZACHARIAH STACY. Shortly after their marriage, they moved to Hawkins County, where they lived about three years. Then Zachariah ran off to avoid apprehension and punishment for passing counterfeit money. Sarah returned with her two children to her father's house in Greene County. About three or four years after she returned to Greene County, a "respectable" citizen of said county gained her affections and promised to marry her. He had illicit intercourse with Sarah, which resulted in the birth of twins. Petition is signed by 30 persons, including David Morelock.
5-1833

MORGAN, JOSIAH   1831   GREENE COUNTY
Statement by William Johnson that Josiah and his wife, JEMIMAH MORGAN, had been parted six years or more. Jemimah told Johnson that she'd had a child by John Morris. The child died at Johnson's house, and Jemimah sent to Morris for burying clothes. Morris sent them to her.
Statement by Nancy Johnson that Jemimah had lived with John Morris and intended to live with him her lifetime.
Statements by George Houston and Mary Houston.
267-1831

MORGAN, MASSEY   1827   no county stated
Massey Morgan, wife of PETER MORGAN, is granted the privileges of a feme sole.
Acts of TN, 1827

MORRIS, JINCY   1832   HARDIN COUNTY
Jincy was married to ISAAC MORRIS in 1818 in Tennessee. They moved to Hardin County about 1825. In 1829 he left her. Before he left her, he was guilty of adultery. He has been out of the county for 18 months. He caught a venereal disease in Florence, Alabama.
Petition includes the signatures of 29 persons.
38-1832

MORRIS, NANCY   27 August 1821   SUMNER COUNTY
Nancy was married 10 May 1818 in Sumner County to JOSEPH MORRIS. They lived together six months. A few weeks after their marriage he began to treat her unkindly and cruelly. She became fearful for her life, and when she told her husband, he tied up her clothes and told her to leave, which she did. Since she left him, he has lived with Mary Richmond for two years.
Statement by Benjamin Grissum.
Statement by Jemima Lovel that Mary Richmond had had two children since living with Joseph Morris.
37-1821

MORRIS, SAMUEL   1827   BEDFORD COUNTY
The marriage is to be dissolved between Samuel and his wife, MALINDA MORRIS, upon proof that Malinda lived separately from Samuel and dissolutely.
Acts of TN, 1827, p.211

MOSS, JOHN   1 September 1829   ANDERSON COUNTY
John Moss has been a citizen of Anderson County for 27 years. In 1813 he was married to BETSEY HAGGARD. They had one child. She then took up with another man. When questioned, she admitted her guilt, then took up with John's brother, Thomas Moss, and ran off with him and lived with him 14 or 15 months, and then returned to John.
Statement by Thomas HAgler that he saw Betsey Moss and Thomas Moss in the act of adultery.
Petition is signed by 51 persons, including Daniel Moss.
191-1829

MURPHREE, RHODY   15 November 1831   CARROLL COUNTY
Rhody was married in 1812 to NIMROD MURPHREE. He left her many times, and her with a "small and helpless family." In September 1829 he left her and four children. She has not seen or heard from him since. She has been informed he is in Nashville. He left her in Carroll County.
262-1831

MURPHREE, RHODA   1831   CARROLL COUNTY
Rhoda Murphree, the wife of NIMROD MURPHREE, is granted the privileges of a
feme sole, except that of intermarrying with another man.
Acts of TN,1831

MURPHY, RHODY   1833   CARROLL COUNTY
The marriage bonds are hereby dissolved between Rhody and her husband, NIMROD
MURPHY. Rhody is hereby restored to all the privileges of a feme sole.
Acts of TN, 1833, p.20

MURRAH, JEREMIAH   1833   SUMNER COUNTY
Jeremiah is husband of LUCY MURRAH. She left him about 12 months ago in
Sumner County.
Petition includes signatures of 17 persons.
Statement 4 September 1832 by Lucy A. Murray in Logan County, Kentucky saying
that she agrees to be divorced from Jeremiah.
196-1833

MURRELL, JAMES   September 1821   HAWKINS COUNTY
James was married at the age of 17, to NANCY WILLIAMS alias NANCY LAWSON.
They "lived together in tolerable harmony til the time of the late war."
James returned from serving a tour of duty in the militia and caught Nancy in
adultery with Christian Pearson. James did not want to cohabit with Nancy
anymore, but was willing that she should still live in his house with her
children in peace. She left James, bought goods on credit in his name at two
stores and became pregnant (not by James). When the child was about a year
old, she brought it to James' house and then she left. James said they were
lifelong residents of Hawkins County.
Statement by Peggy Winsted that Nancy has been gone about 3 years and left
James with seven children.
Petition includes signatures of 7 persons.
Statements by Capt. David S. Rogers, George Rogers, Howel Brewer, and John
Green, saying that the child Nancy had in April 1820 was named Calven and that
Nancy left it at James Murrell's house.
70-1821

MUSGROVE, LUCY   September 1826   CAMPBELL COUNTY
Lucy is wife of WILSON MUSGROVE. He beat her and committed adultery.
Petition includes signatures of 15 persons supporting Lucy's character.
Statement by Jonathan Dagley and Mary Dagley that in about 1824 they saw
Wilson Musgrove and Lucy, and Jonathan had to get Wilson away from Lucy to
keep him from beating her.
Statement by James Grant and William Hancock supporting Lucy's good character.
Statement by Rachel Clowd that she'd (Rachel) lived with Rachel Musgrove for
the past two years and saw Wilson try to kill her several times.
Statement by Wilson Musgrove that he gave his voluntary consent to his wife's
petition,dated 28 October 1826.
53-1826

MYERS, JUDAH   1 October 1823   WILLIAMSON COUNTY
Juday was married to JOHN MYERS on 16 January 1819. On the March following,
he left her. He was a foreigner by birth. She was left in a state of pregnancy.
Petition includes signatures of 27 persons.
67-1823

NETTLES, ABIGAIL   1827   JACKSON COUNTY
Abigail, wife of JOSEPH NETTLES, is granted the privileges of a feme sole,
except that of intermarrying with another man.
Acts of TN, 1827

NICHOL, JOHN   1820   no county stated
The marriage is hereby dissolved between Nancy and her husband, JOHN W. NICHOL. Nancy was formerly NANCY ANDERSON.
Acts of TN, 1820, p.95

NIGHT, NANCY   12 October 1829   LAWRENCE COUNTY
Nancy is wife of RICHARD NIGHT. He left about 1827-1828. She wishes to be divorced and have her name restored to NANCY W. ELYEA.
7-1829

NOBLE, MARK   1799   ROBERTSON COUNTY
Mark Noble was married 13 December 1792 to CATY ELLIOTT. THey have had 2 children. She left him.
Statement by William Noble that Mark and wife have not lived together since August 1797, this statement dated 24 November 1798.
10-2-1799

NOBLE, MARK   1799   ROBERTSON COUNTy
"Be it enacted, that Mark Noble ..and his wife CATY,....be, and are hereby dissolved from the bonds of matrimony, to all intents and purposes; and it shall and may be lawful for either of the said parties again to marry, in the same manner as if neigher of them had ever been married; provided nothing herein contained shall be construed to bastardize the issue ...of Mark Noble and Caty his wife..."
Acts of TN, 1799, p.53

NOWLEN, DAVID   1826   BEDFORD COUNTY
The marriage bonds between David Nowlen and his wife MARY ANN V., are to be dissolved upon proof of desertion by Mary Ann V.
Acts of TN, 1826, p.35

NULL, JOHN   16 June 1820   LAWRENCE COUNTY
John's first wife died within 6 months after their marriage. He remarried, to CATHERINE MIRES, widow of John Mires, dec'd. Two or three months after this marriage, Catherine left. They had no children.
Statement concerning Null's good character signed by John Null and 37 other persons.
29-1820

ODAN, JAMES   1833   no county stated
James is husband of MARY ODAN. James lost his leg, so she left him and took up with Wilson Nichols and is living with Nichols in Alabama as man and wife. Petition includes signatures of 55 persons.
114-1833

OGLE, MALINDA   18.22   BLEDSOE COUNTy
Malinda Ogle, otherwise MALINDA COALTE, was married in Bledsoe County in May of 1821 to JAMES OGLES. About 2 June 1822 he left her and she is informed he went to the White River country. He left a few words: "It isn't worthwhile to follow me, for neither men nor devils could bring me back."
114-1822

OLIVER, ELIZABETH   1822   ROANE COUNTY
Eizabeth Oliver, the wife of JOHN OLIVER, is granted the privileges of a feme sole.
Acts of TN, 1822

OLIVER, ELIZABETH   1827   ROANE COUNTY
A divorce is to be granted to Elizabeth Oliver, wife of JOHN OLIVER, upon proof of the desertion of John.
Acts of Tn, 1827, p.210

OLIVER, SUSANNAH   19 September 1821   KNOX COUNTY
Susannah was married to THOMAS OLIVER on 4 July 1817 in Jefferson County. He brought her to Knoxville and left her on the second day, and she never heard from him again.
Statements by James McMillan and Alexander McMillan.
Statement by James McMillan, Justice of the Peace, that Susannah had lived with him the greater part of the four years she'd been in Knoxville.
66-1821

ORTTO, ELIZABETH   1813   no county stated
Elizabeth was married on 2 July 1805 to FREDERICK ORTTO. In NOvember 1805 he left her. She heard he is in a distant region and has taken another wife. He left her with many debts.
16-2-1813

ORTTO, ELIZA   1813   no county stated
This file contains a bill presented to the General Assembly regarding the petition of Eliza Ortto asking for a divorce from her husband, FREDERICK ORTTO. Record Group 60, Box 14, Folder 35, Manuscripts Division

OSBORN, JOHN   22 October 1845   MARSHALL COUNTY
John's second marriage took place on 29 June 1841. His wife (name not given) has a bad temper. They had two children.
17-1844

OWENS, REBECCA   1827   RUTHERFORD COUNTY
Rebecca was married ca 1797 to FRANCES OWENS and lived with him 20 years. They "had several children 12 or 15 years since the said Francis moved to Tennessee, Warren County, bringing your petitioner with him, where they lived some time together..." Francis treated her cruelly, threatened her life and abused her. He did not provide her and the family with life's necessities, so she abandoned him to live with strangers. She is informed he is married to another woman and lives with her in Warren County.
Petition includes signatures of 107 persons.
31-1827

OWENS, REBECCA   1829   RUTHERFORD COUNTY
The marriage is to be dissolved between Rebecca and her husband, THOMAS OWENS, upon proof that he abandoned his wife for a space of two years.
Acts of TN, 1829, p.220.

PAINTER, JANE   12 June 1822   SULLIVAN COUNTY
Jane was married to JACOB P. PAINTER more than six years ago in Sullivan County. He was guilty of harsh treatment of her within 2 years of their marriage. He would beat her, he was adulterous, and he would strip Jane of her clothes and call to passersby to come in and look at her. She had to sleep at times outside.
Her petition is witnessed by George Burkhart, J. P.
Statement by William Stuffle and by Elizabeth Miller, a "neighbor."
112-1822

PALMER, LEE   2 October 1829   CARROLL COUNTY
Lee was married in 1816 to Lucy. In January 1827 she left and refuses to live with him. She left him two children.
142-1829

PARK, SARAH   12 September 1832   KNOX COUNTy
Sarah, a resident of Knox County, was married in November 1825 to ALFRED PARK in McMinn County. After their marriage he did not support her and got indebted. Every dollar's worth of her property was sold to satisfy his debts except that rescued by law. He then sold her property to get whiskey. He beat and abused her when he was drunk. On 30 May 1831 he left on board the steamboat "Knoxville" and has not returned. She asks to again become a feme sole.
Petition includes signatures of 39 persons, "residents of Knoxville and vicinity," including that of William Park.
165-1833

PARK, SARAH   1832   KNOX COUNTY
Sarah Park, wife of ALFRED PARK, is granted the privileges of a feme sole.
Acts of TN, 1832

PARKER, NATHAN   September 1831   JACKSON COUNTY
Nathan on 19 January 1829 was married to SUSANNAH DOSS. He found out she was unfaithful and he tried to get a divorce through Jackson County Court, but she was able to erase the process until some of the papers were lost, so a regular divorce couldn't be gotten. He calls her a prostitute.
Statement by John Houston that Nathan and his wife separated on 15 June 1829. John said Nathan was a widower before his marriage to Susannah, and that Susannah was guilty of adultery with a neighbor, Thomas Heatherly. "Affiant and Parker left for a while to Crawford County, Indiana, where they have lived ever since. It is said and believed that the said Susannah now lives in Louisville, Kentucky...."
Nathan and Susannah were married in Jackson County, Tennessee.
286-1831

PARRISH, MARY M.   17 September 1832   BEDFORD COUNTY
Mary M. was married in 1824 to SAMUEL B. PARRISH of Bedford County. They lived together about 5 years, during which time he was irritable and disagreeable to his family, stayed intoxicated and provided but little for the family.
 He was arrested 6 January 1829 in Shelbyville in Bedford County on a charge of forging cotton receipts, was found guilty (see judgement below), but escaped and left the county and has been absent more than 2 years.
Petition is signed by 42 "residents of Bedford County."
Judgement of Samuel Parrish: found guilty, fined court costs, to be imprisoned for 10 days, to stand 2 hours in the pillory for 3 successive days, and to receive 30 lashes "well laid upon the bare back," and was to be rendered infamous.
2-1832

PARTEE, DINCY   1820   no county stated
DIncy Partee, wife of HENDERSON PARTEE, "shall in no wise be liable to the payment of debts of said Henderson, or to be disposed of by him in any manner."
Acts of TN, 1820, p.111

PATRICK, ROBERT R.   NOvember 1821   WARREN COUNTY
Robert R. Patrick was married in 1814 to LACE MARS of Warren County. He lived with her for some time. They have not lived together since about 1818. She is guilty of adultery and now lives in adultery with certain individuals in

Warren County and is now pregnant by another man.
Petition includes signatures of 19 persons.
Statement by Daniel Eleazor and Robert Henderson. (They referred to Patrick's wife as LAKEY.) Statement by Wiley Patrick that Robert now lives in Rutherford Cty.
83-1821

          PATTERSON, JAMES   18 September 1817   STEWART COUNTY
James Patterson was married in October 1797 to JENSEY MASSEY. She left 12 December 1816 while he was marrying a couple in the neighborhood, he being a justice of the peace for the county of Stewart. She left with William James to go to the Missouri Territory.
Statements by Henry Edwards, Solomon Grice, and James Latimer.
Petition includes signatures of 42 persons.
22-1817

          PATTERSON, MARY   11 November 1833   DAVIDSON COUNTY
Mary was married in 1827 in Tennessee to FENTON PATTERSON. Shortly afterward, he commenced cruel treatment, threatening her life. In October 1831 he kicked her, with her child in her arms of age 9 months, at her dwelling in town of Nashville and out of the house, and has now desserted her and absented himself from her for two years. The child took sick "that night we were kicked out and died a few days later. Dr. Roone believed it died from the injuries received."
Mary hears that Fenton is now living with a woman in Louisville, Kentucky.
Statements by neighbors: John D. Newgent, Thomas A. Winfrey, and John T. Erwin. and Jacob Rulman.
Statement by William Harwell that Fenton had said he had a woman in Shelbyville and that he lived with her and intended to take her to Lovisville with him. William also heard of a woman Fenton lived with in 1832 by name of Sealy Skidmore.
Statement of John B. West, a partner of G. S. Cooke and Company, where Mrs. Patterson came for sewing, that she lost her house because Fenton had not paid the rent. John said he talked with Patterson's father, who censured Fenton.
142-1833

          PATTERSON, MARY   1833   no county given
The marriage is herebydissolved between Mary Patterson and her husband, FENTON PATTERSON. Mary is restored to all rights and privileges of a feme sole.
Acts of TN, 1833, p.144

          PATTON, WILLIAM   21 September 1821   DAVIDSON COUNTY
WIlliam, a citizen of Nashville, was married ca 1813 to MARTHA MARK, a citizen of Nashville. They were happy until "a few months ago." He then suspected her of adultery with James Monroe, who boarded with them. William found Monroe and MArtha in bed together "August last." William and Martha had children (number not stated).
Petition includes signatures of 24 persons.
ctatement of James Patton, "brother of William."
8-1821

          PEAIRS, ISAAC   2 November 1826   SUMNER COUNTY
Isaac Peairs was married in 1822 to ELIZABETH. Isaac was then about 54 years old, having 13 children. Elizabeth was the widow of Arthur Tinnon, with 5 children. Isaac and Elizabeth separated for nearly two years and then went back together and have been together 12 or 18 months. Isaac has made a provision for Elizabeth that she and her brother, Thomas GLEAVES, Jr., have accepted. Isaac and Elizabeth cannot get along,and want a divorce.
154-1826

PEARCE, ISAAC   1826   SUMNER COUNTY
Isaac Pearce and his wife ELIZABETH PEARCE, have separated by mutual consent.
They are to be divorced upon proof.
Acts of TN, 1826, p.134

PEMBERTON, JESSE   October 1821   WILSON COUNTY
Both Jesse and his wife, RUTH PEMBERTON, agree to and want a divorce, for "causes best known to ourselves."
65-1821

PERRY, NORFLEET   14 September 1819   DAVIDSON COUNTY
Norfleet Perry was married in December 1816 to RACHAEL PERRY of Davidson County. (A search of the Davidson County marriages shows that Rachael's name at the time of her marriage was PERRY.) After 5 or 6 months of marriage, Rachael delivered a mulatto child.
Statement of William Donelson, Justice of the Peace of Davidson County, attesting to the marriage of Norfleet Perry.
Statements by Thomas Walton of Sumner County, Josiah Perry, and Edward Phillips.
47-1819

PERRY, NORFLEET   1819   SUMNER COUNTY
NOrfleet is the husband of RACHEL PERRY. They were married in 1816. Five or six months after the marriage, "...Rachel appeared to have been guilty of acts and deeds which would authorize the interposition of this legislature...."
The marriage is hereby dissolved.
Acts of TN, 1819, p.165

PHILLIPS, WILLIAM   29 September 1827   CAMPBELL COUNTY
William Phillips was married in march 1824 to ELIZABETH STILL. They lived together at her father's, James Still's, for a few months. WIlliam wanted to leave her father's and settle elsewhere, but she refused to go and live with him. Sometime afterward, Elizabeth left her father's and went to live with Caswell Cross, a single man. The two were "indicted and convicted in the court of pleas and quarter sessions of Campbell County for living together in open and notorious lewdness and adultery." The two now plan to leave the country for somewhere else.
Statement by Elizabeth Phillips saying that the facts stated by William Phillips are true.
A second petition by William Phillips states that he has been a citizen of Tennessee for 15 or 16 years.
Statement by Micajah Phillips, Henry Adkins, Asa Dougharty, and Charles Philips.
235-1831

PHILLIPSON, POLLY   1807   KNOX COUNTY?
The marriage bonds are hereby dissolved between Polly and her husband, JOHN PHILLIPSON. Polly was formerly POLLY HALL of Knox County.
Acts of TN, 1807, p.85

PICKETT, LETTY   7 June 1826   McMINN COUNTY
Letty was married on 8 June 1824 to WILLIAM PICKETT, then of McMinn County. During the time they lived together he did not make any attempts to have any sexual relationship with her. She states that "he is wholly impotent and incapable of procreation." He left her.
81-1826

PILLE, JOHN   1829   FENTRESS COUNTY
John is husband of NANCY PILLE, who left him.
Petition includes signatures of 22 persons.
193-1829

PIPPIN, KINCHEN   1831   JACKSON COUNTY
Kinchen Pippin has resided in Jackson County for more than 3 years. He was married in North Carolina ca 1817 to LINNY. They had not been married but six weeks before he found out she was unfaithful. He continued to live with her. About 1828 he moved to Tennessee from North Carolina. She, however, continued in her habit of open adultery.
Petition includes signatures of 46 persons.
284-1831

PISTOLE, SUSAN R.   1831   MAURY COUNTY
Susan Pistole, the wife of DAVID PISTOLE, is granted the privileges of a feme sole.
Acts of TN, 1831

PITT, WINFRED   21 September 1819   SUMNER COUNTY
Petition is written by Winfred's "next friend," A. H. Douglass. She was married ca 1798 or 1799 to DAVIS PITT. She believes her husband was committing adultery with Polly Strother. Winfred became convinced that he had, and Davis said he'd slept with Polly two nights at William Pitts' of this county. On June last, he left and took Polly with him, and they are living together.
97-1820

PITT, WINNIFRED   1820   no county stated
Winnifred is wife of DAVIS PITT. "Be it enacted that her property be exempted from liability of the debts of her husband and from his disposition, and to this end that they be divorced from bed and board."
Acts of TN, 1820, p.111

POE, BARBARY   1826   SULLIVAN COUNTY
Barbary Poe, wife of JOHN POE of Sullivan County, is granted the privileges of a feme sole.
Acts of TN, 1826

PONDER, JAMES   1829   SEVIER COUNTy
James Ponder was married to NANCY MATSON ca 1822. They had four children. She left him ca July 1829. He has been a resident of Sevier County the last 8 or 9 years.
145-1829

PORTER, DINCEY   1820   county unclear
Dincey Porter was the late widow of Esquire Sherman, dec'd. of Maury County. She married again to HENDERSON PORTER, who formerly lived in Smith County. Porter was accused of stealing 2 Negroes in Smith County from Benjamin Porter. He left to escape.
Statements acknowledged in Rutherford County by Robert Sellers, Esq., William Yancey, and Col. Samuel Crawford.
42-1820

PORTER, SALLY   6 September 1825   WHITE COUNTY
Petition is written by her "next friend," Anthony Dibrill. Sally was married ca 1776 to JOHN PORTER. They had 11 children. They have lived in White County nearly 20 years. About 12 months ago, John started abusing and beating

her and was constantly from that time up to this, in the habits of adultery with his own granddaughter and has kept her as a wife in his own house and left Sally. John has a tract of land and other property, valued at $5,000.00. Sally wants a divorce, alimony, and that John be compelled from selling or disposing of his land until a decree can be had.
Petition includes signatures of Samuel Turney, attorney.
(This file also includes the following bond:) 3 November 1825 "Sally Porter, John Yeats, and Samuel Porter, all of White County ...bound to John Porter in the sum of $600.00...the condition is such that Sally Porter has agreed to forever relinquish all claim to the property of said John Porter...."
Statement by JOHN PORTER that the claims his wife made against him in 1825 could not be proven. He agreed at that time to give in fee simple one tract of land containing 68 acres to her son-in-law, George Yates, in trust for her support, use, and benefit for and during her natural life. She agreed to give up all her claims to his property and not bother him. Since then, the land has been sold for $600.00, and he doesn't feel that Sarah will keep her covenant. John says that Sarah left his bed in 1824 and refuses to return. He wants a divorce. (no date on this statement)
273-1829

PRICE, HENRY   September 1823   McMINN COUNTY
Henry says that his wife, RYNAY PRICE, has left him and has taken up with WILLIAM GOSSAGE and has children by the said Gossage.
Statements by Henry bullard, Joseph Bullard, Timothy Philpot, and Patsay Ganlery?.
115-1823

PRIVETT, WILLIS   5 November 1827   SMITH COUNTY
Willis Privett was married in December 1824 in Wake County, North Carolina to DELILA PERRY. They lived together happily for two years. At the end of two years and some before, she began asking him to move to the Western Country, suggesting that her mother had moved to Virginia, that her brother had moved to Tennessee, and that since they were poor, by moving they might better themselves. Last February (1827) they arrived in Smith County in the same neighborhood as her brother, Burrell Perry, and his family. They lived with Burrell but Willis soon found his brother-in-law to be devoted to an idle man named John Boze. Delila ran off with Boze and lives with him.
Petition includes signatures of 5 neighbors who say they have known Willis Privett 9 or 10 months.
27-1827

PUGH, PRUDENCE   1827   HICKMAN COUNTY
Prudence Pugh, wife of JOEL PUGH of Hickman County, is granted the privileges of a feme sole.
Acts of TN, 1827

RAINS, JOHN   1829   COCKE COUNTY
John asks for a divorce from his wife, JANE RAINS. She is living in Warren County. They have been separated nine years (since ca 1820). They lived together 10 or 11 years before he left her. John says she was so ill-natured to him he could not live with her. They had six children. He has resided in Cocke County since about 1822.
Petition includes signatuers of 88 persons, including John Rains and Joel Rains.
11-1829

RALSTON, SAMUEL   1827   FAYETTE COUNTY
Samuel Ralston was married in 1817 to SUSANNA ISAACKS in Lincoln County. They lived together until the fall of 1826. In November of 1826 Susanna "started and did go to her father's in Madison County, Alabama..with William Robertson." On the journey she and Robertson passed for man and wife. She returned to Samuel and said she would not live with him unless he let Robertson live at their house. When Samuel refused, she left with Robertson, headed for Lincoln County. That was 1 January 1827.
Petition includes signatures of 84 citizens of Fayette County supporting Ralston's petition.
35-1827

RAMSEY, ELIZABETH   1827   OVERTON COUNTY
The marriage bonds between Elizabeth Ramsey and her husband, WILLIAM RAMSEY, are to be dissolved upon proof that William has abused or abandoned Elizabeth.
Acts of TN, 1827, p.191

RAMSEY, MARY   1831   no county stated
Mary Ramsey, wife of THOMAS K. RAMSEY, is granted the privileges of a feme sole except that of intermarrying with another man.
Acts of Tn, 1831

RAMSEY, MARGORY   October 1821   SUMNER COUNTY
Margory is wife of SHEWBRIDGE RAMSEY. In August 1817, Margory was taken sick, and Shewbridge treated her cruelly and had done so before her illness. She escaped to her father. She has remained with her father for the past four years. Shewbridge has withheld all her property but one dress, is guilty of adultery with a mulatto Negro woman, and got a venereal disease, and is attending Drs. Jepson and Milliken to be cured. Margory wants a divorce and her name to be changed to MARGORY BRASKIN and be given privileges of being single.
Statement by Jesse Milliken of Simpson County, Kentucky saying he (Jesse) was "...called in to give opinion whether or not ...Subridge Ramsey had the venereal disease or not.... as he called me by his brother John ..."
Petition saying that Shewbridge treated his wife ill is signed by 9 persons.
Statements by Edmund Keen of Simpson County County, Kentucky and by Samuel Jepson.
57-1821

RAYBURN, POLLY   July 1820   BEDFORD COUNTY
Polly is wife of HIRAM RAYBURN. She claims cruel treatment by him, and tells of his intoxication. He left the county about 1818.
Statement signed by Larkin Baker, before a justice of the peace of Rutherford County, that the ill treatment of Polly is true. dated July 1820.
17-1820

RAYBURN, ROSANNA   13 OCTOBER 1821 HICKMAN COUNTY
Rosanna is wife of HODGE RAYBURN. They lived together about 9 months. She had a child, a boy. When the boy was about 4 months old, Hodge left. Rosanna states that Hodge was originally from the state of North Carolina and Haywood County, and that she, ROSANNA HARDIN, was married to him in Dickson County.
Statement by Henry Hardin and Clara Hardin, parents of Rosanna Rayburn, formerly Hardin, that said Rosanna was married to Hodge Rayburn 3 September 1818.
26-1821

RAYMOND, SARAH   1833   PERRY COUNTY
Petition is written by Sarah's father, Burrell BENTON, who says that ca 1826 DAVID B. RAYMOND induced his daughter, SARAH, then being ca 16 years old, to elope with and marry him. David has used no sort of means to support Sarah and has been mostly drunk and has been mean to Sarah. About 8 or 9 months ago, David left Sarah and two children. Burrell thinks David is in state of New YOrk. Sarah has gone back to live with her father, Burrell.
Petition includes signatures of 23 persons.
23-1833

RAYMOND, DAVID B.   1833   PERRY COUNTY
The marriage bonds are hereby dissolved between David B. Raymond and his wife, SARAH.
Acts of TN, 1833, p.147

REESE, NANCY   6 September 1813   BEDFORD COUNTY
Nancy is wife of JESSE REESE. They had numerous problems between them and agreed to separate themselves and their property.
Petition includes signatures of 22 persons.
Statement 1 January 1817 in Laurens District, South Carolina signed by 23 persons states that Nancy is about to leave said district with her mother and her brother, Jonathan YORK, that Nancy's husband abused her and ran off with another woman and was caught by the law. Rather than face the courts, Jesse made over a certain portion of his property to Jonathan York in trust for Nancy and the children.
Laurens District, South Carolina. By deed of trust, Jesse Reese gave Nancy 247 acres on which she was then living, one Negro, and other property. Dated 19 October 18__.
26-3-1813

REYNOLDS, ELIZABETH BIGGS   12 October 1826   HAWKINS COUNTY
Elizabeth was married about 1822 to HIRAM REYNOLDS. About 1825, Hiram left. They have one daughter.
Petition includes the signatures of Thornds? Biggs and Elizabeth Biggs.
71-1826

RICH, JOHN   1829   MAURY COUNTY
John Rich was married to SUSANAH MOORE on 15 November 1827. In February of 1828 she gave birth to a mulatto child.
Petition includes the signatures of 35 persons.
233-1829

ROBERTS, ELIZABETH   9 July 1833   ANDERSON COUNTY
Elizabeth is wife of THOMAS ROBERTS. About 1829 he left her and their children. Thomas remarried &is now living in White County, Tennessee.
Petition includes the signatures of 109 persons.
189-1833

ROBERTS, ELIZABETH   1833   ANDERSON COUNTY
The marriage between Elizabeth Roberts and her husband, THOMAS ROBERTS, is hereby dissolved. Elizabeth is restored the privileges of a feme sole.
Acts of TN, 1833, p.37

ROBESON, JOHN L.   5 September 1829   WEAKLEY COUNTY
John L. Robeson was married in 1824 to NANCY PERY in Kentucky. He lived with her until 1st of November last. She was guilty of adultery with Jacob Rogers.

John and Nancy had three? children.
Statement by Jeremiah Huggins that Nancy had confessed she had "done wrong with Jacob Rogers." 18 September 1829.
Statement by Joseph Wilson that the last child Nancy Robeson had belonged to Rogers.
282-1829

ROBINSON, COMFORD   1827   CLAIBORNE COUNTY
Comford is wife of WILLIAM B. ROBINSON. They were married 16 years ago. William is intemperate and she has had to support herself a great portion of that time by her own industry, but is now becoming old and inform, and having no children to support her, has supported her husband for the last 12 years. For the last 12-18 months he hasn't done any work, and it is all she can do to keep him from selling her housekeeping articles to whiskey sellers.
140-1827

ROCKHOLD, DAWSON B.   21 September 1833   WHITE COUNTY
Dawson B. Rockhold was married 20 April 1826 to LUCINDA MOORE. She was guilty of adultery with Thomas Hopper.
Petition includes signatures of 15 persons.
81-1833

RODGERS, JAMES   18 October 1833   SUMNER COUNTY
James Rodgers was married in Sumner County on 25 April 1833 to POLLY BRAZZEL of Sumner County. He lived with her "until June last." Polly would not permit him to cohabit with her, or "treat him as a wife should treat a husband." She went to Gallatin and took goods in his name up to $100.00 and returned home, took his only horse and saddle and left him. She says she only married him for his property and that she won't live with him. He last heard she was on her way to Nashville. He believes she is guilty of adultery, but has no proof.
269-1833

ROGERS, JAMES   1833   SUMNER COUNTY
The marriage bonds between James Rogers and his wife, POLLY, are hereby dissolved.
Acts of TN , 1833, p.85

ROGERS, SARAH   5 September 1832   HICKMAN COUNTY
Sarah is wife of GEORGE RUGERS. He left her and has been gone 3 years "next December." He beat her before he left and she believes he's in Illinois and is married to another woman. He left her with four small children.
Petition includes the signatures of 33 persons.
25-1832
268-1833

RODGERS, SARAH   1833   HICKMAN COUNTY
The marriage bonds are hereby dissolved between Sarah Rodgers and her husband, GEORGE RODGERS. Sarah is granted the privileges of a feme sole.
Acts of TN, 1833

ROPER, WILLIAM   1812   no county stated
William Roper was married 29 April 1792 to POLLY. She frequently left him. In 1794 he went with her to South Carolina to visit her father. She then refused to return with William. About 12 months later she returned to William's house in Virginia and pursued bad conduct. Early in 1800, William came to Tennessee. She has denied him in bed since April 1810, but has produced two

male children "...without the aid or assistance" of William Roper.
This file includes a statement by Polly Roper who states that she agrees with
the wanting of a divorce.
42-1-1812

ROPER, WILLIAM   1812   no county stated
The marriage bonds are hereby dissolved between William Roper and his wife,
POLLY.
Acts of TN, 1812, p.66

ROSS, CAPT THOMAS   31 October 1831   CARROLL COUNTY
CApt. Thomas Ross was married in 1810 to CATHERINE YOST. They lived together
until 1825. He found out she was guilty of adultery. He separated from his
wife because of this.
Petition includes signatures of 28 persons who state that they have been
acquainted with Capt. Ross since 1825.
261-1831

ROSS, THOMAS   1833   CARROLL COUNTY
The marriage is hereby dissolved between Thomas Ross and his wife, CATHERINE
ROSS.
Acts of TN, 1833, p. 171.

ROUNSEVILLE, BARSHABA   1827   no county stated
Barshaba Rounseville is granted the privileges of a feme sole, except that of
intermarrying with another man. (husband's name not stated)
Acts of TN, 1827

RUTLAND, MILBERRY P.   7 October 1831   WILSON COUNTY
Milberry P. Rutland was married to REDDICK RUTLAND, his first cousin, sometime
in 1818 and lived with him about 2 years. He left her and has been gone 12
years and lives in the state of Georgia.
80-1831

RUTLIN, MEBERRY   1827   WILSON COUNTY
Meberry Rutlin is granted the privileges of a feme sole. (husband's name not
stated.)
Acts of TN, 1827

SANDERS, PRUDENCE   1817   MAURY COUNTy
Prudence is the wife of JAMES SANDERS. She says that he beats her.
Statement 1 September 1817 by William Williams and his wife, Marthen Williams
that Sanders did beat his wife.
58-1817

SANDLIN, ELIZABETH   10 November 1821   WASHINGTON COUNTY
Elizabeth was married ca 1811 to RANDOLPH SANDLIN. They lived together but a
short time before he enlisted in the regular service and left her. He returned
with another woman.
In another statement, Elizabeth says she was married September 1813 and that
Randolph enlisted after they'd been married 6 or 8 weeks. "About three years
ago" Randolph informed Elizabeth by letter that he had married again. She
said she remained in the York District until the spring of 1817 when she
returned in company with her brother and his family to Tennessee, to which

place her parents had in the meantime removed, and with a view of being some
nearer to the place where Elizabeth's husband was stationed.
Petition includes signatures of 13 persons.
This file includes letters:
A Letter from Elizabeth's husband, Randolph Sandlin, 13 July 1818 , from
Belle Fountain Missouri Territory, addressed to Miss Elizabeth Sandlin, West
Tennessee, Leeburge. This letter mentions Randolph's brother, John Sandlin.
Second letter is dated 3 February 1819 from Randolph. He mentions his mother,
and informs Elizabeth he has another companion and gives her privileges to do
the same. He asks her to write to him at Missouri Territory, St Louis, Fort
Osage.
103-1822

SAUNDERS, MARY   24 October 1831   DAVIDSON COUNTY
Mary was married in 1824 to WILLIAM SAUNDERS. On 20 June 1831 he became
outrageous toward her and did her bodily damage and tried to deprive her of
life. He drove her from home and children.
198-1831

SCHOLL, JERUSHA   30 July 1822   DAVIDSON COUNTY
Jerusha was married in the summer of 1815 to MILTON SCHOLL in Williamson
County. They moved to the Duck River and lived there until fall of 1816 and
then he brought her to Davidson County and left her. He returned in the
summer of 1818 and then left again ca March 1820 and went to Kentucky. they
have two children.
Oath by Enoch Ensley.
99-1822

SCOTT, JANE   no date stated   DAVIDSON COUNTY
Jane is wife of JAMES SCOTT of Davidson County. they have been married 16
years. For the last 14 years he has been given to "habits of intemperance,"
and he has spent all her property and has not for the last 9 years made any
provision for her support or her children. He has treated her cruelly and
threatened her life. She, through her industry, has been able to provide a
home for herself and children and by teaching school has supported them. She
asks for rights of a feme sole.
Undated Box, Legislative Petitions, Manuscripts Division

SCOTT, JANE   1827   DAVIDSON COUNTY
Jane Scott, the wife of JAMES SCOTT is granted the privileges of a feme sole,
except that of intermarrying with another man.
Acts of TN, 1827

SCRUGGS, WILLIE W.   1831   WILSON COUNTY
Willie W. Scruggs was married in November 1828 to HARRIET SCRUGGS in Sumner
County. They lived together a short time in Hendersonville, and then permanently settled in Lebanon. He thought she was being unfaithful, and he left
his business in Lebanon, and they moved to St. Louis, Kentucky. He again
returned to Lebanon where her conduct became worse. She left him and went to
Nashville, and he believes she is living as a common prostitute.
Petition includes signatures of 17 persons.
13-1831

SCUDDER, HARRIET PAYNE   1825   TOWN OF SHELBYVILLE
"Harriet Payne Scudder of the town of Shelbyville, may file her petition
before the next circuit court for the county of Bedford, praying to be divorced

from her husband, PHILLIP I. SCUDDER, and it shall be the duty of said court
to dissolve the marriage contract now existing and that she shall hereafter be
known by the name of HARRIET PAYNE WHITNEY, providing 10 days' notice shall be
given to the said Phillip previous to the sitting of said court."
The divorce is to be granted upon proof that Phillip absented himself and
failed to support Harriet.
Acts. of TN, 1825, p.210

   SEALES, ROBERT HENRY 26 September 1831 WILLIAMSON COUNTY
Robert Henry Seales states that he has been a citizen of Williamson County for
many years. In June of 1829 he was married to NANCY YOUNG, who resided at
that time in said county. Nancy lived with him 5 or 6 months, then left him.
She went to Kentucky and has remained there ever since. She has had a child
which he says is not his.
Petition includes signatures of 44 persons.
320-1831

   SELVIDGE, GEORGE 1 July 1820 MONROE COUNTy
George is husband of MARY SELVIDGE. He accuses Mary of adultery in the summer
and fall of 1818. They have 5 children. George lives on Forke Creek in
Monroe County.
Statement signed by Mary Selvidge saying that she wants a divorce.
In a later petition George states that he became suspicious of Mary in the
summer and fall of 1818, suspicious of her conduct with a man of the neighborhood. On 21 November 1818 he told his wife his suspicions, and she confessed.
They separated, and he divided with her some of his goods. He took his
children and moved to Monroe County.
Statement by Nancy Oakes, 6 November 1820.
25-1820
55-1821

   SELVIDGE, NANCY 1825 MONROE COUNTY
Nancy states that in 1818 she and her husband separated. She is seeking a
divorce and says that her husband had sought a divorce several years ago.
20-1825 (Husband's name is not stated.)

   SEVIER, CHARITY 1812 no county stated
The marriage bonds are hereby dissolved between Charity Sevier and her husband,
JOSEPH SEVIER.
Acts of TN, 1812, p.66

   SEVIER, JOHN, JR. 1809 no county stated
The marriage bonds are hereby dissolved between John Sevier, Jr. and his wife,
SUSANNA SEVIER, formerly of Greene County.
Acts of TN, 1809, p.18

   SEXTON, JAMES R. 23 August 1831 BLOUNT COUNTY
James R. Sexton states that he was married in 1827 to ELIZABETH. Within three
months she left him and has finally left the country. He wants a divorce.
Petition includes signatures of 8 persons.
Statement by Mrs. Mary Carson, age 25, who says that "last fall" Elizabeth
Sexton came to Mrs. Carson's father's house and asked Mary where Mary's husband,
Robert Carson, was. Elizabeth stayed, with her child, and when Robert came home
and all were in bed, Mary caught Elizabeth and Robert in the act of adultery.
Statement by Mark Sexton, age 60, Blount County: "I found Able Dockery lying on
the bed with Elizabeth."

Statement by Joseph Duncan, age 40, Blount County: "Elizabeth lived at my
house for some time. She had bad conduct towards men, both married and single."
Statement by James Alexander, age 26, Blount County, that he saw Able Dockery
in private conversation with Elizabeth Sexton.
Statement by David Hamontree, age 35, Blount County, that he saw Thomas Cart-
write "on top of Elizabeth Sexton."
Statement by Thomas Cartwrite, age 23, that he saw Elizabeth with a Samuel
McOnel of McMinn County.
File contains a page with 68 signatures.
216-1831

SHANNON, MARGARET   1823   GREENE COUNTY
Margaret Shannon, "otherwise MARGARET CONNER," a citizen of Greene County,
shall be known as MARGARET SHANNON, and that her children retain the name of
Shannon.. She is granted the privileges of a feme sole except that of inter-
marrying with another man.
Acts of TN 1823.

SHAW, MAHALIA   8 September 1832   WILLIAMSON COUNTY
Mahalia Shaw, "formerly MAHALIA BUGG," was married in December 1831 to a man
who called himself GEORGE W. SHAW. In October of 1831 George Shaw had come to
her neighborhood with his brother, Thomas Shaw, and a man who called himself
Elisha Green and his family. Green was supposed to have married a sister of
Shaw some four days after Green purchased a valuable tract of land for which
he gave his notes due the April following, and Green told her that he and
"the Mrs. Shaw" had carried a drove of horses to South Alabama and sold them,
which money would be collected in time to pay for the land. The Shaws procured
a place and pretended to making arrangements to open a store. George W. Shaw
made several attempts to purchase stores of merchants who were already in
business, and from his appearance seemed he would settle in this part of the
country. Around December1831 Shaw left with his brother and brother-in-law
and family under cover of night. Mahalia states that she is entitled to some
property by her father's will, which she doesn't want Shaw to get. She also
wants her name restored to MAHALIA BUGG.
Petition includes the signatures of 31 persons.
51-1832

SHAW, MAHALA   1832   WILLIAMSON COUNTY
The bonds of matrimony are hereby dissolved between Mahala Shaw and her husband,
GEORGE W. SHAW. "Mahala Shaw .....to be known by her former name, MAHALA
BUGG."
Acts of TN, 1832, p.41

SHEARMAN, GEORGE T.   June 1822   HUMPHREYS COUNTY
George T. Shearman was married 4 February 1821 to MILLY ELIZA CLINTON of
Humphreys County. They lived together until the last of September. Thereafter
Milly left him at that time and will not return.
Petition includes signatures of 59 persons, including Charles Shearman.
Statement by Milly E. Shearman, agreeing to a divorce.
Statement by a neighbor, D. Mims.
Statements by William Wood and Wilson M. Sarrett.
109-1822

SHELL, LEMENTINE   1831   GILES COUNTY
A divorce is to be granted to Lementine Shell, wife of JAMES N. SHELL, upon
proof that James treated her cruelly, deserted her, and made no support for
her.
Acts of TN, 1831, p.223

SHERRILL, EVE   1827   WILSON COUNTY
Eve Sherrill, wife of SAMUEL SHERRILL, is granted the privileges of a feme sole.
Acts of TN, 1827

SHIRLEY, REBECCA   3 September 1825   LAWRENCE COUNTY
Rebecca is wife of GEORGE SHIRLEY. About 1821, George left.
Statements by John A. Hale & Josephus Irvine.
17-1825

SHORT, JANE   1829   no county stated
Jane was a widow with 5 children, the oldest being 10 years old when she was married 12 December 1826 to AARON SHORT. He said he was 59 years old. He stayed with her about 3 months, drunk most of the time, and then left, and she was pregnant.
Petition includes signatures of 24 persons, including Joab Short.
65-1829

SICK, MARY   28 September 1829   CLAIBORNE COUNTY
Mary is wife of JOSEPH M. SICK. They had "several" children. Joseph abandoned her and has since married 2 or 3 times, as she is informed. She wants feme sole.
Petition includes signatures of 16 persons.
229-1829

SICK, MARY   1829   CLAIBORNE COUNTY
Mary Sick, wife of JOSEPH SICK, is granted the privileges of a feme sole, except that of intermarrying with another man.
Acts of TN, 1829

SIMPSON, REUBEN   1807   no county stated
The marriage bonds between Reuben Simpson and his wife, POLLY SIMPSON, are hereby dissolved.
Acts of TN, 1807, p.85

SISK, FAULKNER   1831   LINCOLN COUNTY
Faulkner Sisk, of Lincoln County, was married to MARTHA OWEN of Giles County. Soon after their marriage, Martha separated from him for 3 years and refused to cohabit with him or perform any of the matrimonial obligations, but cohabited with other men and has become the mother of a "spurious offspring."
Petition includes the signatures of 14 persons.
314-1831

SLEEKER, PATSY   1823   WILLIAMSON COUNTY
Patsy Sleeker, wife of GEORGE SLEEKER of Williamson County is granted the privileges of a feme sole except that of intermarrying with another man.
Acts of TN, 1823, p.111

SLEEKER, GEORGE, SR.   no date stated   no county stated
George Sleeker, Sr. is husband of PATSY SLEEKER. They have lived together unhappily as man and wife. At the last session of the General Assembly, Patsy was granted the privileges of a feme sole.
Petition is signed by both George and Patsy Sleeker.
Undated Box, Legislative Petitions, Manuscripts Division

SLOSS, JOSEPH   5 August 1829   RUTHERFORD COUNTY
Joseph Sloss is husband of SALLY SLOSS. She left him February 1826. He was then living in Rutherford County.
Petition includes signatures of 13 persons.
41-1829

SMITH, CATHERINE S.   6 October 1821   WILLIAMSON COUNTY
Catherine was married 22 April 1819 to JOHN P. SMITH. Since she's been living
with him, their house has been open to the worst company who engaged in lewdness
and drunkenness. John has treated her inhumanely. He is guilty of adultery,
even with his slaves.
Statements by Levi H. Reaves and Alfred A. Edney.
Statement of issuance of marriage license16 April 1819 in Franklin, Williamson
County between John P. Smith and CATHERINE D. ROBINSON of Williamson County.
Statement signed by 11 persons called on by Mr. Robinson to certify to the
character of John during his residence in Franklin.
1821-49

SMITH, CATHERINE   no date stated   WILLIAMSON County
Catherine is wife of JOHN SMITH. They have agreed to live separate and have
divided their property which is satisfactory to them and their children. the
circuit court of the state refused to embrace their case so the General Assembly
of Tennessee "passed a bill to divorce them."
Record Group 60, Box 17, Folder 36; Manuscripts Division

SMITH, FREDERICK   11 September 1827   CAMPBELL COUNTY
Frederick Smith of Campbell County was married ca July 1817 to NANCY HOOVER,
who was at that time a widow and had lived in Campbell County for some years
prior to their marriage. Frederick caught Nancy in the woods twice with
another man. Frederick left her for a few months but returned to her, but
before long he caught her with other men. He applied for a divorce with the
circuit court of Campbell County, and she then pledged to do better. He
stayed with her another 6 or 7 months before leaving. Nancy laid in bed all
night with Samuel Crabtree in Frederick's house in Frederick's presence. She
now lives with Samuel Crabtree, who is her sister's son, in Campbell County.
"An indictment was found against them for so living and they refused to be
taken."
272-1827

SMITH, LYDIA   4 October 1821   no county stated
Lydia states that she agrees to be divorced from her husband William Smith.
15-1821

SMITH, MARGARET   19 November 1827   McMINN COUNTY
In 1826 Margaret's husband died, which left her with a number of small children
and but a small estate. Last February she married JOHN SMITH of Monroe County.
"Just a few days past" he left her.   She wants feme sole.
248-1827

SMITH, MARGARET   9 September 1831   McMINN COUNTY
Ca 1827 MARGARET SITZ was married to JOHN SMITH in McMinn County, whe she has
ever since resided. She was a widow with 7 children. A few weeks after their
marriage he would become irritated and threaten to leave her, accusing her of
too great affection for her children. They separated after they lived together
8 months. He left her and has been absent from the state upwards of 3 years.
Petition includes signatures of 8 neighbors.
123-1831

SMITH, MARGARETTA   November 1833   BLOUNT COUNTY
Margaretta, of Blount County, married JOSHUA SMITH "some years ago," he once
of the county of Blount, but has since left. They lived together 10 or 12
years. Ca 1830 Joshua left her and went to McMinnville. She heard he married
again. He is by trade a shoemaker. He left her and her little son.
Petition includes signatures of 25 persons, people of Maryville, where Joshua
lived before he left Margaret and child.
187-1833

SMITH, MILLY   1827   ROANE COUNTY
Milly was married to JAMES H. SMITH of Roane County in April 1823. He left her April last and did not leave support for her and their two children. Petition is signed: "Milly Smith, alias MILLY STOUT."
92-1827

SMITH, ROSEAN   19 December 1829   KNOX COUNTY
Rosean, a citizen of Knoxville, is the daughter of Terence McCAFFREY. She was married in February 1827 to ULYSSES G. SMITH, then of Knoxville. They lived together at her father's house until August 1827 when he induced her to go to West Tennessee to Lebanon. He left for Nashville to get work, returned in September 1827 and then left for Nashville, promising to return soon, but did not. She heard from Nashville he went to Natchez and married again. In the fall of 1828 he went to Louisville and there married Emily E. Oldham. From the LOUISVILLE PUBLIC ADVERTISER, she learned that he went from Louisville to Cincinnati and tried to get married there. Rosean received a letter from Emily of Louisville stating that Ulysses had married her (Emily) and also a letter from Emily's brother-in-law, Jefferson Overstreet, stating same. The LOUISVILLE PUBLIC ADVERTISER of May 27, 1829 showed Smith's marriage and was signed by Jefferson Overstreet, Henry Oldham, and William Oldham. Petition includes signatures of 30 persons.
231-1829

SMITH, ROSANNA   1829   KNOX COUNTy
A divorce is to be granted to Rosanna Smith, wife of ULYSES G. SMITH, upon proof that Ulyses was either married before or since his marriage with her.
Acts of TN, 1829, p.261

SMITH, TEMPERANCE W.   1819   RUTHERFORD COUNTY
The marriage ishereby dissolved between Temperance W. Smith and her husband, THOMAS B. SMITH. Temperance hereafter to be called TEMPERANCE W. BASS.
Acts of TN, 1819, p.30

SNAPP, MAGDALENE   1827   SULLIVAN COUNTY
Magdalene was married ca 1789 in Virginia to JOHN SNAPP now of Sullivan County, Tennessee. She bore him six children. Between ca 1807-1809 John deserted her, leaving her and 5 children. In ca 1816 she moved from Virginia to Sullivan County and has been engaged in tavernkeeping in Blountville and is now pursuing the same business in Paperville(?) and has acquired a comfortable living for her and the two children who are still living with her.
215-1827

SNAPP, MAGDALENE   1827   no county stated
Magdalene Snapp, wife of JOHN SNAPP, is granted the privileges of a feme sole except that of intermarrying with another man.
Actas of TN, 1827

STACY, SARAH   1832   GREENE COUNTY
The marriage between Sarah Stacy and her husband, ZACHARIAH STACY, is to be dissolved upon proof of desertion for space of two years by Zachariah.
Acts of TN, 1832, p.25

STALCUP, RACHEL   1822   JACKSON COUNTY
Rachel Stalcup is granted the privileges of a feme sole. (Husband's name is not stated.)
Acts of Tn, 1822

STEWART, ELIZABETH E.   no date stated   LAWRENCE COUNTY
Elizabeth E. was married to JOSHUA STEWART in Lawrence County in January 1829
when she was 14 years old. He left her after 3 months of marriage. She is
informed he lives with another woman.
Petition includes signatures of 34 persons.
Undated Box, Legislative Petitions, Manuscripts Division

STEWART, WILLIAM   13 September 1824   OVERTON COUNTY
William and his wife, ELIZABETH STEWART separated ca 1817. She was caught in
the bed of adultery.
Petition includes signatures of 52 persons, including John Stewart, Joseph
Stewart, David Stewart, and Hansford Stewart.
61-1824

STOCKARD, SAMUEL   1824   MAURY COUNTY
A divorce is to be granted Samuel Stockard, husband of PHOEBE STOCKARD, upon
proof.
Acts of TN, 1824, p.111

STOKES, ISBEL   6 November 1821   RUTHERFORD COUNTY
Isbel is wife of WILLIAM STOKES. She says he hasn't treated her as a husband
should treat his wife for 12 or 15 years. He has given her little support and
has left her and 5 small children.
Statement by James Sanders who said he lived near the Stokes in 1817.
Statement by Moses Wollen and Elizabeth L. Wollen.
Statement by Henry Cooper, Joshua Barton, and John Bealey, also by Solomon Ren
and Luresay Ren.
44-1821

STONE, DERINDA   7 September 1821   MAURY COUNTY
Derinda is wife of LEMUEL W. STONE. He left her after only 10 days of marriage.
Statement by Lemuel Prewett.
Another statement supporting the facts of the petition is signed by about 10
persons.
Statement by Derinda on 13 September 1823 that Lemuel has been gone 6 years.
Statement by Charnel Russ and Avarilla Green Russ that after Lemuel left
Derinda, he went to NOrth Carolina and married Parthona Brasil and left her
after 12 months.
11-1821
21-1823

STONE, DERINDER   1823   MAURY COUNTy
Derinda, wife of LEMUEL STONE, is granted the privileges of a feme sole.
Acts of TN, 1823

STONE, HANNAH   6 October 1831   HAYWOOD COUNTY
Petition is written by David Huddleston. Ca 10 May 1821 Hannah was married
to THOMAS STONE. HE left her and has been absent for more than two years.
She has heard that he is in MIssissippi or Louisiana. She has two infant
children.
Petition includes signatures signatures of 7 persons of Haywood County.
329-1831

STONE, KIZZIAH   1823   DICKSON COUNTY
Kizziah, wife of WILLIAM STONE is granted the privileges of a feme sole.
Acts of TN, 1823, p.227

STREET, ELIZABETH   16 September 1821   SUMNER COUNTY
Elizabeth was married in 1810 to JAMES STREET. In about 1812 he sold their only
Negro and left Elizabeth. He had other debts., so the rest of the property
was taken by creditors. She was left with one child. James was absent about
6 months. He returned and they lived together again for about 5 years ..."during
which time she has had 4 children." He abused her, left for 2 or 3 weeks at a
time and then left her again. He has now been absent more than 2½ years. Her
father has assisted her in subsisting.
Petition includes the signatures of 27 persons.
56-1821

STUART, REBECCAH   7 September 1813   GREENE COUNTY
Rebeccah was married ca 1799 to William Stuart. In December 1810 William left
her and took with him another woman. Rebeccah heard they live in Rutherford
County.
15-2-1813

STUART, REBECCAH   1813   GREENE COUNTY
This file contains a bill presented to the General Assembly regarding the
petition of Rebeccah Stuart asking for a divorce.
Record Group 60, Box 14, Folder 35; Manuscripts Division

STUNSTON, JAMES   17 September 1829   WEAKLEY COUNTY
James states that his wife, BURNETTEY STUNSTON, left his home in Weakley
County ca 9 October and refuses to return.
Statement by Elizabeth Stunston and Elizabeth Summers that Burnettey had left
James twice and came to the house of Henry Stunston. Burnettey refused to
return to James, saying that she hated him and was forced to marry him.
30-1829

SULLIVAN, ANN ELIZA   July 1820   DAVIDSON COUNTY
Ann Eliza was married in May 1818 to ELISHA SULLIVAN. In August 1818 he
"obliged her to quit his house and refused her admittance there ever after."
She wants a divorce and to be restored to her maiden name of PHILLIPS.
Statement by John Sanford that he heard Elisha say on 16 June 1820 that he
didn't expect ever to live with his wife again.
STatements by John Dennis and John Hartgraves.
Petition includes signatures of 5 persons.
192-1821

SUTTLES, CELA   October 1827   McMINN COUNTY
Cela was married in 1824 to HENRY SUTTLES. He left her shortly after they
married, returned, but left again about 12 months "past." They have children
(number not stated). She believes he now lives in the western part of the
state with another woman in open adultery. She wants a divorce and to be
restored to her former name, CELA HAMRICK, and to be allowed the privileges of
a feme sole.
Petition includes signatures of 10 persons.
Statement by Sealy Suttles that she has just reason to believe that her husband
committed adultery with Susana Richards, by his confession to her. He left
Sealy on 4 November 1826 and moved to Warren County. He is now living with
another woman.
Statement by Samuel Hewbanks, who lived with Sealy and Henry the forepart of
the winter of 1825 and spring of 1826.
181-1827

SWANEY, SARAH R .   8 July 1820   DAVIDSON COUNTY ?
Sarah R. has been married to JAMES N. SWANEY for six months. He was jealous, and in 3 months was taken ill and accused a Negro girl "that my father had sent me." Sarah tells of harsh treatment she received, and of not being allowed to leave the house. Her father-in-law and others of the family live with them. Her father-in-law at one point though James might be violent towards her.
Second petition of Sarah's states that they were married 4 January 1820, and that he treated her in a violent manner. She stayed with him about six months. He has left her without any support.
66-1820
54-1821

SWISHER, ANN   22 October 1827   WILLIAMSON COUNTY
Ann was married 30 January 1823 to MICHAEL SWISHER of Williamson County. After their marriage, they lived in the house with her father, Isaac BATEMAN for two years and worked with her father's hands on the farm. Her father gave Michael one-third of the crop raised on his farm each year. In less than 5 months after their marriage Michael commenced drinking and gambling and spending his part of the crops before it could be raised. In the spring of 1825 they moved and set up housekeeping of their own. Michael continued drinking and gambling. In 9 months they had to move back to her father's. Michael then became involved in forgery and counterfeiting of order and notes of land. When it was likely to come against him, he left for Bowling Green, Kentucky, where he said he had business. She thinks instead he went to Nashville for a few days, then returned to her father's house at night, stole her father's trunk with money and papers in it, took it to Nashville and destroyed the papers. He then returned to her father's house. He was caught a few days later when he tried to draft a $100.00 note which turned out to be one of her father's. He confessed to taking the trunk and money. He escaped and left her and one child in May 1826.
Second petition is a statement by four persons certifying that the charges alleged in Ann's petition are believed to be true.
44-1827
225-1827

SWISHER, ANN   1827   WILLIAMSON COUNTY
The marriage between Ann and her husband, MICHAEL SWISHER, is to be dissolved upon proof of the desertion of Michael and his failure to support his family.
Acts of TN, 1827,p.121

TANNER, SELY   no dated stated   LAWRENCE COUNTy
SELY ODOM was married to JOHN TANNER, both being of Lawrence County. He left her shortly after they married, and one child. She found out at the time of their marriage that John had another wife and children then living in North Carolina.
Petition includes signatures of 19 persons, including a John Tanner.
Undated Box, Legislative Petitions, Manuscripts Division

TATE, ELIZA JANE   1833   McMINN COUNTY
The marriage between Eliza Jane and her husband, JOHN TATE, is hereby dissolved. Eliza Jane is restored to the privileges of a feme sole.
Acts of TN, 1833, p.17

TATUM, HOWEL   1812   no county stated
The marriage between Howel Tatum and his wife, ROSANNAH TATUM, is hereby dissolved.
Acts of TN, 1812, p.21

TAYLOR, JANE   1819   OVERTON COUNTY
A divorce is hereby granted to Jane and her husband, THOMAS TAYLOR.
Acts of TN, 1819, p.181

TAYLOR, MARY   6 July 1822   SULLIVAN COUNTY
About May 1810 Mary was married to SAMUEL TAYLOR. They lived together about 3 years and then he left her. She went to her father's house for protection and support. They have two children.
100-1822

TAYLOR, MARY   1822   SULLIVAN COUNTY
Mary Taylor is granted the privileges of a feme sole. (Husband's name is not stated.)
Acts of TN, 1822

TAYLOR, TEMPLE   22 September 1833   LINCOLN COUNTY
Temple states that he was married to his present wife, JANE OLLIFENT, in 1804 in Mecklenburg County, North Carolina, and then removed from Iredell County, North Carolina to Lincoln County. "We have had 3 children." Then, in Fall of 1828, Jane became insane and so continued to present time. Temple is poor and will be constrained to put her in some asylum where she will be attended to. He still loves her, and is willing to pay all charges for her maintenance. He has no other complaint of her except that she can't be a wife to him. She has become impotent. "Complainant will abide by any decision that your Honorable Body may make either by granting the prayer of the petitioner or by a special reference to the circuit court of Lincoln County for adjudication."
Statements by Wiilliam Cashion, James Brown, William George, James Bracy, and Henry C. Taylor stating that Jane has been deranged the last 4 or 5 years, that she is totally incompetent, and wholly unfit for married life. "Henry C. Taylor is Temple's son."
116-1833

TAYLOR, THOMAS   September 1821   RUTHERFORD COUNTY
Thomas was married in 1819 to NANCY NEUSOM of Bedford County. They lived together 4 months, then she left him. She was taken away the first time by her father and uncle, and afterwards by her uncle. Thomas got her to return, but she stayed only 3 months and left again. She now lives with her father in Bedford County, about 20 miles from Thomas. She treated Thomas with abuse. He had one child by Nancy.
Statement by Thomas Lofton, Larken Johnson, Hardy Miller, and James Higgins.
64-1821

THOMAS, MARGARET   1827   DAVIDSON COUNTY
Margaret Thomas is granted the privileges of a feme sole. (Husband's name is not stated.)
Acts of TN, 1827

THOMAS, PEGGY   1824   HENRY COUNTY
Peggy Thomas, wife of ISAAC THOMAS, both citizens of Henry County, is granted the privileges of a feme sole, except that of intermarrying with another man. Peggy can sue for a divorce, and Henry County is authorized to appoint her as the guardian of her children, "should they think proper."
Acts of TN, 1824, p.143

THOMPSON, AGNESS   2 MAY 1813   JACKSON COUNTY ?
Agness was married to WILLIAM THOMPSON about 11 March 1786. She was informed
that at the time of their marriage he had a wife then living, named Avy Thompson.
Avy is still living.
Petition includes signatures of 14 persons.
Statement from Montgomery County, Virginia 22 January 1803 by Avy Thompson who
stated that she was married to William Thompson in 1783 and that they lived
together some time, and that he lived with her in 1794 or 1795 and then left
her.
Statement by Jonas Medford of Jackson County that in May of 1807 he was sent
for by William Thompson of Jackson County. William wanted him to draw up an
instrument of writing securing his property so that his wife in Virginia could
not recover any of it. 20 September 1809.
8-2-1809

THOMPSON, SUSAN S.   15 September 1833   WILLIAMSON COUNTY
Susan S. was married in 1824 to THOMAS A. THOMPSON, who shortly after became
dissolute and squandered all the fortune which he had acquired by her. She
then worked and provided for them. He would become intoxicated and absent
himself for spells, and threatened violence. He has now been absent more than
three years.
Petition includes signatures of 89 "citizens of Williamson County."
Statement by John F. Smith and J. H. Childress, 16 September 1833.
Statement by Cary White of Williamson County that Susan and Thomas lived in
her house part of one year--1828 or 1829. 16 September 1833.
Letter with heading of 25 September 1833, Covington, and addressed to Major
Joseph Coe and Josiah Hatley and from Thomas A. Thompson says that he read in
the last Nashville papers about a bill introduced by Mr. Martin to divorce
Susan J. Thompson from bonds of matrimony. "This is against my will. I ask
you to prevent it. She refused to go with me when I left Williamson County,
refusing to leave her sisters." He says that HEnry R. W. Hill of Nashville,
R. C. Foster of Williamson County, and James Sparks of Franklin, and Dr.
McPhail can attest that "I have sent her money since I've been here."

THOMPSON, SUSAN L.   1833   WILLIAMSON COUNTY
Susan Thompson is hereby divorced from her husband, Thomas A. Thompson, and is
restored the privileges of a feme sole.
Acts of TN, 1833, p.15

THOMPSON, WILLIAM   1824   WASHINGTON COUNTY
William is hereby divorced from his wife, MARY THOMPSON, upon proof.
Acts of TN, 1824, p.112

THORNBURGH, REBECCA   1807   no county stated
Rebecca is hereby divorced from her husband, ISAAC THORNBURGH.
Acts of TN, 1807, p.85

TILLEY, DIANNA   November 1833   WASHINGTON COUNTY
Dianna Tilley, formerly DIANNA SELLARS, was married ca 1826 to WESTLY TELLEY.
He became involved in dishonesty, forgery, etc. and finally left her more than
2 years ago. He was convicted of felony in North Carolina. She was left with
2 helpless children. She asks to be restored to all the rights which she
possessed as a feme sole.
194-1833

TODD, FLORA M.   1833   MONROE COUNTY
The marriage is to be dissolved between Flora M. Todd and her husband CHARLES W. TODD. Flora is restored to all the privilges of a feme sole.
Acts of TN, 1833, p.134

TODD, SAMUEL   1 November 1833   KNOX COUNTY
Samuel states that his wife, DIANNA TODD, left him ca 1828.
Petition includes signatures of 20 persons.
183-1833

TOWNSEN, ALBERT   1826   OVERTON COUNTy
Albert was married ca 1823 to POLLY LYTLE of Overton county. She ran around with bad company and finally eloped with Reuben Flowers of Kentucky, where they live together as man and wife. Polly left with Albert their infant daughter, the only child that she and Albert had.
STatement by Reuben Flowers   29 September 1826.
5-1826

TOWNSEND, SARAH ANN   1827   WILSON COUNTY
Sarah Ann, wife of RICHARD TOWNSEND, is granted the privileges of a feme sole, except that of intermarrying with another man.
Acts of Tn, 1827

TREADWAY, DANIEL   16 August 1813   JEFFERSON COUNTY
Daniel was married in FEbruary 1807 to REBECCAH EATON. In 1809 he entered into the service of the United States. She lived for nearly 12 months in the camp with him. When their children began to grow in size and number, they concluded she should move back to the plantation in Jefferson County. She committed adultery sometime after that with Benjamin Davis.
Statement in Hawkins County, by Joseph Austin, neighbor, who said that Rachel was pregnant, but not by Daniel.
Statement in Hawkins County by mother of Rebecca, Rachel Eaton.
11-2-1813

TROUSDALE, SALLY   12 September 1833   SUMNER COUNTY
Sally, a citizen of Sumner County and so has been for 30 or 40 years, was married ca 1813 to JONATHAN TROUSDALE in Sumner County. They lived together 4 or 5 years, during which time he drank til he spent all of her property. He then became intolerable. They separated. Some years later he married a ____ (blank) Young, and they moved to Madison County, Alabama.
233-1833

TURNER, ELIZABETH N.   1831   McMINN COUNTy
Elizabeth N. of Athens, McMinn County, was married ca 22 November 1827 to JOHN P. TURNER of same place. They lived together in peace for "some weeks," then he became ill tempered towards her. He proposed moving to Alabama. She consented and in February 1828 they moved to Bellfouts?, Alabama. They later moved to Tuscumbia, then to Mount Pleasant, then to Franklin, Tennessee, then to Nashville, then again to Mount Pleasant, then to Farmington, "where they arrived in the month of July...." They had lived in this last place ca 3 weeks when his conduct towards her became so bad that the local citizens interferred "and confined said Turner." He escaped from custody and left her 1 August 1828 to she knows not where, "except by a letter from his father, who stated that said John P. Turner was there in North Carolina, on his way to Philadelphia and that he never intended returning to Tennessee." She was 150 miles from her relations but did get home to her father's in 1828 and has lived there since.
Petition includes signatures of 4 "citizens of Athens."
133-1831

TURNER, WILLIAM   September 1827   McMINN COUNTY
William was married "2 April last" to RACHEL RIGGINS. She left only a short time after they were married. He believes she has been guilty of adultery since she left him about four months ago. Rachel also said she wanted to poison him.
STatement by Byars Willson.
Petition includes signatures of 40 persons, plus those of John Turner and Samuel Turner.
179-1827

TURNEY, HOPKINS S.   29 September 1823   MARION COUNTY
Hopkins S. Turney was married August 1820 to MARY LEA of White County. (This was how the marriage was celebrated:) "On Saturday about 11 o'clock in the morning....I was invited to the store of...Lewis Fletcher in Sparta, and on my arrival at said store, there was some wine together with some white sugar set on the counter. I was invited to drink, and after drinking there for some time, I became intoxicated, and then some person commenced persuading me to marry said Mary, but I had no intention of doing so, until I became very drunk, and that after some time I was conducted to the house of a certain Joseph Copper where the said Mary lived. When I arrived there, some person who is unknown to me set some wine and sugar on the table, and I was invited to drink, which I did, and after some time some person had went off to the office of the clerk of the county court and obtained the marriage license, and procured a justice of the peace to go with him to the house of said Copper where I was drinking and then..." he married Mary. After two or three days of marriage, he left her and went to Illinois. After he left her, he heard she left White County with Charles Lowery and traveled with him to Illinois, where she remained for two years with said Lowery and his family. Hopkins S. Turney accuses Mary of adultery with Lowery.
66-1823

TYLER, CHARLOTIA T.   19 September 1832 BEDFORD COUNTY
Charlotia T. Tyler, formerly CHARLOTIA T. SHARP, was married 3 August 1831 to CHESTER TYLER. She was 16 years old when they married. He left her about 4 weeks after they married "under pretense of going to Middleton, Rutherford County..." She was supposed to join him when he asked her to come. She found out he left Middleton. In about 1 month she received a letter form him saying he was "confined in the common jail of Franklin County, Tennessee on a charge of petit larceny." On 13 January she received another letter saying he'd been convicted of said charge and sentenced to the state penitentiary for 2 years. He requested her to address his letters by name of Charles T. Broughton.
181-1831

URY, GEORGE   29 June 1820   MONTGOMERY COUNTY
George was married in 1815 to NANCY HARRIS. In October 1817 she left him for 3 or 4 months. She lived with him 2 or 3 months, then in March 1818 she left again and said she'd not return. She took property and furniture as she'd had before their marriage. She was his second wife. He has a large family dependent upon him and has recently become disabled from a dislocation of his right hip. He is 57 years old.
93-1820

VANDEVANTER, REBECCA   1826   SULLIVAN COUNTy
Rebecca is a citizen of Sullivan County. She was born in said county and has been a citizen thereof for more than a year last past. She was married to JOHN VANDEVANTER ca January 1814. She had 7 children by him. She brought with her when they married property worth about $150.00. They lived together

about 10 years. They moved from Sullivan County to Lee County, Virginia, and while there John was guilty of adultery and other acts for which he ran from Lee County to McMinn Cunty, Tennessee and took Rebecca with him. She left him and returned to Sullivan County.
85-1826

    VANDEVENTER, REBECCA 1826 no county stated
Rebecca, wife of JOHN VANDEVENTER, is granted the privileges of a feme sole.
Acts of TN, 1826

    VANDYKE, NANCY 1833 RHEA COUNTY
Nancy Vandyke, formerly NANCY EVES, is hereby divorced from her husband, ISRAEL A. VANDYKE.
Acts of TN, 1833, p.62

    VAUGHN, RACHEL 1832 CARTER COUNTY
Rachel Vaughan, wife of T. VAUGHN, of Carter County, is granted the privileges of a feme sole.
Acts of TN, 1832

    VARDELL, SARAH 1827 RUTHERFORD COUNTY
Sarah was married 1818 or 1819 to THOMAS VERDELL in Rutherford County. They lived together 4 or 5 years, and had 3 children. When the youngest child was still at her breast, Thomas left her. He was cruel to her and beat her and now lives in open adultery with a woman of ill fame in the western section of the state. He has not provided any support for Sarah and her children.
Petition includes isgnatues of "49 citizens of Rutherford County."
Petition is witnessed by John Howell and Henry Linch.
Statement by Wright Gregory that he say Thomas in Henry County living with another woman. Thomas wants a divorce from Sarah so he can marry the other woman.
Statement by Elizabeth Finch, "sister of Sarah Vardell," that she "saw bruises on her sister."
106-1827

    VERNOY, SARAH 31 August 1829 CARTER COUNTY?
Sarah Vernoy was formerly SARAH WAGNER. In 1825, PETER VERNOY, a citizen of Kentucky visited her, a citizen of Carter County, at her father's house. They were married December 1825. She and her possessions were taken to Kentucky by Peter. He treated her cruelly and spent what property she had. He also drank a lot. He kept and supported in the neighborhood several loose women. She found out that he had already been married and divorced. He became intimate again with this ex-wife and she had a child which she said was Peter's. Another female charged him with being the father of her child, begotten and born after the marriage of Sarah and Peter. Sarah had a child and took the child and fled to her father's house in Carter County and has there since remained.
212-1829

    VERNOY, SARAH 1829 CARTER COUNTY
Sarah Vernoy is to be divorced from her husband, PETER VERNOY, if she shall prove that her husband, Peter Vernoy, used her with cruelty or rendered her situation so intolerable asto compel her to withdraw from him, or that he committed acts of adultery, and said court shall grant her a divorce, notwithstanding said circumstances may have happened in the state of Kentucky after they moved from Carter County into said state."
Acts of TN, 1829, p.97

VITITS, DICY   1829   BLEDSOE COUNTY
Dicy Vitits is to be granted a divorce from her husband, JOHN VITITS, upon
proof that John abandoned her and that they have not lived together for a
space of two years.
Acts of Tn, 1829, p.220

WALKER, DR. JAMES   1807   no county stated
The marriage bonds arehereby dissolved between Dr. James Walker and his wife,
HARRIET WALKER. He abandoned her though he remained in Tennessee, for a space
of four years.
Acts of TN, 1807, p.34

WALKER, SAMUEL   June 1832   OVERTON COUNTY
Samuel seeks a divorce from his wife ELIZABETH WALKER.
Statement by Amber Gore that in last of December 1825 or first of January
1826, Amber was in Alabama in Madison County at the house of Michael Gomley
and said Elizabeth was living with said Gomley and said she didnot intend to
live with her husband Samuel anymore.
In a second petition of June 1832, Samuel states that he was married in 1815
to ELIZABETH GREER in Overton County. In 1824 she left Samuel and took up
with another man with whom she continues to live to this day.
Statement by Armsted Walker that he was present when Elizabeth left Samuel in
1825, and says that she took up with a Michael Gomley and that they now live
as man and wife in Alabama.   30 June 1832.
21-1832
76-1832

WALKER, SAMUEL   22 August 1833   WARREN COUNTY
Samuel, at present a citizen of Warren County, was married ca 1815 in Overton
County to ELIZABETH GREER. They lived in Overton ca 7 years. He found out
she was untrue, so he moved them to Madison County, Alabama. About 2 years
after they'd moved to Alabama, he crossed with Michael Gourley who "had
previously separated from his wife and was living with his children in a
house on the plantation." Samuel believes Elizabeth to be guilty of adultery
with Gourley. She left with Gourley and married him soon after Samuel moved
back to Overton County, where he remained til last spring when he moved to
Warren County. He wants a divorce and the rights he would have enjoyed had he
not married.
Statement in Overton COunty by Armsted Walker and Ambrose Gore.
Petition includes signatures of 72 persons.
234-1833

WALKER, SAMUEL   1833   WARREN COUNTY
The marriage bonds arehereby dissolved between Samuel Walker and his wife.
ELIZABETH WALKER.
Acts of TN, 1833, p.147

WALKER, WILLIAM C.   1833   WARREN COUNTy
The marriage bonds arehereby dissolved between William C. Walker and his wife,
SARAH WALKER.
Acts of TN, 1833, p.139

WALSH, ANN   1833   DAVIDSON COUNTY
Ann Walsh is granted the privileges of a feme sole except that of intermarrying
with another man.
Acts of Tn, 1833

WARD, MARGARET M.   14 September 1825   KNOX COUNTY
Margaret was married 30 January 1816 to LEONARD WARD. They lived together about 4 years and had two children. He left her.
40-1825

WARD, WILLIAM   1812   no countys stated
The marriage bonds are hereby dissolved between William Ward and his wife, ELIZABETH WARD.
Acts of TN, 1812, p.66

WATKINS, SARAH   1812   ROBERTSON COUNTy
Sarah was married in 1809 to JOHN WATKINS. They lived together about 9 months. He treated her cruelly, and she left and went home to her father. She filed a petition with the judge of the circuit court of Robertson County for divorce in October 1811. The court found in favor of Sarah, but John protests the divorce.
Her father is Jesse Williams. John's father is Henry Watkins. She and John have one small son.
55-2-1812

WATKINS, SARAH   1812   no county stated
The marriage bonds are hereby dissolved between Sarah Watkins and her husband, JOHN WATKINS.
Acts of TN, 1812, p.66

WATKINS, THOMAS G.   1826   GREENE COUNTY
Thomas is to be divorced from his wife, SUSAN W. Watkins, upon proof.
Acts of TN, 1826, p.40

WATSON, JAMES   13 October 1821   DAVIDSON COUNTY
James seeks a divorce from his wife, MARY WATSON.
Statement by Joseph K. Kane that during February and March "last," he lived for about 6 months with James and Mary Watson. He said James used abusive language toward Mary, did little to support her and did one time turn her out of his house. During her absence, Watson wrote an article of separation and requested Kane to take it to Mary, but he refused to do it. She came back but left again and Watson at first seemed aggravated at her and her father and family but then expressed contrition for his conduct towards her.
Statement by Rev. William Hume, "in the case of MARY M. PAYSIS.(?)"
184-1821

WATSON, MARGARET   12 October 1831   MARION COUNTY
Margaret was married in October 1825 to JOHN WATSON of MARION COUNTY. In the fall of 1826 they moved to McNairy County. He left her for 14 or 15 months after they moved. She was removed from McNairy by her mother to Marion County. She was followed by John, and after living in Marion for 7 months, she went back to John, on his persuasion. They lived together from March til fall of 1827 of same year when John again left her and went to Arkansas Territory, where he remained til a few days ago. She believes he was guilty of horse stealing in Arkansas Territory and was punished by whipping. She wants a divorce and her name changed to MARGARET BRYSON.
140-1831

WATSON, MARY M.   1823   no county stated
Mary M. Watson is granted the privileges of a feme sole, except that of intermarrying with another man. She shall be known by the name of MARY M. POYZER.
Acts of TN, 1823

WEAVER, GEORGE   14 September 1821   WILSON COUNTY
George was married ca 1810 or 1811 to NANCY SPERRY. They had two children "that is alive, the youngest is about 7 years old." Nancy left, had a child by another man. George wants a divorce and to have a law passed that the last child Nancy had is not his and is not entitled to be a lawful heir to his estate.
Petition includes signatures of several persons.
Oaths made by 2 persons of Wilson County, D. Moss and Rebekah Gwyn.
53-1821

WEBB, E. C.   1849   WHITE COUNTY
E. C. Webb was married in 1826 in Rutherford County, North Carolina to ADALINE PORTER. They had nine children. He accuses her of adultery.
49-1849

WEBB, ELIZABETH   14 September 1821   WARREN COUNTY
Elizabeth Webb was formerly ELIZABETH MASTIN. About 1817, while living in Warren County, she was courted by RICHARD WEBB, a Methodist preacher. She married him; he was twice as old as she was; he was a widower and had six children. They moved 12 or 13 times in 3 years of living together. He beat and kicked her. He slept with another woman named Emery in from of Elizabeth.
Elizabeth "slept off from Webb," who had then conveyed her to Jackson County, Alabama. She was then living with her father in Warren County, Tennessee. Statements by Uriah York and William Boyd.
68-1821

WELCH, CHARLES M. K.   4 September 1833   McMINN COUNTY
Charles was married in January 1824 to MARY ATHON. She left him after ca 3 months of marriage. He accuses her of whoredom. When she left him and was caught in the act of whoredom, he came to Tennessee and lived in Tennessee ever since, except for 1 year that he lived in Kentucky. She had 2 children in his absence and "swore the rape against...William Mosby now living in this state...then after which acknowledging that she was persuaded to it and that she had sworn a lie..." Charles is now "nearly 28 years of age." He has not been with Mary since May 1824 though he returned to North Carolina to his father's house in 1830. Seh had left the state and gone to Georgia, he was told.
Petition includes signatures of 47 persosn, who say Charles lived in McMinn County in 1824 and 1825 and after that in Overton County "until these last 2 years during which...he lived in McMinn County."
108-1833

WELLS, MATTHEW   1825   no county stated
Matthew was married to BARBARA in ca 1804 in North Carolina, but has been in Tennessee for 20 years. They had six children, but only one had a lawful birth. They have separated, and both want a divorce.
166-1825

WHALIN, CHINA   1833   FRANKLIN COUNTY
China Whalin, wife of JOHN WHALIN, is granted the privileges of a feme sole.
Acts of Tn, 1833

WHERRY, ANN   1831   WILSON COUNTY (See last page for this omission.)
WHERRY, ANNY   1831   no county stated
Anny Wherry, wife of SIMEON WHERRY, is granted the privileges of a feme sole.
Acts of TN, 1831

WHITE, ELIZA   1826   RHEA COUNTY
Elizabeth White is to be divorced from her husband, WILLIAM WHITE. She is "authorized to file a petition for a divorce in the circuit court ...and the judge...shall hear and determine upon said petition..."
Acts of TN, 1826, p.140

WHITE, ELIZABETH   1821   BEDFORD COUNTY
Elizabeth White, the wife of JAMES WHITE, is granted the privileges of a feme sole except that of intermarrying with another man.
Acts of TN, 1821

WHITE, ELIZABETH   1827   ROANE COUNTY
The marriage bonds are to be dissolved between Elizabeth White and her husband, JAMES White, upon proof of the desertion by James for 3 years.
Acts of TN, 1827, p.210

WHITE, MINERVA FRANCIS   3 October 1831   HENRY COUNTY
Minerva Francis was married in February 1827 to THOMAS J. WHITE in Henry County. Shortly after their marriage, he said he only married her because he thoughthe would get considerable property from her and if he didn't, he would leave her. She married without her father's consent, and her father would not give much property until Thomas proved himself. For 3 years Thomas left her off and on for days or weeks without cause. He finally left her for good with two infant children, because her father did not give her a liberal portion of his property. He left her June 1830 and went to an adjoining county. She took one of her children and went to him. He left her again. She knows not where he went and he's been gone more than one year. In the last will and testament of her grandfather, Henry FREEMAN, she will be entitled ("upon the death of her grandmother, Elizabeth Freeman, who is the widow and relic of Henry Freeman,") to a dividend in her deceased grandfather's estate.
Petition includes the signatures of 16 persons.
Statement by James J. White.
277-1831

WILBOURNE,NARCISSA   1833   no county stated
The marriage bonds arehereby dissolved between Narciss Wilbourne, formerly NARCISSA HESS, and her husband, KINCHEN A. WILBOURNE.
Acts of TN, 1833, p.136

WILLIAMS, ANN   1826   no county stated
Ann Williams, wife of ROBERT WILLIAMS, is granted the privileges of a feme sole.
Acts of TN, 1826

WILLIAMS, ELIZABETH   1809   no county stated
The marriage bonds are herebydissolved between Elizabeth Williams and her husband, NATHANIEL WILLIAMS.
Acts of Tn, 1809, p.18

WILLIAMS, ELIZABETH   1823   WARREN COUNTy
Elizabeth was married in 1821 to NICHOLAS WILLIAMS, who on 26 December following left her. He drank a lot and did little to support them. She was previously married to Albert HOAS(?), who died at New Orleans in the service of his county. She had 3 children by Hoas. She had property before her marriage to Williams;he had nothing. She wants her property to be relieved from the payment of the debts of Williams.
Petition includes signatures of 13 persons.
85-1823

WILLIAMS, ELIZABETH   1823   no county stated
Elizabeth Williams, the wife of NICHOLAS WILLIAMS, is granted the privileges
of a feme sole except that of intermarrying with another man.
Acts of TN, 1823.

WILLIAMS, MARTHA M.   4 October 1825   RUTHERFORD COUNTY
Martha was married to HARRISON WILLIAMS on 23 DECEMBER 1819. He treated her
in a cruel manner by calling her abusive names, and he beat her. On 1 September
1821 he saddled a horse given to her by her father and ordered her to leave
him forever. He then kicked her out because she did not move the instant he
told her to.
Petition includes the signatures of 16 "neighbors of Martha."
She sought protection under her father's roof.
Second petition includes signatures of 24 persons.
95-1825
112-1827

WILLIAMS, MARTHA M.   1827   RUTHERFORD COUNTY
Martha M. WIlliams, wife of HARRISON WILLIAMS, is granted the privileges of a
feme sole, except that of intermarrying with another man.
Acts of TN, 1827

WILLIAMS, MARTHA   1827   RUTHERFORD COUNTY
Martha Williamsis to be granted a divorce from her husband, HARRISON WILLIAMS,
upon proof that he abused and chastised her and wholly ceased to support and
protect her.
Acts of TN, 1827, p.120

WILLIAMS, ROBERT H.   September 1831   SULLIVAN COUNTY
Robert H. Williams, of HAwkins County, lately of Sullivan County was married
in 1825 to ANN NICELY of Sullivan County. They parted after living together
15 months, and shortly thereafter, Ann "applied to the legistlature and obtained
the privileges of a feme sole, and she has never lived with him since. She
has been guilty of adultery and she bore an illegitimate child last spring,
the father generally thought to be Montgomery Erwin. Robert has not had
intercourse with her since 1826.
Petition includes signatures of 80 persons.
Statement by John Fain of Blountville.
331-1831

WILLIAMS, SILAS   24 October 1827   CAMPBELL COUNTY
Silas Williams was married in 1811 to NANCY UMBREESON (WINBREESON?). He
accuses her of adultery. They have children (number not stated). He caught
her with another man. She threatens to destroy his house by fire, particularly
his hatters shop. She also threatens to poison him.
Statement by John E. Wheeler.
216-1827

WILLIAMS, SOPHIA   1825   BEDFORD COUNTY
A divorce is to be granted to Sophia Williams from her husband, JAMES A.
WILLIAMS, upon proof.
Acts of TN, 1825, p.265

WILLIAMSON, LUCY   1827   DAVIDSON COUNTY
The marriage bonds are to be dissolved between Lucy Williamson, wife of
GEORGE WILLIAMSON, upon proof that George deserted her and failed to support
her or their two children.
Acts of TN, 1827, p.186

WILLIAMSON, THOMAS   16 September 1833   WILSON COUNTY
Thomas seeks a divorce from his wife (her name is not stated).
Petition includes the signatures of 50 persons.
248-1833

WILSON, ELIZABETH   16 November 1826   SUMNER COUNTY
Elizabeth Wilson, formerly ELIZABETH PENN, was married in 1822 to JOSEPH P.
WILSON of Sumner County. She possessed when they married 53 acres on Cumberland
River, 2 Negroes worth $400.00, and other small articles. In less than 2
years, all they had was sold to pay the debts he had incurred. About 1824 he
left her and their one child.
87-1826

WILSON, GEORGE   October 1833   DAVIDSON COUNTY
George Wilson was married in October 1832 to MARY ANN RICHARDSON. Soon after
he took her to his residence she expressed dissatisfaction at his two sons
continuing to live in his family. One had just finished studying law, and
he left. The other was in college, and arrangements
were made for him, too. Then Mary wanted his 2 young daughters to be sent
away. She wanted to leave since he would not send his daughters away, but
friends persuaded her to stay. She did leave, however, ca beginning of March.
He thinks she was close to insanity.
Mary Ann said that previous to her marriage to George, he told her his son
Rhea Wilson "would go to FAyetteville to join his brother in the practice of
law..." She denies asking or demanding either the sons or daughters to be
sent away.(This statement for Mary Ann Wilson is made by William Livingston.)
139-1833

WILSON, GEORGE   1833   no county stated
The marriage bonds are hereby dissolved between George Wilson and his wife,
MARY ANN WILSON. She is to resume her maiden name, and is granted all rights
of a feme sole. Her maiden name is RICHARDSON.
Acts of TN, 1833, p.33

WILSON, JUDITH   27 September 1831   WILLIAMSON COUNTy
Judith in 1825, she possessing " a competency of property," was married to
WILLIAM WILSON. They lived together less than 3 years, during which time he
spent all of her property and reduced them to beggars. He left her then while
she was "far advanced with a second child."
Statement of Frances Gunter and Felix Gunter that William married JUDITH
CLARK, and left her in 1828.
Statement by John F. Smith and John W. Miller that Judith had lived in the
town of Franklin for more than 2 years.
Statement by George White.
318-1831

WISE, MARY   September 1827   LAWRENCE COUNTY
Mary Wise, formerly MARY CAWSON, was married 21 August 1809 to JAMES WISE in
Blount County. About 7 January 1825 he beat her and drove her from the house
and refuses to live with her or provide for his family, consisting of six
children.
Petition includes signatures of 12 persons.
Statement by Alex Miller that in February 1816 James and Mary came to Giles
County, Big Creek, and stayed about a year, then moved to Maury County for
about a year, then moved to Lawrence County.
Statement by Daniel Bellar.
276-1827

WOMACK, JAMES   30 October 1833   JACKSON COUNTY
James Womack is husband of JANE WOMACK, formerly JANE SADLER. She left him ca 4 or 5 years ago.
Petition includes signatures of 10 persons.
270-1833

WOODALL, JOHN   12 November 1829   SUMNER COUNTY
John Woodall was a minor in 1825 when he was married to JUDAH KERBY. Judah left after six months and has been gone since.
Petition includes signatures of 34 persons, including Christopher Woodall, William M. Woodall, Jr, and James Woodall.
71-1829

WOODS, ELIZABETH CARSON   1812   SULLIVAN COUNTY
Elizabeth was married 8 January 1807 to JOHN WOODS. After 10 months of marriage John took up with another woman, Agness Tarbut, who has three children by him.
Petition is signed by eight witnesses.
File includes a letter from John Woods dated 15 January 1811, agreeing to divorce.
36-1-1812

WOODS, ELIZABETH   1812   WASHINGTON COUNTY
The marriage bonds arehereby dissolved between Elizabeth Woods and her husband JOHN WOODS, late of Washington County.
Acts of TN, 1812, p.21

WOODS, IGNATIUS F.   1833   BEDFORD COUNTY
Ignatius F. Woods was married 1826 to SUSAN THOMPSON in Bedford County. They lived together for 6 years in peace; from that time til December 1831 they quarreled, then separated. She left, but not before throwing a pot of boiling water in his face, putting out one of his eyes and disfiguring him.
Petition includes signatures of 5 persons.
111-1833

WOODS, DORCAS L.   1826   RUTHERFORD COUNTY
Dorcas is to be divorced from her husband, ARCHIBALD WOODS, upon proof that "...he drove her from his home and would not again receive her, that her said husband left the state of Tennessee more than 6 years "since," and has never returned..."
Acts of Tn, 1826, p.89

WOODS, WILLIAM   1829   GIBSON COUNTy
A divorce is to be granted to William Woods and his wife, NANCY WOODS, upon proof. "...Either William or Nancy may prefer a petition to the ...court ...for a divorce..."
Acts of Tn, 1829, p.61

YOUNG, POLLY   26 September 1821   WILSON COUNTY
Polly is wife of ARCHIBALD YOUNG. He has not provided for his family for the past 3 years. He has left her and his family for the past 12 months. She states that Archibald Young became guardian for her children that she had by her first husband, Robert KNIGHT, who was killed in the army. Archibald drew the money that was coming for her former husband's service and stayed until he spent it, then left.
Petition includes signatures of 35 persons, including Absalom Knight, Margaret

Knight, Samuel Knight, Malinda Knight, Thomas Knight, and Sarah Knight.
Statements by Sampson Conner, Pryer Lasson, and a statement by Elizabeth Beshears accusing Archibald of adultery.
Statement by Rebecka Hopkins that she lived with Archibald Young when he and his wife were living together and that Archibald "offered impoliteness to me in the way of cohabiting with him..."
69-1821

YOUNT, MARY   1 October 1833   BLOUNT COUNTY
Mary, of Blount County, was married in March 1832 to PETER YOUNT of said county. About 2 months after their marriage he beat and abused her and she left him. Since then she believes he is keeping other women.
Petition includes signatures of 34 residents of Blount County.
Statement by John Woods and Eliza Woods that Mary had lived with them since her separation from her husband.
Mary asks that if her divorce is granted, for her name to be MARY PAYNE.
188-1833

OMISSIONS:

JARRETT, ELIZABETH A.   12 November 1833   BEDFORD COUNTY
Elizabeth A. was married in Bedford County in 1824 to GEORGE L. JARRETT. They lived in Wilson County. She lived with him til latter part of 1827. He had to leave the state because of some criminal activity, so she returned to her parents' house, where she had lived since December 1827.
Petition includes signatures of 33 persons.
244-1833

WHERRY, ANN   1831   WILSON COUNTY
Ann was married to SIMON WHERRY "some years since." They lived together until about 5 years ago, at which time he had wasted and squandered all his property by dissipation. He left her, with 5 small children to support. He has been living in different neighborhoods in Wilson County, drinking and "spending his labor." She asks for privileges of feme sole.
Petition includes signatures of 40 persons.
83-1831

INDEX

Note:
Capitalized given names are those of petitioning husbands, wives, their spouses, and if listed in the petitions, also the maiden or former names of females.

Aaron, JOHN 1
Aaron, RACHEL 1
Adams, MARTHA 1
Adams, MARTIN, 1
Adams, NANCY 1,9
Adams, Peter 9
Adams, TODD R. 1
Adams, William 5
Adkins, Henry 76
Aithley, ELIJAH 1
Aithey, SARAH 1
Alexander, James 85
Alison, MISS POLLY 60
Allen, ANN 1
Allen, CALLOWAY 1
(see Calloway, ALLEN)
Allen, FANNY H. 31
Allen, GEORGE WASHINGTON 1
Allen, John 21
Allen, JOHN W. 1
Allen, LEVI P. 1
Allen, LUCY W. 1
Allen, POLLY D. 1
Allen, SARAH 1
Alley, MARY 1
Alley, WILLIAM 1
Allison, James 60
Anderson, Doc 2
Anderson, EDMUND R. 2
Anderson, ELIZA 2
Anderson, ELIZABETH 2
Anderson, FANNY 2
Anderson, HENRY 2
Anderson, NANCY 72
Anderson, SALLY 2
Anderson, SARAH 2
Anderson, Susana 59
Anderson, WILLIAM 2
Anderson, WILLIAM L. 2
Anthony, Alfred 10
Anthony, POLLY 10
Almstead, Elizabeth 22
Archer, LAVINA 54
Armstrong, James 27
Ash, JANE 23
Ashburn, JOHN 2
AAshburn, REBECKA 2
Ashley, ___ (male) 68
Ashlock, SARAH 21

Athon, MARY 99
Atkins, Charles 69
Atkinson, Elizabeth Jr. 54
Atkins, Margaret T. 69
Ausborn, Rebeccah 18
Austin, Joseph 94

Babb, Alsa 3
Babb, ELIZABETH 3
Babb, Jesse 3
Babb, WILLIAM 3
Bacon, ANN 3
Bacon, CHARLES 3
Badgett, James Jr. 4
Bailey, CATHERINE 3
Bailey, ___ 60
Baker, CHARLOTTE 3
Baker, Larkin 79
Baker, Rev. ROBERT 3
Baker, ROBERT 4
Baker, Zimri 3
Balch, Robert 64
Baldwin, Edward 61
Ball, ANN 4
Ball, EVELINA 4
Ball, JAMES 4
Ball, WILLIAM 4
Ballard, ELIZABETH A. 4
Ballard, JAMES R. 4
Ballenger, Hannah 19
Ballenger, William 19
Balling, REBECCA 56
Banty, NANCY 4
Banty, PETER 4
Barefoot, DILLON W. H. 4
Barefoot, NANCY CHOATE 4
Barham, ARRILLA CAROLINE 4
Barham, JOHN A. 4
Barker, ALEXANDER B. 5
Barker, ELIZABETH 5
Barker, BRIGGS 5
Barker, Howell W. 5
Barker, REBECCA 5
Barnes, Polly 28
Barrott, John 46
Barton, ANDERSON 5
Barton, CYNTHIA 5
Barton, Joshua 89
Bass, TEMPERANCE W. 88

Batte, AMERICA R. ELIAM 5
Batte, Frederick, Sr. 5
Batte, Robert 5
Batte, WILLIAM P. 5
Bateman, ANN 91
Bateman, Isaac 91
Bayles, RICHARD 5
Bayley, JOHN 3
Bealey, John 89
Beard, Richard 4
Beasley, Josiah 67
Beason, NANCY 6
Begly, Philie 48
Bell, ELIZABETH C. 6
Bell, John 63
Bell, Dr. Joseph E. 36
Bell, JOSEPH M. 6
Bell, William M. 50
Bellar, Daniel 102
Beesley, DELILAH 56
Bembridge, LYDIA 6
Bembridge, PETER W. 6
Benton, Burrell 80
Benton, SARAH 80
Berry, FRANCIS 6
Berry, PATSEY SELLERS 6
Beshears, Elizabeth 104
Bidwell, REBECCA 13
Bigby, Mrs. 2
Bigham, William H. 3
Biggs, Elizabeth 80
Biggs, Thornds? 80
Biles, ISABELLA 6
Biles, JAMES 6
Billingsley, ELIJAH 7
Billingsley, POLLY 7
Bishop, Henry 61
Bishop, JAMES 7
Black, BENJAMIN 7
Black, SUSANNAH 7
Blake, Samuel 20
Blakemore, John 20
Blalock, SARY 7
Blalock, WILLIAM 7
Blankenship, POLLY 31
Blevins, ARMISTEAD 7
Blevins, KITTURA 7
Bond, FRANCES 8
Bond, JESSE Jr. 8
Bond, JOHN 8

Bond, SUSAN 8
Borin, DARIAS 59
Borin, JOshua 59
Bose, Martha 19
Boswell, James 26
Boswell, Susannah 26
Bowman, COSBY 8
Bowman, ELIZABETH 8
Boyers, MARGARET 8
Boyers, MICHEL 8
Boyd, William 99
Boze, John 78
Bracher, NANCY 9
Bracher, WILLIAM 9
Bracy, James 92
Bradford, HENRY 8
Bradford, James H. 28
Bradford, REBECCA 8
Bradley, JOHN 8
Bradley, MARGARET 8
Brasil, Parthona 89
Braskin, MARGORY 79
Brassfield, SALLY 9
Brassfield, THOMAS 9
Brazzel, POLLY 81
Breechen, HENRIETTA 11
Breeden, JANE 9
Breeden, LINSEY O. 9
Brewer, Howell 71
Brewington, JAMES 9
Brewington, SARAH 9
Brewton, HESIAH 36
Bugg, MAHALIA 85
Briggs, JOhn 26
Brison, EASTER 9
Brison, GEORGE 9
Britton, JOHN 9
Britton, SARAH 9
Britton, Capt. William 28
Brooks, ELIZABETH 10
Brooks, JOAB 10
Brooks, SARAH 10
Brooks, WILLIAM 10
Broughton, Charles T. 95
Brown, AGNESS 62
Brown, ANNA 41
Brown, E. W. 10
BRown, ELIZABETH 10
Brown, FRANKLIN M. 10
Brown, GABRAEL R. 10
Brown, George 29
Brown, HENRIETTA 11
Brown, Jacob Sr. 53
Brown, Jacob 3
Brown, James 92
Brown, JANE H. 51
Brown, Jesse 3

Brown, Joseph 51
Brown, Katherine 10
Brown, Mary Jane 51
Brown, NANCY 29
Brown, PHILLIP 11
Brown, POLLY 10,11
Brown, Sally 3
Brown, Solomon 53
Brown, THOMAS 11
Brown, William 19
Bruington, JAMES 11
Bruington, SARAH 11
Bryant, LUCRETIA 29
Bryson, MARGARET 98
Buchannon, JOhn 22
Buckhannon, James 7
Buckhannon, JOHN W. 11
Buckhannon, OBEDIENCE 11
Buckner, DANIEL 11
Buckner, JULIANA 12
Buckner, POLLY 11
Buckner, VIRGIL 12
Bullard, Henry 78
Bullard, JOSEPH 12
Bullard, Joseph 78
Bullard, LUCY 12
Bullfin, MARY 12
Bullfin, THOMAS 12
Bullock, DANIEL 12
Bullock, LYDIA 12
Bunch, Charles 33
Burford, ELIZABETH 66
Burkhart, George 73
Burleson, CELIA 12
Burleson, HELKIEN 12
Burns, SALLY 12,21
Burns, WILLIAM 12
Burrus, MICHAEL 12
Burrus, POLLY 12
Burton, ELIZABETH 13
Burton, SALLY 10
Burton, THOMAS 13
Burton, USILLER 13
Burton, William 13
Butler, SALLY 13
Butler, EDWARD L. 13
Butler, WILLIAM HENRY 13
Buzby, MARY 13
Buzby, THOMAS 13
Byrns, RHODA 46

Cabler, JOHN L. 13
Cahal, JAMES 13
Cahal, REBECCA 13
Cain, ALLEY 40
Cain, William 40
Caldwell, DAVID 13

Caldwell, ELIZABETH 13
Caldwell, SINDERELLA 13
Caldwell, WILLIAM B. 13
Caldwell, William H. 14
Callaway, ALLEN 14
(see Calloway Allen)
Callaway, Joseph 13
Callaway, SARAH 14
Callis, ABEL 14
Callis, MARTHA (PATSY) 14
Campbell, JOHN 14,35
Campbell, MARGARET J. 14
Campbell, MARY 14
Campbell, Robert 18
Campbell, WILLIAM 14
Camron, Mrs. Susanna 16
Cannon, DORCAS 35
Cannon, JAMES A. 14
Cannon, MARY A. M. 14
Cantrell, ANNY 14
Cantrell, benjamin 14
Cantrell, Elijah 33
Cantrell, Francis 47
Cantrell, James 14
Cantrell, JOHN 14
Cantrell, Moses 14
Cantrell, Peter 14
Cantrell, Sampson 14
Cantwell, JANE 15
Cantwell, JEAN 15
Cantwell, LEWIS 15
Caperton, POLLY B. 15
Caperton, HUGH 15
Caps, BENJAMIN 15
Caps, FRANCIS 15
Caps, SALLY 15
Caps, SARAH 15
Capshaw, Josiah 47
Card, ELIZABETH 15
Card, WILLIAM 15
Cadrwell, ELIZABETH 15
Cardwell, WILLIAM E. 15
Carmichael, JOHN 15
Carmichael, Margaret 15
Carnahan, William 15
Carney, MARY L. 36
Carpenter, John 25
Carper, ADAM 16
Carper, SUSANNA 16
Carr, SUSAN D. 16
Carr, William P. 20
Carroll, ANN 16
Carroll, NATHAN 16
Carruthers, MARY 16
Carruthers, WILLIAM 16
Carson, CYNTHIA 16
Carson, JOhn Sr. 16

Carson, JOHN 16
Carson, Mrs. Mary 84
Carson, Robert 84
Carson, Sally 57
Carson, William 16
Carver, BENJAMIN 16
Carver, NANCY W. 16
Cartwright, POLLY 16
Cartwright, WILLIAM 17
Cartwrite, Thomas 85
Casey, CHINA 17
Casey, NATHANIEL 17
Cash, JOhn 25
Cashion, William 92
Cavell, LUCY 12
Cawson, MARY 102
Chambers, JOEL 17
Chambers, MARGARET 17
Champlain, Elizabeth Sr. 36
Chaplain, ELIZABETH 17
Chaplain, MOSES 17
Chealley, GEORGE 20
Cheek, James 38
Cherny, JOHN 17
Cherny, SARAH 17
Chesney, JOHN 17
Chesney, SARAH 17
Childers, Betsy 21
Childress, SUSAN 50
Childers, William 32
Childress, J. H. 93
Childress, NATHANIEL G. 17
Childress, SARAH 17
Childress, Stephen 50
Chisholm, JOHN 18
Chisholm, PATTY 18
Christian, Nancy 26
Chowning, JOHN Sr. 18
Chowning, MARY 18
Chumley, Lewis 35
Chumley, Malinda 35
Chumley, Mary 35
Clabough, Charles 19
Claiborne, Thomas 2
Clark, Benjamin 8
Clark, ELIZABETH 18
Clark, JOHN G. 18
Clark, JUDITH 102
Clark, SAMUEL 18
Clark, Tillman 25
Clark, WINNEY 18
Clay, MARTHA A. S. 18
Clay, SAMUEL 18
Clements, FLORINDA 18
Clements, LUTHER M. 18
Clendennen, ELIZABETH 18
Clendennen, JOHN 18,19

Clevenger, Elizabeth 19
Clevenger, George 19
Clevenger, SARAH 19
Clevenger, THOMAS S. 19
Cliborn, John 67
Clifford, BRIDGET 19
Clifford, PATRICK 19
Clinton, Ezekiel 61
Clinton, MILLY ELIZA 85
Close, NANCY 19
Close, SAMUEL 19
Clowd, Rachel 71
Coalte, MALINDA 72
Cobb, GEORGE 20
Cobb, SARAH 20
Cochran, Daniel 53
Cockrill, John Sr. 53
Cockrell, MARTHA A. R. 53,54
Coe, Major Joseph 93
Coen, ELEANOR 40
Cole, David R. 2
Cole, John 28
Collier, David 3
Collins, David 26
Combs, John 26
Commins, HANNAH 55
Compton, JOHN 20
Compton, SARAH 20
Conner, HANNAH 20
Conner, John B. 20
Conner, MARGARET 85
Conner, Sampson
Conway, FANNY 20
Conway, FRANCES 20
Conway, Col. Henry 59
Conway, SUSANNAH, 59,60
Conway, THOMAS 20
Conway, THOMAS Jr. 20
Cook, G. S. and Co. 75
Cook, Henry 35
Cook, JOHN 21
Cooke, JOHN F. 21
Cooke, JOseph 42
Cook, Mary 21
Cook, Sally 21
Cook, SARAH 21
Cook, WILLIAM 21
Cooper, CELIA 21
Cooper, EDWARD 21
Cooper, Henry, 34,89
Cooper, JAMES 21
Cooper, JOHN Sr. 21
Copper, JOseph 95
Cooper, NANCY, 21
Cooper, PEGGY 21
Cooper, SARAH 21
Cooper, WILLIAM 21

Corban, BENNET B. 21
Corban, ELIZABETH 21
Corbitt, CHRISTIANA 13
Corbitt, MIchael 22
Cording, JACOB 22
Cording, MARY 22
Covington, William 5
Cotton, Noah 44
Coulter, John 42
Courts, JOHN 22
Courts, RACHEL 22
Cox, Absolom 31
Cox, JOHN 22
Cox, Judith H. 31
Cox, PHEBE 22
Cox, William 31
Crabtree, Samuel 87
Craig, David 46
Crawford, rebecca 40
Crawford, Col. Samuel 77
Crawford, SAMUEL 22
Creacy, JOHN 22,23
Creacy, NANCY 22,23
Crenshaw, DANIEL 23
Crenshaw, ELIZABETH L. 23
Crenshaw, HARRIET P. 23
Crisp, BETSY H. 57
Crisp, Tilman A. 46
Cross, Caswell 76
Cunningham, ELIZABETH 23
Cunningham, JOHN 23
Cunningham, John N. 61
Curl, William 37
Currin, R. 56
Currins, Robert P. 22

Daft, LANEY 23
Daft, JOHN 23
Dagley, Mary 71
Dagley, Jonathan 71
Dail, James 17
Dalton, Aseaneaia 20
Dalton, Sally 46
Davault, Abraham 58
Davault, CATHERINE 58
Davenport, JANE 23
Davenport, JOHN 23
David, Sampson 9
Davidson, H. M. 28,
Davis, benjamin 94
Davis, ELIZABETH 24
Davis, James 19
Davis, JOHN 24
Davis, John 46
Davis, John M. 46
Davis, JESSE 24
Davis, LITTITIA 24

Davis, MARY 24
Davis, NANCY W. 24
Davis, Polly 46
Davis, ROBERT C. 24
Davis, THOMAS C. 24
Davis, Thomas 46
Davis, William R. 34
Dawson, DAVID B. 24
Dawson, ESTER 24
Deaderick, GEORGE MICHAEL 24
Deaderick, POLLY 24
Deatheridge, Dianah 24
Deatheridge, RUSSELL 24
Dear, GOODALL 24
Dear, NANCY 24
Dearee, Jonathan 24
Dennis, AZARIAH 25
Dennis, ELIZABETH 25
Dennis, John 90
Denson, MARTHA 38
Denson, William 38
Denton, EDWARD 25
Denton, SUSAN 25
Denton, Susannah 25
Depriest, CHARLES C. 25
Depriest, POLLY T. 25
Dew, MARIA 35
Dew, MATTHEW 35
Deweese, AGNES 25
Deweese, MORGAN 25
Dibrell, Anthony 77
Dickson, ANN 26
Dickson, John 59
Dickson, SAMUEL 26
Dicus, MAHULAY 64
Dilliard, GABRIEL 26
Dillehay, POLLY 26
Dillehay, STERLING 26
Dilliard, SARAH J. 26
Dishawn, ELIZABETH 42
Dickery, Able 84
Dodd, JOHN 26
Dodd, SARAH 26
Dodson, David 22
Dodson, Elijah 27
Dodson, Elizabeth 27
Dodson, FORTUNE 26
Dodson, JEHU 26
Dodson, Martin 27
Dodson, NANCY 26
Dodson, PATIENCE 26
Donelson, William 76
Donnelly, Hezekiah 35
Donnelly, ISABELLA 31
Donnelly, Nancy 35
Doolen, Jordan 27

Doolen, SUSAN 27
Doolen, THOMAS J. 27
Dooley, MOURNING 27
Dooley, WILLIAM 27
Doss, SUSANNAH 74
Dossett, MOSES 27
Dossett, RHODA 27
Dougharty, Asa 76
Dougherty, CORNELIUS R. 27
Dougherty, MARGARET S. 27
Dougherty, R. E. C. 4
Doughty, ____(male) 41
Douglass, A. H. 77
Doyle, BETSY S. 28
Doyle, Capt. H. 28
Doyle, HARDY 28
Doyle, John L. 3
Doyle, Samuel H. 28
Drake, JOHN 28
Drake, SARAH 28
Dugan, SUSAN 8
Duncan, ELIZABETH 28
Duncan, JOHN 28
Duncan, Joseph 85
Duncan, MARY 28
Duncan, RAWLY 28
Dunkin, LUcinda 65
Dunn, WILLIAM 28
Dunn, POLLY H. 28
Dyer, AHASMERUS 29
Dyer, LUCRETIA 29
Dyer, MARTHA ANN 29
Dyer, Thomas 17
Dyer, WILLIAM H. 29

Earl, William 36
Earl, William H. 50
Easley, JOhn 38
Easley, Warham 4
Easterly, Polly 59,60
Eaton, Rachel 94
Eaton, REBECCA 94
Eaves, Andrew 29
Eaves, CLARK 29
Eaves, DAniel 28
Eaves, ESTHER H. 29
Eaves, William 29
Edwards, Henry 75
Edwards, John W. 29
Edwards, Lewis 29
Edwards, MARTHA 18
Edwards, MARY 29
Edwards, NANCY 29
JEdwards, POLLY TURLEY 25
Edmiston, James 61
Edney, Alfred A. 87

Eldridge, FRANKY 29
Eldridge, SAMPSON 29
Eleazor, Daniel 75
Eliam, AMERICA R. 5
Eliam, Edward 5
Eliam, Jane 5
Ellin, S. F. 49
Elliott, AMOS 29,30
Elliott, CATY 72
Elliott, SARAH 29,30
Elyea, NANCY W. 72
Embree, ELIHU 40
Embrey, B. 48
Embry, John 45
Embry, Patsy 45
Embry, REBECCA 44
Emery, ____(female) 99
Emtree, ANNIS 30
Emtree, ELISHA 30
England, JESSE 30
England, MATILDA 30
English, ELIZABETH 30
English, William 30,58
ENsley, Enoch 83
Erving, NARCISSA 30
Erving, William 30
Erwin, Francis 7
Erwin, John T. 75
Erwin, MOntgomery 101
Essary, JOSEPH 30
Essary, SALLY 30
Essex, ELIZABETH C. 6
Estes, John 50
Evans, ALFRED 30
Evans, ELIZABETH 30
Evans, Walter 66
Everitt, SIMEON 30
Everitt, SUSANNAH 30
Eves, NANCY 96
Ewell, Dabney 68

Fagan, ELEANOR 30
Fagan, JAMES 30
Fain, John 101
FALLS, MARTHA 31
Falls, THOMAS 31
Falvey, Hugh 31
Falvey, ISABELLA 31
Falvey, JOHN F. 31
Faris, NANCY 1
Farless, James 39
Farless, NANCY 39
Farmer, ELIJAH 31
Farmer, FANNY H. 31
Farmer, JOHN 31
Farmer, POLLY 31

Farney, SAMUEL 31
Farney, SUSAN 31
Farr, ELEANOR 31
Farr, GEORGE 31
Farrar, RACHEL P. 32
Farrar, WILY 32
Farris, Isaac A. 35
Farrow, JOHN G. 32
Farrow, LUCINDA 32
Farrow, Sabrina 11
Ferguson, Alexander 15
Ferguson, Elizabeth 15
Ferguson, William 17
Fettle, Samuel 9
Fickle, ABRAM B. 32
Fickle, MARGARET 32
Fickle, Robert P. 32
Field, PATIENCE 26
Fields, Bennett 26
Fields, DENSON 33
Fields, LUCINDA 33
Fields, RACHEL 33
Figures, MARTHA H. 57
Finch, Elizabeth 96
Finch, Thomas 27
Finnie, ELIZABETH D. 33
Finnie, JAMES 33
Firestone, SARAH 33
Firestone, WILLIAM 33
Fisher, BENJAMIN 33
Fisher, Dr. 19
Fisher, PEGGY 33
Fisher, SARAH 41
Fisk, Celia 3
Fitchjearl, ELIZABETH 3
Flanery, Elijah 59
Flemiker, Samuel 4
Fleming, Samuel 5
Fletcher, EDMOND 33
Fletcher, Lewis 95
Fletcher, POLLY 33
Flowers, Reuben 94
Fly, CALEB 33,34
Fly, MARY 33,34
Fonville, EVELINA 34
Fonville, JOHN B. 34
Ford, LOID 34
Ford, MARY 34
Fornwalt, AMELIA 34
Fornwalt, AURELIA 34
Fornwalt, JOHN B. 34
Fornwalt, JOHN H. 34
Fornwalt, NANCY B. 34
Fornwalt, William B. 34
Forrest, Richard 64
Fort, Elias, Jr. 36
Foster, DORCAS 35
Foster, EDWARD 35

Foster, Ephraim H. 28
Foster, JEMIMA 35
Foster, John 10,35
Foster, NANCY 35
Foster, Polly 10
Foster, R. C. 93
Foster, THOMAS 35
Fowler, William 17
Francis, Hugh 7
Fraser, CAROLINE 47
FRaser, D. N. 47
Fraser, J. H. 47
Freeling, JOHN H. 35
Freeling, LUCY 35
Freeman, ELIZABETH 35,100
Freeman, HAMLEN 35
Freeman, Henry 100
Freeman, JANE 35
Freeman, JOHNSON 35
Freeman, JOSEPH P. 35
Freeman, MARIA 35
Fry, LETITIA 36
Fry, MARTIN 36
Fullterton, AGNES 36
Fullerton, WILLIAM 36
Fulser, Peggy 50
Fussell, SUSAN 36
Fussell, HARRISON 36

Gabbort, Dr. Michael 25
Galbraith, James 48
Gallaher, MARY ANN 36
Gallaher, WILLIAM 36
Ganlery?, Patsy 78
Gardenhire, GEORGE 36
Gardenhire, NANCY 36
Gardner, HENRY 36
Gardner, MARY L. 36
Garrard, Daniel 58
Garrott, BENJAMIN 36
Garrott, ELIZABETH 36
Gartin, DAVID 36
Gartin, HESIAH 36
Gassaway, ELEANOR 31
Gattis, ELIZABETH 51
Gely, RACHEL 39
George, JESSE 37
George, RACHEL 37
George, William 92
George, William Steel 37
Gibbs, John 28
Gibbs, Thomas 64
Gibson, DENNIS 37
Gibson, HARRIET 37
Gibson, HARRIET H. 37
Gibson, HENRY 37
Gibson, PRISCYLLA M. 37
Gilbreath, ANN 50

Gilliam, James 68
Giman, REBECCA 8
Ginnings, Elizabeth 27
Ginnings, Jesse 27
Ginnings, Leah 27
Ginnings, Obediah 27
Gladdin, JOHN 37
Gladdin, REBECCA BALL 37
Gleaves, Thomas Jr. 75
Glenn, G. H. 67
Golden, LUCINDA 37
Golden, WILLIAM 37
Goldsby, Elizabeth 52
Goldsby, James 52
Gollahan, SARAH 62
Gomley, MICHAEL 97
Gordon, POLLY 37
Gordon, THOMAS 37
Gore, AMBER 97
Gossage, William 78
Gosset, SARAH 50
Gourley, Michael 97
Gower, ELISHA 38
Gower, JEMIMA 38
Gowen, John 27
Grace, DAVID 38
Grace, ELIZABETH 38
Graham, Margaret C. 55
Graham, NANCY 38
Graham, REUBEN P. 38
Grant, James 71
Green, DANIEL 38
Green, Elisha 85
Green, John 71
Green, MARTHA SMITH 38
Green, MARY 38
Green, THOMAS C. 38
Greenwood, BETSY 39
Greenwood, ____ (female) 39
Greenwood, JOHN 39,56
Greenwood, NANCY 56
Greer, Caswell 39
Greer, ELIZABETH 97
Greer, GEORGE 39
GREER, James C. 39
Greer, NANCY 39
Greer, RACHEL 39
Gregory, Edward 5
Gregory, Wright 96
Grice, Solomon 75
Griffin, ____ (male) 62
Griffin, JESSE W. 40
Griffin, SARAH 40
Griggs, SARAH 40
Griggs, WILLIAM 40
Grissum, Benjamin 70
Groom, Nelly 54

Grooms, SALLY 52
Groves, HIRAM 40
Groves, SARAH 40
Grubbs, LENA 40
Grubbs, SINE 40
Grubbs, THOMAS 40
Guin, Briant 39
Gulley, Robert Johnson 61
Gunter, JClaybourne 57
Gunter, Felix 102
Gunter, JFrances 102
Gurthry, ELEANOR 40
Guthery, ALLEY 40
Guthery, WILLIAM 40
Guttrey, PEYTON H. 40
Guttry, POLLY 40
Gwyn, JINCY C. 40
Gwyn, Rebekah 99
Gwyn, THORNTON P. 40

Hackney, JACOB 41
Hackney, SARAH 41
Haggard, BETSY 70
Hagler, Thomas 70
Haile, Cage 69
Hale, ANNA 41
Hale, JOHN 41
Hale, John A. 86
Hale, JOseph 31
Hall, HOPY 41
Hall, James 42
Hall, Michael C. A. 41
Hall, PHEBE 41
Hall, POLLY 42, 76
Hall, SAMUEL 42
Hall, WILLIAM 41
Hallum, MORRIS 42
Hallum, NANCY 42
Hamilton, MARGARET 27
Hamilton, NANCY 42
Hamilton, REBECCA 55
Hamilton, Robert 67
Hamilton, widow 6
Hamilton, WILLIAM 42
Hamlet, CYNTHIA 42
Hamlet, WILLIAM 42
Hammond, ELIZABETH 42, 43
Hammond, GEORGE 42, 43
Hammons, John 14
Hamontree, David 85
Hampton, POLLY 44
Hamrick, CELA 90
Hancock, Dr. R. C. 60
Hancock, William 71
Handy, ELIZABETH 43
Handy, ISHAM 43

Hanks, FRANCES F. 43
Hanks, JOHN A. 43
Hanks, Lucy 43
Hardaman, MARY ELIZABETH 43
Hardeman, JOHN 43
Hardin, CATHERINE 43
Hardin, Clara 79
Hardin, Henry 79
Hardin, ROSANNA 79
Harlin, JEREMIAH 43
Harlin, NANCY 43
Harmon, GILLY 43
Harmon, LEWIS 43
Harmon, JANE 41
Harmon, JOHN 44
Harp, MARIA 44
Harp, NATHANIEL 44
Harper, Alexander T. 44
Harper, ELIZABETH 44
Harper, Harriett, 44
Harper, James L. 44
Harper, John M. 44
Harper, Joseph 44
Harper, Mary 44
Harper, Nancy 44
Harper, Sophia 44
Harper, Talitha 44
Harper, Zelda 44
Harrelsoon, J. G. 29
Harrelson, William 29
Harris, AMEY 44
Harris, ANDREW 44
Harris, Anna 45
Harris, Archibald 21
Harris, GEORGE E. 45
Harris, JOURDAN 44
Harris, JULIA G. 45
Harris, MARY 45
Harris, NANCY 95
Harris, REBEKAH 45
Harris, RICHARD C. 45
Harris, Robert 45
Harrison, Edward C. 5
Harrison, Josiah 52
Hartgraves, John 90
Harwell, William 75
Hassell, Penelope 59
Hasten, Benjamin 21
Hatley, Josiah 93
Haynes, Jonathan 69
Haynes, George 53
Hawes, TABITHA T. 45
Hawes, WILLIAM 45
Hay, A. 9
Hayworth, ABSALOM 45
Hayworth, SARAH 45

Hearn, GEORGE Jr. 45
Hearn, MILLEY 45
Heatherly, Thomas 74
Heatherly, William 27
Helton, LUCY 64
Henderson, JOHN 45
Henderson, JOSEPH Jr. 46
Henderson, POLLY 45,46
Henderson, Robert 46,75
Henderson, SARAH 46
Hendry, CHLOE 46
Hendry, WILLIAM 46
Henley, RHODA 46
Henley, ISAAC 46
Herndon, ELIZABETH 18,19
Herrelson, ESTHER 29
Hess, NARCISSA 100
Heston, MARY 3
Hewbanks, Samuel 90
Hicks, Phoebe 35
Hickerson, ELLINOR 46
Hickerson, EZEKIEL 46
Hickerson, Joseph 27
Hciklin, AVERY M. 46
Hicklin, MARY T. 46
Hicklin, POLLY 46
Hickman, MILLY 47
Hickman, POLLY 47
Hickman, SNODEN 47
Hickman, WILLIAM 47
Hicks, Henry 47
Hicks, Isaac 66
Hicks, JANE 47
Hicks, STEPHEN 47
Hill, ALFRED 47
Hill, BENNET 47
Hill, CAROLINE 47
Hill, Dan 22
Hill, ELIZABETH 47
Hill, Harry R. W. 22
Hill, Henry r. W. 93
Hill, Lewis 48
Hill, Martha 22
Hill, NANCY 22
Hill, Robert 47
Hill, SEINA 48

Hill, Sucky 50
Hill, Thomas 28
HInds, Jane 17
Hinds, William 17
HInes, ELIZABETH 48
Hines, JOHN B. 48
Hoas, ALBERT 100
Hobson, Adcock 31
Hodges, Rowland 53

Hogan, JANE 48
Hogan, WILLIAM 48
Holdway, HUGH B. 48
Holdway, J. W. 48
Holdway, REBECCAH 48
Holland, Benjamin 11
Holland, John 57
Holley, CELIA 48
Holley, David 48
Holley, JOHN 48
Holley, Mary 48
Holley, Sion 48
Holley, William 48
Hollingsworth, William A. 67
Holloway, James 10
Holson, James 45,46
Holt, JOSEPH 48
Holt, SARAH 48
Honeycut, ELIZABETH 48
Honeycut, ROBERT 48
Hookins, MARY 48
Hookins, WILLIAM 48
Hooper, CLARENDER 49
Hooper, MARY S. 49
Hoover, NANCY 87
Hopkins, Jason 29
Hopkins, Rebecca 104
Hopkins, William 56
Hopper, Thomas 81
Hopson, HARROD 49
Hopson, SALLY 49
Hornberger, ALICE 49
Hornberger, PHILIP 49
Horton, PATSY (MARTHA) 49
HOrton, WILLIAM 49
Houston, George 70
Houston, John 74
Houston, Mary 70
Howard, Alexander 49
Howard, BENJAMIN 49
Howard, ELIZABETH 8
Howard, FLORINDAH 18
Howard, James 8 ,49
Howard, MAHALY 49
Howard, Peggy 44
Howard, Rebecca 59
Howard, Reubin 49
Howard, Thomas 18
Howard, William 27
Howell, John 96
Howell, William L. 28
Howeth, Aquilla 49
Howeth, John 49
Huddleston, David 89
Huff, ANN 50
Huff, JOHN 50

Huffaker, Hannah 35
Huggins, Jeremiah 81
Huggins, POLLY 42
Hughlett, JOHN 50
Hughlett, TEANY 50
Hull, MARGARET 17
Hulme, SUSAN 50
Hulme, THOMAS 50
Hume, Rev. William 98
Humphreys, JESSE 50
Humphreys, MARY 50
Humphreys, Stockley 38
Hunt, Nathaniel 28
Hunter, Henry W. 47
Hunter, Isaac 67
Hunter, MARY T. 46
Hunter, POLLY 47
Hurt, ELIZABETH 50
Hurt, ISAAC 50
Huston, RACHEL 50
Huston, WILLIAM 50
Hutchinson, AMBROSE 50
Hutchison, JANE 44

Irick, JAMES 51
Irick, JANE N. 51
Irvine, Josephus 86
Isaacs, ELIZABETH 51
Isaacs, JOHN W. 51
Isaacks, SUSANA 79
Isom, George 17
Jack, JEREMIAH 51
Jack, CATHERINE 51
Jack, Thomas 28
Jackson, ISABELLA 51
Jackson, JOHN 51
James, Buckhannon 57
James, WINNEY 18
James, William 22
James, William 75
Jameson, HOSEA 51
Jameson, NANCY 51
Jarrett, ELIZABETH A. 52
Jarrett, GEORGE S.(L.?) 52
Jenkins, JEREMIAH 52
Jenkins, SARAH 52
Jennings, AGNES 52
Jesson, Dr. 79
Jesson, Samuel 79
Jett, JOHN F. 52
Jett, MARY Ann F. 52
Jiams, SALLY 52
Jiams, WILLIAM L. 52
Jiles, William 52
Johnson, Abner 15
Johnson, ANNEY 14

Johnson, ASHLEY 52
Johnson, C. 53
Johnson, CALVIN 52
Johnson, John 53
Johnson, Mary 15
Johnson, Martha 52
Johnson, Nancy 70
Johnson, SARAH 15,52
JOhnson, SOPHRONIA 52
Johnson, Thomas 15
Johnson, William 52
Johnson, William 70
Johnston, Asa 54
Johnston, John 53
Johnston, M. 3
Johnston, NARCISSA 53
Joiner (Jamor?), Richard 12
Jones, ALEXANDER A. 53
Jones, Alexander W. 54
Jones, CATHERINE 53
JOnes, DAVID 54
Jones, DEMPSEY 53
Jones, ELIZABETH 53
Jones, Gabriel 41
Jones, JAMES 53
Jones, JANE 53
Jones, JOEL 53
Jones, JULIA 53
Jones, LEWIS 54
Jones, MARTHA A. R. 53,54
Jones, NANCY 21
Jones, Philip 26
Jones, Polly 41
Jones, POLLY 54
Jones, SARAH J. 26
Jones, Stephen 21
Jones, SUSUNAH 54
Jones, RHODA 54
Jones, Richard 21
Jones, William 53
Jordan, LUCRETIA 54
Justice, ESTHER 54
Justice, WILLIAM 54

Kane, Joseph K. 98
Kearney, Col. 39
Kearney, Henry G. 54
Kearney, Lucy D. 54
Keasley, ELIZA 65
Keeling, LAVINA 54
Keeling, THOMAS S. 54
Keen, Edmund 79
Kelley, William 18
Kelly, Jesse 55
Kelly, REBECCA 55
Kennedy, Andrew 36

Kennedy, ELEANOR 55
Kennedy, HANNAH 55
Kennedy, HUGH 5
Kennedy, JAMES 55
Kerby, JUDAH 103
Kersee, CHAMPNESS 55
Kersee, ELIZABETH L. 5
Key, MARGARET C. 5
Key, STROTHER 55
Keye, DELILAH 56
Keye, TANDY 56
Kimbro, SARAH 19
Kimbrough, ANNE 56
Kimbrough, THOMAS 56
Kirby, David 53
Kinnard, DAVID C. 56
Kinndard, HANNAH 56
Knight, Absalom 103
Knight, Malinda 103
Knight, Margaret 103
Knight, Robert 103
Knight, SAmuel 103
Knight, Sarah 103

Lampkins, Elizabeth 14
Lane, Ill? 10
Lasson, Pryor 104
Latimer, James 75
Lattimore, SARAH 33
Lauderdale, NANCY 56
Lauderdale, William 55
Lawrence, REBECCA 56
Lawrence, WILLIAM R. 56
Lawson, NANCY 71
Lawson, USILLER 13
Lea, MARY 95
Lee, JACOB 56
Lee, MOURNEN 56
Lester, Fountain 34
Leuty, David, 57,63
Leuty, Elizabeth 57,63
Lewis, MARTHA H. 57
Lewis, MARY 29
Lewis, SALLY 57
Lewis, Dr. SAMUEL 57
Lewis, Samuel Jr. 57
Lillard, Abraham 52,59
Lilliard, Jeremiah 57
Lilliard, sarah 57
Linch, Henry 96
Lindsey, BETSY 57
Lindsey, JEFFERSON 57
Lindsey, NANCY 57
Lindsy, GREEN LEE 57
Line, ELEANOR 58
Line, WILLIAM 58

Linn, BETSEY 58

Linn, ELIZABETH 58
Linn, JACOB 58
Livingston, William 102
Lloyd, Lucinda 32
Lofton, Thomas 92
Logan, CATHERINE 58
Logan, DAVID B. 58
Logue, DAVID 58
Logue, MARY 58
Lon, AGNES 25
Long, JUDITH R. 58
Long, Margaret 66
Long, NICHOLAS I. 58
Long, SARAH 45
Loudermilk, Adam 59
Loudermilk, DARIAS 59
Loudermilk, JACOB 59
Loudwich, Nancy 39
Lovel, Jemima 70
Lowery, Charles 95
Lowry, John 10
Lowry, William 10
Lucas, Peter W. 55
Lumpkin, BETSY S. 28
Lumpkin, EDMUND 59
Lumpkin, NANCY 59
Lusk, HANNAH 59
Lusk, SAMUEL 59
Lynch, POLLY 60
Lyncy, Mary 27
Lynn, CHARLOTTE C. 3
Lyon, John 35
Lytle, POLLY 94

MacRae, MARY 66
MacRae, ALEXANDER 66
Madding, Champness 3
Maddux, ANNY 59
Maddux, NATHANIEL 59
Mahon, HENRY 59
Mahon, MIRANDA 59
Mahon, William 42
Malgrew, William 27
Malony, HUGH 59,60
Malony, SUSANNAH 59,60
Manchester, MARY 60
Manchester, WILLARD 60
Manly, CHAPMAN 60
Manly, LAURA 60
Mark, MARTHA 75
Marlow, JOSEPH 60
Marlow, POLLY 60
Marr, Milton H. 20
Mars, LACE 74

Marsh, DANIEL 60
Marsh, NANCY 60
Marshall, JULIA G. 45
Marshall, SARAH G. 60
Marshall, WILLIAM 60
Martin, JOSEPH J. 61
Martin, MARY 60,61
Martin, Mr. 93
Martin, SALLY 61
Martin, SAMUEL N. 60,61
Mason, BENNETT 61
Mason, David 56
Mason, FRANCES F. 43
Mason, MARTHY 61
Massengale, HENRY Sr. 61
Massengale, MARY 61
Massey, JINSEY 75
Mastin, ELIZABETH 99
Matlock, Benjamin 35
Matson, NANCY 77
Mathews, Isaac 61
Matthews, John, Sr. 61
Matthews, JOHN 61
Matthews, Rebeccah Sr. 61
Matthews, REBECCA 61
Matthews, TEPPINS 61
Matthews, TOPPENAS 61
Matterson, william J. 68
Matticks, Jane 65
Mauldin, SALLY 15
Maxey, Bennett 3
Maxwell, Capt. JAMES J. 61
Maxwell, ELIZABETH 61
Maxwell, Elizabeth Jr. 62
Maxwell, JAMES I. 62
Maxwell, JANE 62
Maxwel, John w. 62
Maxwell, Lydia 62
May, JAMES 62
May, SARAH 62
May, Temperance 61
McAdams, JACOB 62
McAdams, SARAH 62
McAdow, Finley S. 62
McAdow, PATSY 62
McAdow, SAMUEL 62
McAlpin AGNESS 62
McAlpin, THOMAS 62
McCabe, ELIZABETH 62
McCabe, STARK 62
McCaffrey, ROSEAN 88
McCaffrey, Terence 88
McCardle, JOHN 63
McCardle, SINA 63
McCawly, MARY 38
McClannathan, LEWIS 63

McClannathan, NANCY 63
McClure, CHARLES C. 57,63
McClure, ELIZABETH 57,63
McClure, James 63
McClure, REBECCA 63
McClure, WILLIAM 63
McComac, MAHALY 49
McConnel, Andrew Jackson 63
McConnel, Charlotte Matilda 63
McConnel, JAMES 63
McConnel, POLLY 63
McConnico, Garner 22
McCubbins, PHEBE 63
McCubbins, WILLIAM 63
McCurry, JAMES 63
McCurry, POLLY 63
McCutchen, JANE 63
McCutchen, JOHN 63
McDonald, Archibald 64
McDonald, LUCY 64
McDonald, JOHN 64
McDonald, MILLY 64
McDonald, NORMAN 64
McGavock, R 39
McGee, CLENDENAN 64
McGee, JOhn 21
McGee, MARTHA 64
McGinnis, ARTHUR 64
McGuire, ELIZABETH 64
McGuire, MERRIMAN 64
McGregor, JAY 27
McIntosh, JANE 64
McIntosh, NIMROD 65
McIntosh, REBECCA 65
McIlroy, MARTHA 64
McInturff, John 65
McKearley, JAMES 65
McKearley, PERMELIA 65
McKee, ELIZA 65
McKee, JOHN 65
McKiver, Anguish 9
McLemore, James 41
McLinn, ANN 65
McLinn, WILLIAM 65
McMahon, Jonathan 19
McMillan, Alexander 73
McMillan, James 73
McMinn, JOSEPH 65
McMinn, NANCY 65
McNabb, DAVID 65
McNabb, JEMIMA 65
McNabb, John 59
McNabb, PEGGY 65
McNAbb, SHAWNEY 65
McOnel, Samuel 85
McPhail, Dr. 93

McRhea, MARGARET J. 14
McWhirter, Dr. S. C. 25
Meaders, Nancy 47
Meaders, Nazareth 47
Medford, Jonas 93
Medley, BENONI 66
Medley, MILLY 66
Mennes, ELIZABETH C. 66
Mennes, WILLIAM 66
Merritt, Cynthia 49
Midkiffe, KIMBLE E. 66
Midkiffe, NANCY 66
Miller, Alex 102
Miller, ALICE 66
Miller, ANN 26
Miller, CYNTHIA 42
Miller, Elizabeth 73
Miller, HANNAH 56
Miller, HOSSEA C. 67
Miller, Hugh 26
Miller, James 42
Miller, Jane 42
Miller, JOhn W. 102
Miller, NImrod 27
Miller, NOAH 66
Miller, SALLY 67
Milliken, Jesse 79
Mullins, Barnett L. 17
Mills, BIRD 67
Mills, John 55
Mills, NANCY 67
Milton, ELIZABETH 28
Mims, D. 85
Mitchell, DELANEY 67
Mitchell, HENRY 67
Mitchell HENRYETTA 67
Mitchell, James Sr. 68
Mitchell, JANE 68
Mitchell, John 58
Mitchell, ROBERT 67
Mitchell, WILLIAM 68
Mires, CATHERINE 72
Mires, JOHN 72
Misingo, CHARLES 67
Misingo, SALLY 67
Monroe, James 75
Moody, MRS. MARY 66
Moore, ANN E. 69
Moore, Benjamin 31
Moore, CHARLES 68
Moore, EDWIN S. 68
Moore, ELIAS 68
Moore, ELIZABETH 68
Moore, JOHN 68
Moore, LUCINDA 81
Moore, NIMROD 68,69

Moore, PERLINA 68
Moore, POLLY 68
Moore, PERMILIA 68
Moore, ROBERT 69
Moore, SALLY 68,69
Moore, SAMUEL 69
Moore, Samuel B. 28
Moore, SARAH HAILE 69
Moore, SUSAN 31
Moore, SUSANNAH 80
Morelock, DAvid 69
Morelock, SARAH 69
Morgan, JEMIMA 70
Morgan, JOSIAH 70
Morgan, MASSEY 70
Morgan, PETER 70
Morris, ISAAC 70
Morris, JINCY 70
Morris, John 70
Morris, JOSEPH 70
Morris, MALINDA 70
Morris, NANCY 70
Morris, SAMUEL 70
Morrison, NANCY 42
Mosby, William 99
Mosely, Hannah 40
Moss, BETSY 70
Moss, Daniel 70
Moss, D. 99
Moss, JOHN 70
Moss, Thomas 70
Murphy, Daniel R. 19
Murphy, R. 50
Murphy, Robert 62
Murphree, NIMROD 70,71
Murphree, RHODY 70,71
Murrah, JEREMIAH 71
Murrah, LUCY A. 71
Murray, Lucy A. 71
Murrell?, Calven 71
Murrell, JAMES 71
Murrell, NANCY 71
Murry, Thomas 69
Musgrove, LUCY 71
Musgrove, WILSON 71
Myers, JOHN 71
Myers, JUDAH 71

Nave, John 35
Neal, Thomas 29
Neil, JohnT. 11
Nelson, John 21
Nettles, ABIGAIL 71
Nettles, JOSEPH 71
Newman, David 26
Neusom, NANCY 92

Newgent, John D. 75
Newport, REBECCAH 48
Nicely, ANN 101
Nichol, JOHN W. 47,72
Nicholds, Mathies 66
Nichol, NANCY 66
Nichols, Lawrence 62
Nichols, WILSON 72
Night, NANCY 72
Night, RICHARD 72
Noble, CATY 72
Noble, MARK 72
Noble, William 72
Norman, MARY 22
Norwood, Polly Ann 51
Nowlen, DAVID 72
Nowlen, MARY ANN V. 72
Null, CATHERINE 72
Null, JOHN 72

Oakes, Nancy 84
Odan, JAMES 72
Odan, MARY 72
Odleby, JEMIMA 35
Odom, SELY 91
Odum, CELIA 48
Ogle, JAMES 72
Ogle, MALINDA 72
Oldham, Emily E. 88
Oldham, Henry 88
Oldham, William 88
Oliver, ELIZABETH 72,73
Oliver, JOHN 72,73
Oliver, SUSANNAH 73
Oliver, THOMAS 73
Ollifent, JANE 92
O'Neal J. W.(N.?) 11
Orange, Elizabeth R. 31
Orange, Zephaniah 31
Ortto, ELIZABETH 73
Ortto, FREDERICK 73
Osborn, JOHN 73
Overstreet, Jefferson 88
Overton, John 1
Owen, MARTHA 86
Owens, FRANCES 73
Owens, REBECCA 73
Owins, William 65

Painter, JACOB P. 73
Painter, JANE 73
Palmer, LEE 74
Palmer, LUCY 74
Park, ALFRED 74
Park, SARAH 74
Park, William 74

Parker, Miss Betsy 39
Parker, Elisha 39
Parker, John 49
Parker, NATHAN 74
Parker, SUSANNAH 74
Parks, ANN E. 69
Parks, Melinda 6
Parrish, MARY M. 74
Parrish, SAMUEL B. 74
Parrott, PRISCILLA M. 37
Partee, Abner H. 60
Partee, DINCY 74
Partee, HENDERSON 74
Pasinger, George 41
Pate, Kinchen 5
Pate, POlly 5
Patrick, LACE 74
Patrick, LAKEY 75
Patrick, Robert R. 31
Patrick, ROBERT R· 74
Patrick, Wiley 75
Patterson, FENTON 75
Patterson, James 34
Patterson, James 75
Patterson, JEMIMA 38
Patterson, JINSEY 75
Patterson, MARY 75
Patton, James 25,75
Patton, John 25
Patton, MARTHA 75
Patton, ROBERT 25
Patton, WILLIAM 75
Payne MARY 104
Paysis, Mary.M. 98
Peairs, ELIZABETH 75, 76
Peairs, ISAAC 75,76
Pearson, Christian 71
Pearson, P. F. 56
Peatry, George 67
Peete, Ben 2
Peete, ELIZA 2
Pemberton, JESSE 76
Pemberton, RUTH 76
Perenpile, NANCY 66
Perkins, ARRILLA CAROLINE 4
Perry, Allen 41
Perry, Burrell 78
Perry, DELILA 78
Perry, Josiah 76
Perry, MILLY 64
Perry, NANCY 80
Perry, NORFLEET 76
Perry, RACHEL 76
Peterson, 9
Petree, Jacob 67
Petty, RACHEL 33

Pettypool, Thomas 21
Pharis, Delilah 9
Pharis, James 9
Pharis, JANE 9
Pharis, JOhn 9
Pharis, william 9
Phillips, ANN ELIZA 90
Phillips, Charles 76
Phillips, Edward 76
Phillips, MIcajah 76
Phillips, WILLIAM 76
Phillips, ELIZABETH 76
Phillipson, JOHN 76
Phillipson, POLLY 76
Philpot, Timothy 78
Pickett, LETTY 76
PIckett, WILLIAM 76
Pille, NANCY 77
Pille, JOHN 77
Pippin, KINCHEN 77
Pippin, LINNY 77
Pistole, DAVID 77
Pistole, SUSAN R. 77
Pitman, Michael 5
Mitt, DAVIS 77
Pitt, WINFRED 77
Poe, BARBARY 77
Poe, JOHN 77
Ponder, JAMES 77
Ponder, NANCY 77
Pool, Joel 30
Pool, LUCRETIA 54
Pope, Hardy 21
Pope, Wiley 61
Popejoy, Lydia 17
Porter, Benjamin 77
Porter, SALLY 77
Porter, DINCEY 77
Porter, HENDERSon 77
Porter, JOHN 77
Porter, Samuel 78
Porter, SARAH 29
Poteet, FRANCES 20
Powell, Joseph Sr. 32
Powell, POLLY 63
Poyzer, MARY M. 98
Prewett, Lemuel 89
Price, HENRY 78
Price, RYNAY 78
Prigmore, Ephraim 31
Privett, DELILA 78
Privett, WILLIS 78
Proffitt, David 63
Pryor, John C. 28
Pugh, JOEL 78
Pugh, PRUDENCE 78

Purkeypile, Elizabeth 66
Purkepile, Rachel 66
Pursell, John 43
Pursell, MARY ELIZABETH 43
Pugsley, Dr. 19

Queener, Daniel 9
Queener, SALLY 9

Rains, JANE 78
Rains, Joel 78
Rains, JOHN 78
Rains, Philip 59
Ralston, SAMUEL 79
Ralston, SUSANNA 79
Ramsey, ELIZABETH 79
Ramsey, MARY 79
Ramsey, MARGORY 79
Ramsey, SHEWBRIDGE 79
Ramsey, THOMAS K. 79
Ramsey, WILLIAM 79
Rayburn, HIRAM 79
Rayburn, Hodge 79
Rayburn, POLLY 79
Rayburn, ROSANNA 79
Raymond, DAVID B. 80
Raymond, SARAH 80
Reaves, Levi H. 87
Reed, EASTER 9
Reese, JESSE 80
Reese, NANCY 80
Ren, Luresay 89
Ren, Solomon 89
Reves, John 47
Reynolds, HIRAM 80
Reynolds, RACHEL P. 32
Rhea, MARGARET 32
Rhea, Robert Preston 33
Rhea, Samuel, J. P. 33
Rice, ALEY 66
Rice, John 15
Rich, JOHN 80
Rich, SUSANNAH 80
RIchards, Susana 90
Richardson, MARY ANN 102
Richeson, Frances 41
Richeson, Giles 41
Richmond, Mary 70
Riggins, RACHEL 95
Roberts, ELIZABETH 80
Roberts, James 65
Roberts, PERMELIA 65
Roberts, Ridley 65
Roberts, Silas 65
Roberts, THOMAS 80
Robertson, Alfred 25
Robertson, Joanna 25

Robertson, William 79
Robeson, JOHN L 80
Robeson, NANCY 80
Robinson, CATHERINE D. 87
Robinson, COMFORD 81
Robinson, WILLIAM B. 81
Rockhold, DAWSON B. 81
Rockhold, LUCINDA 81
ROdgers, JAMES 81
ROdgers, POLLY 81
Rogers, Capt. david S. 71
Rogers, George 71
Rogers, GEORGE 81
Rogers, Jacob 80,81
Rogers, John 8
Rogers, SARAH 81
Roland, MARY ANN 52
Roone, Dr. 75
Roper, POLLY 81,82
Roper, WILLIAM 81,82
Rose, Bazel 52
Rose, SARAH 52
Ross, Capt. THOMAS 82
Ross, CATHERINE 82
Ross, THOMAS 82
Ross, William 41
Rounseville, BARSHEBA 82
Rulman, Jacob 75
Runnells, ___ 38
Runnulds, Anderson 21
Russ, Avarilla Green 89
Russ, charnel 89
Rutherford, EVELINA 34
Rutland, MILBERRY P. 82
Rutland, REDDICK 82
Rutledge, James 22
Rutlin, MEBERRY 82
Russey, James 28
Russey, Polly 28
Rybourn, Mathew 1
Rynolds, ELIZABETH BIGGS 80

Sadler, JANE 103
Samples, Elizabeth 31
Sanders, James 82,89
Sanders, PRUDENCE 82
Sandlin, ELIZABETH 82,83
Sandlin, John 83
Sandlin, RANDOLPH 82,83
Sanford, John 90
Sarrett, Wilson M. 85
Saunders, MARY 83
Saunders, WILLIAM 83
Scaggs, Charles 17
Scaggs, Elizabeth 17
Scaggs, Moses 17
Scaggs, SARAH 17

Scholl, JERUSHA 83
Scholl, MILTON 83
Scoggins, D. C. 18
Scoggins, Marthy 18
Scott, JAMES 83
Scott, JANE 83
Scudder, HARRIET PAYNE 83
Scudder, PHILLIP I. 84
Scruggs, HARRIET 83
Scruggs, WILLIE W. 83
Seales, NANCY 84
Seales, ROBERT HENRY 84
Seamore, Elizabeth 17
Sellars, DIANNAH 93
Sellars, Robert 6,77
Sellars, Samuel 56
Sellers, Dickson 22
Sellers, James 22
Sellers, MARY 22
Selvidge, GEORGE 84
Selvidge, MARY 84
Sevier, CHARITY 84
Sevier, JOSEPH 84
Sevier, JOHN, Jr. 84
Sevier, SUSANNA 84
Sexton, ELIZABETH 84
Sexton, JAMES R. 84
Sexton, Mark 84
Shannon, MARGARET 85
Sharp, Abby 28
Sharp, CHARLOTIA T. 95
Sharp, James 17
Sharp, John Jr. 28
Sharp, Robert 25,28
Shaw, GEORGE W. 85
Shaw, MAHALIA 85
Shaw, THomas 85
Shearman, Charles 85
Shearman, GEORGE T. 85
Shearman, MILLY ELIZA 85
SHell, JAMES W. 85
Shell, LEMENTINE 85
Shelton, David 27
Shelton, Samuel 27
Shelton, Zebedee 27
Sherley, Thomas 25
Sherman, Esquire 77
Sherrill, EVE 86
SHerrill, SAMUEL 86
Shirley, GEORGE 86
Shirley, REBECCA 86
Short, AARON 86
Short, JANE 86
Short, Joab 86
Shumaker, JANE 68
Sick, JOSEPH M. 86
Sick, MARY 86

Simcock, HOPY 41
Simcock, Mr. 41
Simes, Ann 61
Simpson, John W. 54
Simpson, POLLY 86
Simpson, REUBEN 86
Sims, J. G. 5
Sims, Margaret 5
SIsk, FAULKNER 86
Sisk, MARTHA 86
Sitz, MARGARET 87
Skidmore, Sealy, 75
Slagle, George 65
Sleeker, GEORGE Sr. 86
Sleeker, PATSY 86
Sloss, JOSEPH 86
Sloss, SALLY 86
Smith, CATHERINE S. 87
Smith, FREDERICK 87
Smith, JAMES H. 88
Smith, John F. 93,102
Smith, JOHN P. 87
SMith, JOHN 87
Smith, JOSHUA 87
SMith, LYDIA 87
Smith, MARGARET 87
Smith, MARGARETTA 87
Smith, MILLY 88
Smith, NANCY 87
Smith, REBECCA 63
Smith, ROSEAN 88
Smith, TEMPERANCE W. 88
Smith, Thomas B. 88
Smith, Ulysses G. 88
Smith, WILLIAM 87
Snapp, JOHN 88
Snapp, MAGDALENE 88
Sparks, James 93
Sperry, NANCY 99
Springfield, ELIZABETH 61
St. Clair, Hugh 36
Stacy, SARAH 69,88
Stacy, ZACHARIAH 69,88
Stalcup, RACHEL 88
Standfield, Abraham 13
Stanford, Edward 59
Steel, RACHEL 37
Steel, William 37
Steward, Peterson 20
Stewart, DAvid 89
Stewart, ELIZABETH E. 89
Stewart, Hansford 89
Stewart, John 89
Stewart, Joseph 89
Stewart, JOSHUA 89
Stewart, WILLIAM 89

Spencer, Elizabeth 22
Spillman, CYNTHIA 16
Smith, ANN 56
Smith, Bowling 41
Smith, Catherine 48
Smith, David 17
Smith, George L. 57
Smith, James 33
Smith, Samuel H. 46
Smith, SUSAN 25
Smith, SUSAN D. 16
Smith, William 40
Slapp, Akellis 13
Still, ELIZABETH 76
Still, James 76
Stockard, PHOEBE 89
Stockard, SAMUEL 89
Stokes, ISBEL 89
Stokes, WILLIAM 89
Stone, DERINDA 89
Stone, HANNAH 89
Stone, KIZZIAH 89
Stone, LEMUEL W. 89
Stone, THOMAS 89
Stone, WILLIAM 89
Stout, MILLY 88
Street, ELIZABETH 90
Street, JAMES 90
Strother, POLLY 77
Stuart, REBECCAH 90
Stuart, WILLIAM 90
Struffle, William 73
Stunston, BURNETTEY 90
Stunston, Elizabeth 90
Stunston, Henry 90
Stunston, JAMES 90
Sullivna, ANN ELIZA 90
Sullivan, ELISHA 90
Summers, Elizabeth 90
Suttles, CELA 90
Suttles, HENRY 90
Swaner, Voelit 65
Swaney, JAMES N. 91
Swaney, SARAH R. 91
Swisher, ANN 91
Swisher, MICHAEL 91
Talley, Zachariah 26
Tanner, JOHN 91
Tanner, SELY 91
Tarbut, Agness 103
Tarpley, Stith T. 67
Tarrent, Leo C. 28
Tashley, NANCY 59
Tate, ELIZA JANE 91
Tate, JOHN 91
Tatum, HOWEL 92

Tatum, ROSANNAH 92
Taylor, Henry C. 92
Taylor, Isaac 8
Taylor, JANE 47,92
Taylor, MARY 92
Taylor, NANCY 92
Taylor, SAMUEL 92
Taylor, TEMPLE 92
Taylor, THOMAS 92
Taylor, William L. 33
Telley, WESTLEY 93
Thomas, C. T. 31
Thomas, Elizabeth 31
Thomas, ISAAC 92
Thomas, Katherine Mrs. 16
Thomas, MARGARET 92
Thomas, NANCY 38
Thomas, Peggy 92
Thomas, POLLY 45
Thompson, AGNESS 92,93
THompson, Avy 93
Thompson, George 33
Thompson, MARY 93
Thompson, POLLY 11
Thompson, SUSAN 103
Thompson, SUSAN S. 93
THompson, SUSAN L. 93
Thompson, THOMAS A. 93
Thompson, William 11
Thompson, WILLIAM 93
THornburgh, ISAAC 93
Thornburgh, REBECCA 93
TIlley, DIANNA 93
TInnon, ARTHUR 75
Tittle, ELIZABETH 30,43
Todd, CHARLES W. 94
Todd, DIANNAH 94
Todd, FLORA M. 94
Todd, SAMUEL 94
Torrell, Robert W. 32
Totty, Robert Jr. 50
Townsen, ALBERT 94
Townsen, POLLY 94
Townsend, James 39
Townsend, Nathaniel 24
Townsend, RICHARD 94
Townsend, SARAH ANN 94
Treadway, DANIEL 94
Treadway, REBECCA 94
Trousdale, JONATHAN 94
Trousdale, SALLY 94
Trowell, LANY 23
Truett, Elijah 47
Turnage, OBEDIENCE 11
Turner, ELIZABETH N. 94
Turner, JOHN P. 94

Turner, JOHN P. 94
Turner, John 95
Turner, RACHEL 95
Turner, Samuel 95
Turner, WILLIAM 95
Turney, HOPKINS S. 95
Turney, MARY 95
Turney, Samuel 78
Turpen, Matthew 62
Turpen, Nancy 62
Tyler, CHARLOTIA 95
Tyler, CHESTER 95

Umbreeson?, NANCY 101
Underwood, Nancy 40
Underwood, Thomas 34
Ury, GEORGE 95
Ury, NANCY 95
Usrey, William 25

Vaden, Burwell 67
Vandevanter, REBECCA 95
Vandevanter, JOHN 95
Vandeventer, REBECCA 96
Vandeventer, JOHN 96
Vandyke, ISRAEL A. 96
Vandyke, NANCY 96
Vaughn, RACHEL 96
Vaughn, T. 96
verdell, SARAH 96
Verdell, THOMAS 96
Vernoy, SARAH 96
Vernoy, PETER 96
Vitits, DICY 97
Vitits, JOHN 97
Vinson, William 59

Wagner, SARAH 96
Walke, Anthony 12
Walke, POLLY 12
Walker, ANN 1
Walker, Armsted 97
Walker, ELEANOR 55
Walker, Elias 63
Walker, ELIZABETH 97
Walker, HARRIET 97
Walker, Dr. JAMES 97
Walker, John 1
Walker, LETITIA 36
Walker, MILLY 66
Walker, SARAH 97
Walker, SAMUEL 97
Walker, WILLIAM C. 97
Wallis, Harvey 17
Walsh, ANN 97
Walton, Thomas 76

Ward, ELIZABETH 98
Ward, LEONARD 98
Ward, MARGARET M. 98
Ward, WILLIAM 98
Warner, John 5
Watkins, Henry 98
Watkins, James 14
Watkins, JOHN 98
Watkins, SARAH 98
Watkins, SUSAN W. 98
Watkins, THOMAS G. 98
Wats, William 47
Watson, JAMES 98
Watson, JOHN 98
Watson, MARGARET 98
Watson, MARY 98
Wassington, Joanna 59
Wassington, MIRANDA 59
Weaver, GEORGE 99
Weaver, NANCY 99
Webb, ADALINE PORTER 99
Webb, E. C. 99
Webb, ELIZABETH 99
Webb, J. K. S. 60
Webb, Matty 21
Webb, RICHARD 99
Webb, W. S. 29
Weeks, Charles 24
Weeks, ESTER 24
Welch, CHARLES M. K. 99
Welch, MARY 99
Wells, BARBARA 99
Wells, MATTHEW 99
West, John 47
West, John B. 75
Whalin, CHINA 99
Whalin, JOHN 99
Wheeler, CELIA 21
Wheeler, John E. 101
Wherry, ANNY 99,104
Wherry, SIMEON 99,104
White, AURELIA 34
White, Cary 93
White, ELIZA 100
White, ELIZABETH 100
White, George 102
White, JAMES 100
Whie, James J. 100
White, MINERVA FRANCIS 100
White, THOMAS J. 100
White, WILLIAM 100
Whitehead, SUSAN 27
Whiteside, JONATHAN 25
Whitney, Elijah 29
Whitney, HARRIET P. 23
Whitney, HARRIET PAYNE 84

Wilbourne, KINCHEN A. 30,100
Wilbourne, Narcissa 30,100
Williams, ANN 100,101
Williams, E. C. 3
Williams, ELIZABETH 100,101
Williams, HARRISON 101
WIlliams, JAMES A. 101
Williams, Jesse 98
Williams, MARTHA M. 101
Williams, Marthen 82
Williams, NANCY 71
Williams NATHANIEL 100
Williams, NICHOLAS 100,101
Williams, ROBERT 100
Williams, ROBERT H. 101
Williams, SARAH 98
Williams, SILAS 101
Williams, SOPHIA 101
Williams, William 82
WIlliamson, GEORGE 101
Williamson, LUCY 101
Williamson, THOMAS 102
Wills, E. F. 5
Willson, Byars 95
Willson, Samuel 11
Wilson, C. B. 37
Wilson, ELIZABETH 102
Wilson, FRANCES 8
WIlson, GEORGE 102
WIlson, Jacob 81
Wilson, JAMES 27,57
Wilson, James H. 21
Wilson, JOSEPH P. 102
Wilson, JUDITH 102
Wilson, MARY ANN 102
Wilson, William 100
Wimberley, Lewis 14
Wimberley, MARY A. M. 14
Winbreeson?,NANCY 101
WInfrey, Thomas 75
Winsted, Peggy 71
Wisdom, NANCY 57
Wise, JAMES 102
Wise, MARY 102
Wood, John D. 28
Wood, William 85
Woodall, Christopher 103
Woodall, James 103
Woodall, JOHN 103
Woodall, William M. Jr. 103
Woods, ARCHIBALD 103
Woods, DORCAS 103
Woods, Eliza 104
Woods, ELIZABETH CARSON 103
Woods, IGNATIUS F. 103
Woods, JOHN 103

Woods, NANCY 103
Woods, SUSAN 103
Woods, WILLIAM 103
Wollen, Elizabeth L. 89
Wollen, Moses 89
Womack, JAMES 103
Womack, JANE 103
Wrinkle, SOPHRONIA 52
Wyly, C. R. 5

Yancey, William 77
Yates, George 78
Yeats, John 78
York, Jonathan 80
York, Uriah 99
Yost, CATHERINE 82
YOung, ARCHIBALD, 103
Young, POLLY 103
Young, NANCY 84
Young, _____ (female) 94
Yount, MARY 104
Yount, PETER 104

Zimmerman, POLLY 63

_____, Jacob 35

INDEX OF TENNESSEE COUNTIES

ANDERSON: 21,22,28,48,65,70,80
BEDFORD: 2,5,10,11,15,24,27,30,48,52,62,66,70,72,74,79,80,83,92,95,100,101,103,104
BENTON: 4
BLEDSOE: 1,7,19,44,68,69,72,97
BLOUNT: 1,10,13,21,31,42,52,84,87,104
CAMPBELL: 27,36,58,67,71,76,87
CARROLL: 3,4,42,49,67,70,71,74
CARTER: 21,30,35,38,50,59,65,96
CLAIBORNE: 8,35,38,49,58,63,67,81
COCKE: 1,11,14,15,59,78
DAVIDSON: 1,2,4,6,11,13,15,16,17,19,20,22,28,33,36,38,44,53,54,56,60,62,64,75,76,83,90,91,92,97,98,101,102
DICKSON: 8,15,38,43,79,89
DYER: 1
FAYETTE: 47,79
FENTRESS: 36,54,77
FRANKLIN: 10,15,18,23,24,27,28,41,42,47,57,60,95,99
GIBSON: 30,34,103
GILES: 12,17,29,34,47,59,60,85,86,102
GRAINGER: 13,17,38,63,66,67
GREENE: 24,26,36,37,44,46,48,51,59,60,63,65,69,70,84,85,88,90
HAMILTON: 49,69
HARDEMAN: 6,35,57,60
HARDIN: 6,17,59,64,70
HAWKINS: 14,38,53,61,66,69,71,80,94,101
HAYWOOD: 9,89

```
HENDERSON:    30,40
HENRY:        8,14,20,28,39,40,42,92,96,100
HICKMAN:      23,43,50 65,78 79,81
HUMPHREYS:    5,12,23,26,30,49,67
JACKSON:      9,44,45,52,65,71,74,77,88,93,103
JEFFERSON:    9,11,19,37,56,57,73,94
JOHNSON:      48
KNOX:         4,14,18,23,34,41,51,52,55,62,73,74,76,88,94,98
LAUDERDALE:   56
LAWRENCE:     33,57,72,86,89,91
LINCOLN:      11,20,43,48,51,52,60,68,79,86,92
MADISON:      3,35
MARION:       1,15,31,66,68,95,98
MARSHALL:     73
MAURY:        2,4,6,13,14,16,22,31,32,33,34,42,45,46,47,51,54,58,60,63,66,77,80,
              82,89,102
McMINN:       26,27,33,37,39,56,64,74,76,78,85,87,90,91,94,95,96,99
McNAIRY:      57,62,98
MONROE:       5,13,16,56,57,61,65,84,87,94
MONTGOMERY:   1,15,21,22,29,36,50,63,95
MORGAN:       28,46,48
OVERTON:      2,20,24,25,26,29,33,36,41,44,79,89,92,94,97,99
PERRY:        9,48,49,80
RHEA:         13,18,30,39,57,63,96
ROANE:        7,18,31,36,49,69,72,73,88,100
ROBERTSON:    3,18,36,46,50,52,53,72,98
RUTHERFORD:   1,9,12,18,21,29,31,40,41,43,45,53,61,62,68,69,73,75,77,79,86,88,
              89,90,92,95,96,101,103
SCOTT:        48
SEVIER:       43,77
SMITH:        6,12,16,28,30,31,35,43,77,78
STEWART:      1,5,37,75
SULLIVAN:     30,32,33,34,40,61,73,77,88,92,95,96,101,103
SUMNER:       4,6,13,14,20,26,29,40,42,44,46,52,53,55,67,68,69,70,71,75,76,77,
              79,81,90,94,102,103
WARREN:       8,9,10,14,18,19,26,42,45,46,47,50,53,55,57,64,68,73,74,78,90,
              97,99,100
WASHINGTON:   15,40,46,55,59,82,93,103
WAYNE:        29,54,56,59,64
WEAKLEY:      17,42,80,90
WHITE:        1,8,12,22,25,30,42,50,64,65,77,80,81,95,99
WILLIAMSON:   4,5,6,11,12,22,23,25,29,37,38,39,50,56,57,58,60,61,71,83,84,85,86,
              87,91,93,102
WILSON:       6,10,14,16,24,25,33,35,45,47,48,54,57,64,67,68,76,82,83,86,94,99,
              102,103,104
```

INDEX OF MENTIONS OF TENNESSEE TOWNS/PLACES/RIVERS/ETC.

Athens: 94
Big Creek: 102
Blountville: 32,40,88
CHerokee Nation: 13
COlumbia 2,22
Cumberland Mountain: 68
Cumberland River: 6,102

Duck River: 83
East Tennessee: 8,26
Fayetteville: 11,102
Franklin: 22,32,87,93,94
Forke Creek: 84
French Broad: 35
Gallatin: 81
Greeneville: 65
Hendersonville 83
Hurricane Creek: 26
Indian Nation:
Jasper: 68,69
Jonesboro: 33
Kingston: 31,38
Knoxville: 4,9,18,41,43,74,88
Lebanon: 35,83,88
Leeburge: 83
McMinnville: 68,87
Mt. Pleasant: 4,94
Manchester: 55
Maryville: 87
Middleton: 95
Murfreesboro: 53
Nashville: 2,10,19,26,32,38,
67,70,81,88,91,93
Newport: 15

Obine River: 28
Paperville: 88
Pleasant Cove: 55
Pulaski: 34
Purdy: 62
Reynoldsburgh: 26
Roaring River: 6
Rogersville: 38
Rutledge: 38
Sequatchie Valley:
Shelbyville: 74,75,83
Smiths Crossroads: 39
Sparta: 95
Stone Fort: 28,41
Stones River: 46
Summerville: 47
Western District: 5,32,44,45,90,96
Winchester: 28

STATES MENTIONED OTHER THAN TENNESSEE

ALABAMA: 18,34,51,53,57,66,72,85,94

   Bellfouts? 94
   Florence: 70
   Huntsville: 31
   Jackson County: 99
   Limestone County 2
   Madison County 79,94,97
   Mobile 45
   Tuscumbia 94

ARKANSAS TERRITORY: 4,44,98

   White River: 72

GEORGIA: 19,28,43,82

   Augusta: 45
   Washington County: 61

ILLINOIS: 23,35,49,63,68,81,95

   Gallatin County: 31

INDIANA: 20

   Crawford County: 74

LOUISIANA: 8,89

   New Orleans: 53,67,100

KENTUCKY: 4,6,8,13,15,37,46,48,49,56,63,
68,80,83,84,94,96,99

   Bowling Green: 91
   Caldwell County: 42
   Christian County: 29
   Clay County: 58
   Farmington: 94
   Goose Creek: 58
   Hazelpatch: 15
   Hopkins County: 61
   Logan County: 3,71
   Louisville: 74,75
   Morganfield, Union County: 39,56
   Simpson County: 79
   St. Louis: 83

MISSISSIPPI: 30,37,41,89

   Hinds County: 41
   Natchez: 21,39,88

"the MISSOURI: 11,46,51,52,54,75

    Belle Fountain: 83
    Fort Osage: 83
    St. Louis: 32,83

NEW YORK: 67

NORTH CAROLINA: 11,29,47,48,54,69,77,
                89,91,93,94,99

    Asheville: 15
    Beaufort County: 22
    Granville County: 24
    Haywood County: 79
    Iredell County: 92
    Mecklenburg County: 92
    Rutherford County: 99
    Wake County: 78
    Wilkesboro: 65

OHIO: 53

    Cincinnati: 88

PENNSYLVANIA

    Carter County: 65
    Philadelphia: 94

SOUTH CAROLINA: 32,45,81

    Laurens District: 80
    Pendleton District: 55
    York District: 82

TEXAS: 32

VIRGINIA: 15,31,38,54,55,67,78,
          81,88

    Buckingham Cjounty: 43
    Campbell County: 43
    Halifax County: 58
    Henry County: 20
    Lee County: 96
    Montgomery County: 93
    Norfolk: 31
    Prince Edward County: 43
    Wythe County: 9

PLACES:

OHIO RIVER: 48,58,67
MISSISSIPPI RIVER: 48